STUDYING TEACHERS' LIVES

Studying Teachers' Lives examines the background and personal experiences of teachers and the direct and indirect influences their individual situations have on their life and work. In an attempt to provide insights into perceptions of teaching, this book covers a wide range of issues from the importance of teacher socialization to the question of teacher dropout.

Drawing on their diverse experience, the contributors identify collective themes which run across many teachers' lives and reflect on the social structure in which their lives are embedded. The studies employ a range of different methodologies allowing the reader to assess their varying strengths and weaknesses, but throughout they re-affirm the centrality of the teacher in educational research.

Ivor F. Goodson is Professor of Education at the University of Western Ontario. He also runs the Research Unit on Classroom Learning and Computer Use in Schools (RUCCUS) where he is directing a range of projects pursuing his longstanding interest in curriculum and culture. He is currently a Visiting Professor at King's College London and is about to take up a position as Warner Visiting Professor at the University of Rochester. He is the author of *School Subjects and Curriculum Change* (1987), *The Making of Curriculum* (1988) and with Rob Walker of *Biography Identity and Schooling* (1991). He is the founding editor of the *Journal of Education Policy* and a national editor of *Qualitative Studies in Education*.

Forthcoming

TEACHERS' VOICES FOR SCHOOL CHANGE
Andrew Gitlin, K. Brinhurst, M. Burns, V. Cooley, B. Meyers,
K. Price, R. Russell and P. Tiess

STUDYING TEACHERS' LIVES

Edited by
Ivor F. Goodson

Teachers College, Columbia University
New York and London

Published by
Teachers College Press, 1234 Amersterdam Avenue, New York,
NY 10027

Library of Congress Cataloging-in-Publication Data
Studying Teachers' Lives/Edited by Ivor Goodson
Includes bibliographical references and index
1. Teachers–History 2. Teachers–Biography 3. Women
teachers–History 4. Women teachers–Biography 5. Biography as a
literary form
I. Goodson, Ivor
LB1775.S75   1992
371.1'0092'2—dc20
[B]

ISBN 0–8077–3155–2
ISBN 0–8077–3154–4

CONTENTS

FIGURES AND TABLES

FIGURES

TABLES

PREFACE

The original aspiration of the new series of books on *Investigating Schooling* is to scrutinize those everyday aspects of schooling which have tended to be taken for granted and to treat these as objects for investigation and study. One of the most neglected aspects of the taken for granted reality of schooling is the importance of teachers' lives. As many of the chapters in this volume testify the overall impact of new initiatives to reform and restructure schools often run counter to the everyday realities of teachers' lives and the priorities grounded therein.

This is certainly not the first volume which concerns itself with the teacher's life and work. There have recently been a number of studies of teacher biography, narratives and of teachers' stories. However, to date the work on teachers' lives has largely reflected 'the stories of action': studies which locate these lives in their full context have been much less common.

The chapters in this volume provide both substantive and methodological support for studies of teachers' lives which seek to tell 'stories of action within a theory of context'. In particular, those chapters which employ life history methods seem best able to embrace these two integrated aspects of analysis.

Ivor Goodson
University of Western Ontario

CONTRIBUTORS

Richard Butt is a Professor in the Faculty of Education, University of Lethbridge. His interests include curriculum praxis, professional development, classroom change, science education and multiculturalism. The common theme across these different areas is an interest in emancipatory forms of education and research. Currently, he uses autobiographical inquiry as research in understanding the sources, evolution and nature of teachers' knowledge. Parallel to this he works with teachers using autobiography for the purposes of professional development.

Kathleen Casey is Assistant Professor of Curriculum Theory and Educational Foundations at the University of North Carolina-Greensboro. She holds an MA from the University of Leeds, England, and a PhD from the University of Wisconsin-Madison; she has taught in Britain, Africa and the United States. Her doctoral dissertation focused on women teachers who were political activists, and she continues to collect and analyse life-history narratives of contemporary teachers.

David Dwyer is currently directing ACOT, the Apple Classroom of Tomorrow, research project. This is a national field study of computer-saturated school environments for the Apple Computer Company, Cupertino, California.

Ivor F. Goodson is Professor of Education at the University of Western Ontario. He also runs the Research Unit on Classroom Learning and Computer Use in Schools (RUCCUS) where he is directing a range of projects pursuing his longstanding interest in curriculum and culture. He is currently a Visiting Professor at

King's College London and is about to take up a position as Warner Visiting Professor at the University of Rochester. He is the author of *School Subjects and Curriculum Change* (1987), *The Making of Curriculum* (1988) and with Rob Walker of *Biography Identity and Schooling* (1991). He is the founding editor of the *Journal of Education Policy* and a national editor of *Qualitative Studies in Education.*

Paul Kleine is currently on the faculty at the University of Oklahoma's School of Education. Here he is teaching general research methods and qualitative inquiry. He is also continuing research into innovation with life-history methods.

J. Gary Knowles is a Teacher Educator at the University of Michigan and received his PhD from the University of Utah. Gary is involved in research in teacher development and socialization and has written a forthcoming book with R.V. Bullough and N. A. Crow called *Emerging as a Teacher* (Routledge, 1992). Recent articles can be found in the *Journal of Education for Teaching, Teachers College Press,* and the *Journal of Experiential Education.*

Lynda Measor was a Research Fellow at the the Open University, UK, for five years where the research that this chapter is based on was done. She is now a Senior Lecturer in Social Policy at Brighton Polytechnic.

Glenda McCue is currently teaching within the Lethbridge School District No. 51. She has accepted a position involving consulting work with parents, children and teachers who have multicultural and English as a Second Language backgrounds.

Sue Middleton is a Senior Lecturer in the Education Department at the University of Waikato, Hamilton, New Zealand, where she also teaches in the Centre for Women's Studies. Previously she taught in primary, intermediate and secondary schools in multi-cultural communities. Her previous research has focused on the life-histories and strategies of feminist teachers and the development of feminist pedagogies. Currently she is involved in a research team investigating the restructuring of school administration in New Zealand. She has published widely in New Zealand, Australia and Britain, edited *Women and Education in Aotearoa* (Allen & Unwin, 1988) and (with John Codd and Alison Jones) edited *New Zealand Education Policy Today: Critical Perspectives* (Allen & Unwin, 1990).

Margaret K. Nelson is Professor of Sociology at Middlebury College. She has written on childbirth, schoolteaching and women's work of caring. She is the co-editor (with Emily K. Abel) of *Circles of Care* (SUNY Press, 1990) and the author of *Negotiated Care: The Experience of Family Day Care Providers* (Temple University Press, 1990).

John Prunty is currently a Project Director and Manager for Maritz Communications Company. Here he is doing needs assessment, curriculum development, conference teaching and consulting for businesses in Chicago, Illinois.

Danielle Raymond is at the Faculté d'Education, Université de Sherbrook, Canada. Her interest in the study of teachers' life histories stems from earlier work on the limited impact of pre-service training on experiential knowledge of teaching and learning. Her current research combines ethnographic and biographical approaches to the understanding of teachers' knowledge of pupils and classroom processes.

Pat Sikes was Lynda Measor's Co-researcher on the Teachers' Careers Project, based at the Open University, UK. She is presently employed as Lecturer in Education at the University of Warwick. Her current research interests are the socialization of teachers, and the use of life-history and biographical approaches in initial teacher education.

Louis Smith has been at Washington University for over thirty years, moving from quantitative measurement concerns in educational psychology to qualitative studies of teachers, classrooms and curricula to studies of Schools and school districts and the problems of innovation and change from ethnographic, biographical and historical modes of inquiry. He is author of *Complexities of the*

Urban Classroom (1968) and *Anatomy of an Educational Innovation* (1971).

Lloyd Yamagishi is a Teacher in the Lethbridge School District No. 51. He has recently been appointed Vice-principal of a junior high school.

1

STUDYING TEACHERS' LIVES
An Emergent Field of Inquiry

Ivor F. Goodson

INTRODUCTION

In 1973 I was travelling on a train in Yorkshire in the North of England. One of the joys of train travel is eavesdropping other people's conversations. Two men were sitting in their working clothes opposite each other, both smoking pipes:

A. I gather your Janet's walking out with a fella.
B. Aye, that's right . . . looks like they might get married.
A. I did hear something about him being . . . a teacher (said meaningfully, a little conspiratorially, hints of 'I won't tell anyone').
B. More's the pity.
(Pause)

A. Never could understand folk like that. They're a rum bunch of buggers by a' large . . . sort of a race apart.
(Long pause)

B. Aye, they leave a lot to be desired.

Now gathered within this conversation are of course a number of themes. Some clearly recognizable, others not. Older Yorkshire working men would be likely to feel at best ambivalent about the group of people implicated in their passage into a harsh working world: their passage into the mines, the mills, the factories of the Yorkshire hinterland where they would spend up to fifty years of their working life. But over and above this ambivalence there seems to be another kind of bemusement, which links with wider ways of knowing and talking and writing. The feeling that one way

1

or another, teachers constitute a separate species. A species that is to some degree apart and unknown to other mortals.

In the literature on schooling, this tendency is also apparent. It is perhaps most evident in those studies using a primarily anthropological method. Here schools are seen as very special and unusual environments. As Philip Jackson says in his germinal *Life in Classrooms*, the life that is experienced in schools is unusual because 'classrooms are special places'. In these special places it is almost as if a separate species of life exists. Yet it is a separate world that remains familiar to all of us:

> Even the odours of the classroom are fairly standardized. Schools may use different brands of wax and cleaning fluid, but they all seem to contain similar ingredients, a sort of universal smell which creates an aromatic background that permeates the entire building. Added to this, in each classroom, is the slightly acrid scent of chalkdust and the faint hint of fresh wooden pencil shavings. In some rooms, especially at lunch time, there is the familiar odour of orange peels and peanut butter sandwiches, a blend that mingles in the late afternoon (following recess) with the delicate pungency of children's perspiration. If a person stumbled into a classroom blindfolded, his nose alone, if he used it carefully, would tell him where he was.[1]

Jackson's world of classrooms is instantly recognizable: if we try we can recall the smell and some of the substance of our own schooldays (only the peanut butter strikes a European as unrecognizable!). But as ordinary people we do our period of service in classrooms and then pass on. While we are at school we may take on features of a separate species of person but ultimately we move into the 'real world'. But what of the people that stay on, who live their lives in those special places? Certainly there is evidence in this volume that they come to see themselves as different. A woman teacher in Vermont saw that 'teachers were a thing apart', 'you couldn't do anything that other people did'. Do teachers then come, in any sense, to constitute a 'separate species', to see themselves as a separate race? Seeking an answer to this question is itself an important reason for studying teachers' lives.

THE TEACHER IN RESEARCH STUDIES

In his book *Schoolteacher* (1975), Dan Lortie summarized the relationship between teachers and educational research studies in the United States:

> Schooling is long on prescription, short on description. That is nowhere more evident than in the case of the two million persons who teach in the public schools. It is widely conceded that the core transactions of formal education take place where teachers and students meet. ... But although books and articles instructing teachers on how they should behave are legion, empirical studies of teaching work – and the outlook of those who staff the schools – remain rare.[2]

The general point with regard to knowledge/power that Lortie makes has been a continuing one in the research discourse as related to teachers: a good deal of prescription and implicit portrayal but very little serious study of, or collaboration with, those prescribed to or portrayed. Yet while there is continuity, there are also changes over time which exist at the intersection with social, political and economic history.

Introducing the book *Teachers' Lives and Careers* (1983), Stephen Ball and I argued that British research on teachers had moved through a number of contemporary phases. 'In the 1960's teachers were shadowy figures on the educational landscape mainly known, or unknown through large scale surveys or historical analysis of their position in society, the key concept in approaching the practice of the teaching was that of role.'[3] Teachers, in short, were present in aggregate through imprecise statistics or were viewed as individuals only as formal role incumbents mechanistically and unproblematically responding to the powerful expectations of their role set.

In the late 1960s and early 1970s this approach changed somewhat (but from the point of view of the teacher not necessarily for the better). Case study researchers began to examine schooling as a social process, particularly in the manner through which school pupils were 'processed'. 'The sympathies of the researchers lay primarily with the pupils, working class and female pupils in particular, who were the "under dogs" in the classroom, teachers were the villains of the piece.' By the late 1970s we discerned a

3

further shift: 'attention began to be directed to the constraints within which teachers work . ... Teachers were transformed from villains to victims and in some cases, "dupes" of the system within which they were required to operate.'[4]

But this latter characterization of teachers finally opened up the question of 'how teachers saw their work and their lives'. Writing in 1981, I argued that researchers had not confronted the complexity of the schoolteacher as an active agent making his or her own history. Researchers, even when they had stopped treating the teacher as numerical aggregate, historical footnote or unproblematic role incumbent still treated teachers as interchangeable types unchanged by circumstance or time. As a result new more contextually sensitive research was needed which stressed life history methods:

> The pursuit of personal and biographical data might rapidly challenge the assumption of interchangeability. Likewise, by tracing the teachers' life as it evolved over time – throughout the teachers' career and through several generations – the assumption of timelessness might also be remedied. *In understanding something so intensely personal as teaching it is critical we know about the person the teacher is.* Our paucity of knowledge in this area is a manifest indictment of the range of our sociological imagination.[5]

In the event, while the argument for studies of teachers lives and careers now began to be more generally pursued in the educational research community, political and economic changes were moving into a period of conservative reaction. In 1979, the era of Thatcherism began in Britain and this presaged an attack on most forms of socially-curious (let alone critical) educational research. As Measor and Sikes, using a beginning quote from Hargreaves, diplomatically (and perhaps wisely!) understate:

> It may not be enough in Britain in the 1980s to say that sociological investigation is itself evidently desirable. There has been 'A decline in government interest in investing in independent questioning and self criticism. ...' We need to take care to ensure that we do not imply that we see teachers as deprived underdogs, nevertheless teachers do work in a context which currently threatens their working autonomy

and their conditions of employment and choice over the ways they teach children (p. 229).

Likewise in North America more conservative patterns of educational reform emerged during the Reagan years when William Bennett was Education Secretary; Aronowitz and Giroux provide a critical summary:

> Bennett's education offensive stubbornly insisted that 'throwing money' at schools, even those with leaky roofs and broken boilers, was not the solution to what he termed the 'crisis of excellence'. Rather, he urged a massive curriculum revision, the central features of which were resuscitating math and science education, concentrating on transmitting the canonical works of Western civilization as a required part of the undergraduate curricula of elite colleges and universities, and emphasizing values such as respect for authority, especially in the family, as well as patriotism and other aspects of moral education, in the early grades. Bennett's curriculum strategy was more than a way to avoid frequent demands for more federal financial support for schools; it was a profound attack on many reforms of the 1960s, when students obtained from reluctant administrators more curriculum choice than was enjoyed by any generation of secondary and university students in recent educational history. [6]

As part of the general reversal of 1960s patterns, the change in the patterns of political and administrative control over teachers have been enormous in the 1980s. In terms of power and visibility in many ways this represents 'a return to the shadows' for teachers in the face of new curriculum guidelines (in Britain an all-encompassing National Curriculum), teachers' assessment and accountability, a barrage of new policy edicts and new patterns of school governance and administration.

THE CONTEXT OF RESEARCH STUDIES

The conservative political renaissance of the 1980s rapidly effected the context of educational research. One of the incidental side-effects on studies of teachers' lives and careers was that work on

5

the 'context' of the teacher's work became less common and certainly less fundable (although some work continued to be funded by teacher unions). As a result, contextualist studies of teachers' lives particularly from a fuller life history perspective became more difficult. Having reached such a promising plateau in the early 1980s, and with serious life history work beginning, the promise and potential of such work was rapidly affected by the new climates in which educational research had to be undertaken.

The crucial focus for life history work is to locate the teacher's own life story alongside a broader contextual analysis, to tell in Stenhouse's words 'a story of action, within a theory of context'. The distinction between the life story and the life history is therefore absolutely basic. The life story is the 'story we tell about our life'; the life history is a collaborative venture, reviewing a wider range of evidence. The life story teller and another (or others) collaborate in developing this wider account by interviews and discussions and by scrutiny of texts and contexts. The life history is the life story located within it's historical context. By making contextual research more difficult, the new climate of research meant that in many cases life history work and collaborative intertextual and intercontextual inquiry was discouraged while more individual and specific life story work could none the less continue. A great deal of valuable work on teacher's stories or narratives was carried out in the 1980s by academics but much of it did not embrace contextual or intercontextual analysis.

In the new climate of the 1980s, the teacher life story teller was therefore located between the power of resurgent political bureaucracy on the one side and the mediating power of the academy through whom their stories were transmitted on the other. To say the least, this is a peculiar 'place of tension' in which to undertake the intimate and ethically perilous collaboration through which the teacher's life might be reconstructed and made textual.

Critics indeed have argued that in the existing political 'moment' life story work is deeply problematic; some certainly hint that it may be best to abandon the whole enterprise. The work in this volume accepts the problematic nature of the enterprise but does not take the view that we should withdraw from the field and thereby leave conduct of life story work to those who do not accept or explore such problematics. Rather it argues for facing squarely the dilemmas of studying people's lives; to build both methodological procedures and value systems which will respect those lives and collaborative patterns which will widen and deepen understandings. The chapters in this volume all share a concern to broaden the manner in which we study teachers' lives from a sole focus on stories or narratives towards a range of more exploratory and contextual procedures and processes.

The problematics of studying people's lives are part of a wider context of social relations, priorities and provisions. Lasch, for instance, has scrutinised the historical trajectory of private lives in *Haven in a Heartless World*. In his history of modern society he discerns two distinct phases. In the first phase he argues that the division of labour which accompanied the development of individual capitalism deprived ordinary people of control over their work, making that work alienating and unfulfilling. In the second phase Lasch argues that liberalism promoted a view that, while work might be alienated under capital, all could be restored in the private domain. 'It was agreed that people would be freed to pursue happiness and virtue in their private lives in whatever manner they chose. The work place was thus severed from the home and the family became the "haven in the heartless world".' [7] No sooner was this equation established, Lasch argues, than liberalism reneged.

Private life was opened up to the 'helping' professions: doctors, teachers, psychologists, child guidance experts, juvenile court officers, and the like. The private domain was immediately made prey to these quasi-official 'forces of organized virtue' and 'the hope that private transactions could make up for the collapse of communal traditions and civic order'[8] was smothered by the helping professions.

Interestingly Denzin has recently argued that ethnographers and biographers represent the latest wave in this 'penetration' of private lives, and that this is to be expected at a time when we see 'the emergence of a new conservative politics of health and morality, centring on sexuality, the family and the individual'. Hence he argues:

> The biography and autobiography are among Reagan's legacy to American society. In these writing forms the liberal and left American academic scholarly community reasserts a commitment to the value of individual lives and their accurate representation in the life story document. The life story thus becomes the left's answer to the repressive conser-

vative politics of the last two decades of American history. With this method the sorrowful tales of America's underclass can be told. In such tellings a romantic and political identification with the downtrodden will be produced. From this identification will come a new politics of protest; a politics grounded in the harsh and raw economics, racial, and sexual edges of contemporary life. This method will reveal how large social groupings are unable to either live out their ideological versions of the American dream, or to experience personal happiness.[9]

And further:

In reinscribing the real life, with all its nuances, innuendoes, and terrors, in the life story, researchers perpetuate a commitment to the production of realist, melodramatic social problems texts which create an identification with the downtrodden in American society. These works of realism reproduce and mirror the social structures that need to be changed. They valorize the subjectivity of the powerless individual. They make a hero of the interactionist-ethnographer-voyeur who comes back from the field with moving tales of the dispossessed. They work from an ideological bias that emphasizes the situational, adjustive, and normative approach to social problems and their resolutions, whether this be in the classroom, the street, or the home.[10]

The problem is well stated in the following section where Denzin argued that a dual myth is perpetuated:

The life story project, with its roots in the Chicago School suffers, then, from the following flaws. It presupposes a body of textual work that keeps the private/public division alive and well. Two myths are perpetuated. First, that urban, modern man, woman and child have enclaves of privacy that the complex urban society cannot touch. Second, the skilled ethnographer-biographer can make sense of these worlds and in so doing bring to life the sacred inner worlds of experience of the oppressed subject. Such work will then show that the inner/private life endows the subject with the cherished values of democracy, namely honor, pride, individualism, heroism and dignity in the face of great obstacles.

But in making the sacred visible, in a pornography of excess which leaves no secret uncovered, the biographical text, in a single, swift stroke, erases the boundaries between the public and the private while it ceremonializes that which it has just exposed. In so doing it perpetuates the myth that the private life and its inner meanings still exists. But in practice this is no longer the case. Our methods have severed the boundaries between the public and the private. Unwittingly, we have made the personal political. However we have failed to articulate a politics that takes this position seriously, for a moral and social theory of democracy can no longer presume a sacred sphere of social life.

In making the personal public the biographer follows a textual politics which valorizes the subjects in question. This heroic gesture diverts attention away from the social structures that have done the oppression. It shifts, that is, attention away from the structure and makes the individual the focus of attention. At the same time it tells their story within a framework that conforms to publicly acceptable conceptions of persons, their lives and the meanings of these lives. These conceptions are embedded in Western literary conventions and have been present since the invention of the biographical form.[11]

Denzin raises a number of important points with regard to the use of life story and biography as methods for studying teachers' lives. There are two points to note, however. First, he is wrong when he asserts that the life story is the 'left's answer' to repressive conservative politics. This is far too sweeping a generalization. Certainly some leftist scholars have employed this methodology but so too have a large body of less overtly political scholars besides some of a conservative orientation. Indeed, it could be argued that one of the side effects of life story work (I think Denzin would take this view) is to de-politicize our inquiry. By locating our study at the individual level, thereby cutting us off from the wider social forces and more collective milieux, it does indeed 'valorize the subjectivity of the powerless individual'.

Second, Denzin is specifically indicting the life *story* and biography. Much of his critique would not stand if we move to a more broadly contextualizing life history or collaborative intercon-

9

textual approach. By pointing out the deficiencies of those approaches which celebrate 'stories' and 'narrative', Denzin's critique is itself an exhortation to pursue a wider structural frame of inquiry.

STUDYING TEACHERS' LIVES: A RESTATEMENT

Denzin's blitzkrieg is, I think, a timely reminder of the dangers involved in studying teachers' lives. It seems almost a call for abandonment of the project and is, at times, a persuasive one. There are, I think, a number of reasons to resist wholesale evacuation of this field of study. First, the negative argument: I don't think 'wholesale' evacuation is a meaningful option. The field is already well occupied with people who produce teachers' stories and narratives. This work will continue and, indeed, Denzin's argument assumes such continuance in arguing the often unintended congruity between this way of studying teachers' lives and present political modalities. Hence, if the field of enquiry is going to continue it behoves us to build up more systematic consideration of context and better ethical procedures and methodologies. Second, there remain powerful rationales for studying teachers' lives if we can succeed in explicating and developing our values, ethics and methodologies.

In one sense the project of 'studying teachers' lives' should represent an attempt to generate a counter-culture which will resist the tendency to 'return teachers to the shadows'; a counter-culture based upon a research mode that above all takes teachers seriously and seeks to listen to 'the teacher's voice'. 'The proposal I am recommending is essentially one of reconceptionalizing educational research so as to assure that the teacher's voice is heard, heard loudly, heard articulately.'[12]

A number of the chapters speak eloquently on this issue which provides the overall rationale for this volume. Butt *et al.*, for instance, argue that:

> The notion of teacher's voice is important in that it carries the tone, the language, the quality, the feelings, that are conveyed by the way a teacher speaks or writes. In a political sense the notion of the teacher's voice addresses the right to speak and be represented. It can represent both the unique

individual and the collective voice; one that is characteristic of teachers as compared to other groups (p. 57).

The sponsoring of this kind of teacher's voice is thus counter-cultural in that it works against the grain of power/knowledge as held and produced by politicians and administrators.

Yet if the economic and political times are inauspicious, on the other side, the current 'postmodernist movement' provides an emergent climate of support, certainly at the level of research. Michel Foucault has been hugely influential in encouraging researchers to retrieve and represent the voices of their 'subjects'. Likewise, Carol Gilligan's superb work, *In a Different Voice*, exemplifies the power of representing the voices of women previously unheard. Above all the postmodern syntagm sponsors: 'The idea that all groups have a right to speak for themselves, in their own voice, and have that voice accepted as authentic and legitimate.' [13] Beyond the general sponsorship of the teacher's voice the studies in this volume represent a range of other rationales for studying teachers' lives.

First, studying teachers' lives will provide a valuable range of insights into the new moves to restructure and reform schooling, into new policy concerns and directives. A number of the chapters address this 'crisis of reform' (see, for example, Butt *et al.* pp. 51–98) or more specifically 'crisis of prescription'. I have recently examined the importance and salience of the belief in curriculum as prescription (CAP):

> CAP supports the mystique that expertise and control reside within central governments, educational bureaucracies or the university community. Providing nobody exposes this mystique, the two words of 'prescriptive rhetoric' and 'schooling as practice' can co-exist. Both sides benefit from such peaceful co-existence. The agencies of CAP are seen to be 'in control' and the schools are seen to be 'delivering' (and can carve out a good degree of autonomy if they accept the rules).

However, there is a substantial downside to this 'historic compromise':

> There are costs of complicity in accepting the myth of prescription: above all these involve, in various ways, acceptance of established modes of power relations. Perhaps

11

most importantly the people intimately connected with the day-to-day social construction of curriculum and schooling – teachers – are thereby effectively disenfranchised in the 'discourse of schooling'. To continue to exist, teachers' day-to-day power must remain unspoken and unrecorded. This is one price of complicity: day-to-day power and autonomy for schools and for teachers are dependent on continuing to accept the fundamental lie. [14]

In addressing the crisis of prescription and reform, it becomes imperative that we find new ways to sponsor the teacher's voice.

As an example, Kathleen Casey's study (pp. 187–208) provides a valuable rationale for studying teachers' lives to understand the much discussed question of 'teacher drop-outs'. She notes that a certain set of taken-for-granted assumptions control the way in which the problem of teacher attention has normally been defined; one which presumes managerial solutions. She notes how the language confirms this direction referring to 'teacher defection', 'teacher turnover' and 'supply and demand'.

This belief in managerialism and prescription is underpinned by the research methods employed within the academy. She finds that:

A limited number of research strategies have been employed in investigating this topic. Former members of the teaching profession have often been traced statistically, rather than in person, and information has typically been collected from such sources as district files, state departments of public instruction, or through researcher-conceived surveys (pp. 187–8).

The results of the research paradigms employed in the academy have powerful implications for our understanding of the management of educational systems.

The particular configuration of selectivities and omissions which has been built into this research frame slants the shape of its findings. By systematically failing to record the voices of ordinary teachers, the literature on educators' careers actually silences them. Methodologically, this means that even while investigating an issue where decision-making is paramount, researchers speculate on teachers' motivations, or at best, survey them with a set of forced-choice options.

12

Theoretically what emerges is an instrumental view of teachers, one in which they are reduced to objects which can be manipulated for particular ends. Politically, the results are educational policies constructed around institutionally convenient systems of rewards and punishments, rather than in congruence with teachers' desire to create significance in their lives (p. 188).

Again and again in this volume the testimonies expose the shallowness of the managerial, prescriptive view of schooling. It is, in truth, not difficult to see in whose interests the teacher's voice has been suppressed and in whose interests academics have embraced less 'curious' research modes. Louis Smith, a psychologist by training, concludes (p. 158):

Behavioural objectives, time on task, mastery learning, school effectiveness, are sounds that emanate from drums and drummers distant from the language and perspectives of the innovator we have studied and the language and theory we have chosen to couch our own interpretations and speculations.

Likewise, the studies in Chapter 3 provide eloquent testimony on this point. For instance, the examination of this point with regard to Lloyd who initially studied his curriculum guides like 'the Bible' speaks volumes. But perhaps the most eloquent epitaph for the believers in managerialism and prescriptions comes from the study of Glenda. 'The teachers' guide was closed and the students' workbooks were returned to the bookroom. The culture and knowledge within the classroom was infinitely more exciting' (p. 84). R.I.P., Q.E.D.

Another rationale for studying teachers' lives is evidenced in this book and develops from the literature on teacher socialization. One major tradition in this literature has designated the period of pre-service teaching training and early in-service teaching as the most formative socializing influence. An alternative tradition, however, has insisted with accelerating force that it is far more complicated than this. Many studies in the 1970s and 1980s have focused on the teachers own experience *as pupils* which is seen not only *as* important as the training periods but in many cases *more* important. (It should be noted that while this book focuses on teachers, it also argues that future work be conducted on pupils' lives and their relationship to their school experiences.) Dan Lortie refers to this pupil period as an 'apprenticeship of observation'. Teacher socialization, then, occurs through the observation and internalization of particular models of teaching as experienced by the recipient pupil. Lortie argues that these models, these latent models, are activated during the training period having often been, so to speak, 'carried in suspension' over a period of time, particularly the undergraduate years. One way to follow up on this alternative tradition in teacher socialization research requires that we examine those socializing influences relevant to the formation of the teacher over the full life experience.

Knowles in Chapter 4 takes this view and argues for a quite focused and specific notion of teacher biography. He argues that 'understanding the origins of student teacher perspectives is largely a product of understanding the impact of biography – those experiences that have directly influenced an individual's thinking about teaching and schools' (p. 102).

A third rationale for studying teachers' lives is articulated in Sue Middleton's work. Work on teachers' lives will provide vital insights into teaching as a gendered profession (as well as the associated and specific aspiration in this chapter of providing a substantive account of the production of one feminist teacher's pedagogy within the specific socio-cultural setting of post-Second World War New Zealand). Other work pursues the experience of women's lives in teaching: Margaret Nelson's attempt to reconstruct the experiences of women teachers in Vermont in the first half of the twentieth century and Kathleen Casey's investigation of why progressive women activists leave teaching. Nelson's work provides a fascinating vindication of the oral history approach. She notes that, 'Numerous studies have shown that there is a gap between what we can discover when we rely on published accounts of some historical event and what we discover when we ask questions of the on-site participants of those same events. This gap looms larger when we are looking at women's history because of the private nature of so much of women's lives.' She adds later, 'Public history often ignores minority views. But women's lives are further hidden because important information is overlooked, consciously avoided, or distorted.'

Middleton argues that, 'Writing one's autobiography becomes, in this framework, in part a process of deconstructing the discursive practices through which one's subjectivity has been constituted.' Butt, Raymond, and Yamagishi, in some senses, pursue similar objectives through their work on collaborative autobiography. Their work, which relates to the earlier discussion about managerialism, reflects a fourth rationale for studying teachers' lives: the desire to produce teacher-centred, professional knowledge. I have recently pursued this argument at length elsewhere but, put briefly, the issue is to develop a modality of educational research which speaks both within and to the teacher.[15] This will require a major reconceptualization of educational research paradigms, but the emerging work on teacher thinking, teacher journalling, teachers' practical knowledge, as well as the new corpus of work on reflective practitioners and action research is, I think, a harbinger of new modalities of research. To date, much of the educational research employed in teacher training has been developed by scholars writing within their own contexts and resonates with their own career concerns in a 'publish or perish' environment. The audience is mainly their academic peers who are addressed through scholarly journals. In the profoundest sense, the knowledge they produce is, from the teacher's point of view, decontextualized. As Woods has argued, 'such knowledge is not under their control. It is produced "out there" and "up there" on an apparently superior plane in forms and terms with which they cannot engage. Further, much of this knowledge appears to be critical of teachers. ...'[16]

Studying teachers' lives will, I suspect, never become mainstream, for such study seeks to understand and to give voice to an occupational group that have been historically marginalized. Yet, as a group, teachers retain considerable power, and as is often the case much truth resides in the margins. This mode of study will undoubtedly contribute to the understanding of the educational endeavour but the use of such study has to be patrolled with extraordinary care.

Studying Teachers' Lives provides insights into the deeply intimate and personal aspects of identity. Plainly, all too plainly, such data could be misused by those who employ, manage, control and direct teachers. Several of the chapters deal with this issue and, in the endpiece, I shall return to the questions of collaboration and ethical procedures. Researching teachers' lives is an enterprise fraught with danger but the alternative is, I think, more dangerous: to continue in substantial ignorance of those people who, in spite of the many historical shifts and cycles, remain central to achievement in the educational endeavour.

The study of teachers' lives depends for its viability and desirability upon teachers themselves. They initially control most of the important data and all those involved in such study must ensure that they continue throughout the process to exercise control and to be actively involved in the negotiation and production of reports. If this is successfully accomplished, we may be developing an important new field for collaborative inquiry. For it remains clear that, in the accounts they give about life in schools, teachers constantly refer to personal and biographical factors. From their point of view, it would seem that professional practices are embedded in wider life concerns. We need to listen closely to their views on the relationship between 'school life' and 'whole life' for in that dialectic crucial tales about careers and commitments will be told. It remains true that the balance of commitment between teaching and life may be precariously affected by educational cuts and changes in public esteem. Studying teachers' lives helps us monitor this most crucial of all equations.

NOTES

1 Jackson, P. (1968) *Life in Classrooms*, New York: Holt, Rinehart and Winston, p. 7.
2 Lortie, D. (1975) *Schoolteacher: A Sociological Study*, Chicago: University of Chicago Press, p. vii.
3 Ball, S. and Goodson, I.F. (eds) (1985) *Teachers' Lives and Careers*, London, Philadelphia and New York: Falmer, p. 6.
4 ibid., p. 7.
5 Goodson, I.F. (1981) 'Life history and the study of schooling', *Interchange*, Ontario Institute for Studies in Education, Vol. 11, No. 4, p. 69.
6 Aronowitz, S. and Giroux, H.A. (1991) *Postmodern Education: Politics, Culture, and Social Criticism*, Minneapolis: University of Minnesota Press, p. 5.
7 Menaud, L. (1991) 'Man of the people', a review of *The True and Only Heaven* by C. Lasch, *New York Review of Books*, Vol. XXXVIII, No. 7, 11 April.
8 Lasch, C. (1977) *Haven in a Heartless World*, New York: Basic Books, p. 168.
9 Denzin, N. K. (1991) 'Deconstructing the biographical method', paper presented at the AERA Conference in Chicago, April 1991, p. 2.

10 ibid., pp. 2–3.
11 ibid., pp. 3–4.
12 Goodson, I.F. (1991) 'Sponsoring the teacher's voice', *Cambridge Journal of Education*, Spring, p. 36, and in Fullan, M. and Hargreaves, A. (eds) *Understanding Teacher Development*, London: Cassells and New York: Teacher's College Press (forthcoming).
13 Harvey, D. (1989) *The Condition of Postmodernity: An Inquiry into the Origin of Cultural Change*, Oxford and Cambridge, Mass.: Blackwell, p. 48.
14 Goodson, I.F. (1900) 'Studying curriculum: towards a social constructionist perspective', *Journal of Curriculum Studies*, Vol. 22, No. 4, p. 300.
15 Goodson, I.F. (1991) 'Sponsoring the teacher's voice', pp. 35–45.
16 Woods, P. 'Life histories and teacher knowledge' in Smyth, J. (ed.) (1987) *Educating Teachers: Changing the Nature of Pedagogical Knowledge*, London, Philadelphia and New York: Falmer, p. 121.

2

DEVELOPING A RADICAL PEDAGOGY

Autobiography of a New Zealand sociologist of women's education

Sue Middleton

Since the late 1960s, feminism has re-emerged as a mass social movement. Education has been crucial in this resurgence: as an object of feminist demands, as a source of ideas, as a means of employment, and as a site for political activism. While liberal feminists have focused on the attainment of equal access for women to existing curriculum subjects and positions of seniority in education, those of more radical persuasions have challenged the very nature of educational institutions – in particular, the selection, social organization and teaching strategies of what counts as 'academic' knowledge.[1] Such challenges have been strong in many universities, where feminists have introduced feminist critiques and theories within their various disciplines and departments as well as starting separate women's studies programmes.

Feminists who are involved with programmes of teacher education, such as those teaching in university 'education' departments, aim to empower their students to develop radical pedagogies – styles of teaching which help make visible to pupils the structural social inequalities which constrain their lives. In this, their strategies may be twofold. Liberal feminists will focus on teaching their students feminist curriculum *content*: transmitting classical feminist 'grand theories' and research findings as 'received knowledge'.[2] In addition, those with more radical perspectives will challenge the hegemony of dominant authoritarian teaching practices by designing for their students alternative forms of classroom experience.[3] Such approaches use various consciousness-raising techniques which developed within the earlier stages of second wave feminism. The pioneers of university women's studies found the style of 'starting with the personal' a useful means of 'making knowledge', since few records had been kept of women's intellectual past and existing social theories and research were criticized as androcentric – reflecting the situation of men and rendering women invisible or marginal.

In developing radical teaching styles, many feminist (and other 'left wing') educators have found life-history approaches useful. For example, Giroux has argued that student teachers 'must be given the opportunity to use and interpret their own experiences in a manner that reveals how the latter have been shaped and influenced by the dominant culture. Subjective awareness becomes the first step in transforming those experiences'.[4] In other words, teachers, as well as their students, should analyse the relationship between their individual biographies, historical events, and the constraints imposed on their personal choices by broader power relations, such as those of class, race and gender. As C. Wright Mills and others have expressed it, 'biography, history and social structure' become the object of analysis.[5] These should be taken into account in the process of curriculum theorizing, or developing a radical pedagogy. As a contribution towards that end, this chapter offers a socialist feminist analysis[6] of how my own experiences of education – as a student and as a teacher – have influenced my praxis as a 'sociologist of women's education'[7] – a teacher and researcher – in an education department in a New Zealand university. In doing this I raise questions about the relationship between education and the processes of political radicalization in teachers and in pupils.

The chapter has two related aims. The first is to give a substantive account of the production of one socialist feminist teacher's pedagogy within the specific socio-cultural setting of post-World War Two New Zealand. The second is to exemplify for teachers a *process* of curriculum theorizing which may be of value to them in theorizing their own teaching practice. As Giroux has argued:

> Teaching must be viewed, in part, as an intensely personal affair. This suggests that prospective teachers be given the concepts and methods to delve into their own biographies, to look at the sedimented history they carry around, and to learn how one's cultural capital represents a dialectical interplay between private experience and history.[8]

19

In developing such 'concepts and methods to delve into our own biographies', discourse theory is useful. Within this framework, one's autobiography is viewed sociologically within the context in which it is produced: 'biography, history and social structure' are studied holistically. The individual human 'subject' is seen as constituted in a multiplicity of discourses. Discourses are sets of social practices which are informed by powerful 'knowledges', such as the law, medicine, demography, psychiatry, psychology and academic disciplines. Such discursive practices shape people's lives, for example, constituting them as 'normal or deviant', 'law-abiding or criminal', 'sane or mad', 'healthy or sick', 'bright or dull', 'successful or unsuccessful'. Such classifications are important in the constitution of a person's 'identity'.

Within such perspectives, schooling has been seen as a crucial site of social regulation.[9] For example, schools monitor pupils' 'progress' according to the criteria established within various discourses, (such as 'IQ testing', or 'developmental psychology'). Schools exchange information about children (and their families) with other agencies, such as the justice system, the police, the social welfare agencies, the health system, employers and psychologists. In schools people are constantly regulated and classified so that 'normalization is disseminated throughout daily life through surveillance and monitoring'.[10] Writing one's autobiography becomes, in this framework, in part a process of deconstructing the discursive practices through which one's subjectivity has been constituted: what specific power/knowledge relations have shaped and regulated one's life? However, people are not mere passive victims of their regulation and monitoring within discourse, but are creative strategists whose everyday realities – at both conscious and unconscious levels – are also their own idiosyncratic constructions.

This chapter offers a sociological analysis of my educational life history. Sociological inquiries usually begin, as Dorothy Smith[11] and others have argued, 'with the conceptual organization of relevances of the sociological discourse', namely, location of the inquiry within the theoretical debates and paradigms of what constitutes sociology as an academic discipline. Smith and other feminists have argued that sociology – like other disciplines – is made up of the terms and relevances of (white middle-class academic) men. The theories, concepts and relevances of sociology have rendered women invisible or marginal, positioning man as subject, woman as 'other'. Women are therefore alienated from social theory. To recover ourselves as sociological subjects, women must theorize from our own experience and thereby 'make the actual practices visible so that we can locate our inquiry in an everyday world'.[12] Only then can we begin to create a sociology which is authentic for women's lives. A woman's 'direct experience' becomes 'the ground of her knowledge'.[13]

I will analyse my 'direct experience' in so far as I understand it to shape, or have shaped, my feminist pedagogy. Direct experience, however, by its very nature, cannot be communicated, but is always interpreted. What I choose to include, then, will inevitably be shaped by conventions of the discourses within which my writing is produced. For example, while participants in sociological studies may be guaranteed anonymity, an autobiography provides no such privacy. Material which may be 'sociologically relevant' may be 'too personal' to share in a public forum such as an academic textbook. My academic production, then, takes place in a context which limits, regulates and shapes it. My account is also structured by *what I perceive* as formative of my feminism and my pedagogy. Since the early 1970s, feminists have developed 'woman-centred' social theories and there is now a 'body of feminist sociological knowledge' – a set of feminist sociological discourses. This chapter offers a socialist feminist reading of my life, i.e. it locates it within the discourse of the 'sociology of women's education'. As a socialist feminist sociologist writing this for an academic text, my 'sense of relevance' will be structured by the very feminist sociological theories my personal account seeks to explain. I therefore make these explicit and begin my analysis 'within the sociological discourse' by sketching what socialist feminist writers have identified as the key historical and structural influences in the resurgence of feminism amongst 'educated' women in the post-World War Two years. This provides both a historical 'context' and a set of theoretical tools to assist my autobiographical account.

THE SOCIAL ORIGINS OF POST-WAR FEMINIST TEACHING: SOME GUIDELINES FROM THE LITERATURE

The reasons for the emergence of the first and second waves of feminism as mass social movements have been widely discussed by feminist scholars. Such writers have argued that modern Western

21

feminism developed when women became conscious that their unnamed 'sense of something wrong' with their lives as women was more than a mere 'personal problem', but was common to other women – a product of broader social inequalities.[14] According to socialist feminists, women's lives in the post-war Western world have been structured by contradictory sets of expectations (experienced as 'conflict' or 'tension'), the origins of which are materially grounded in the dynamics of class, race and gender relations in patriarchal-capitalist societies. Such analyses of post-war Western societies have identified contradictory expectations for women's work and sexuality, and education as an important site for the reproduction of such contradictions.[15]

The dominant liberal ideology of the post-war years promised equality of educational and vocational opportunity, limited only on 'merit'. However, social policies were premised on the assumption that the patriarchal nuclear family (with domesticated wife and male breadwinner) was to be the very basis of post-war society. Married women were to be both equal, and subordinate, to men. Such contradictions were particularly evident in post-war educational policy documents, which expressed aims of educating girls simultaneously for jobs/careers and for domesticity. During the post-war years there were rapid and drastic fluctuations in demand for what Marx called the 'reserve army' of married women's labour. Urged to give up their war-time jobs to returned servicemen, married women were warned that working outside the home could cause 'maternal deprivation', which would lead to delinquency in children. However, labour shortages in the 1950s and 1960s caused employers to demand once more married women's labour, particularly in teaching. Girls at school in the post-war years, particularly those in 'academic' streams, experienced confusing and contradictory images of the 'working woman'.[16]

Similarly, female sexuality embodied contradictions. The traditional sexual double standard constructed two ideal types of women: 'good' women (virgins, then monogamous wives) and 'bad' women (whores or sluts). Sociologists have analysed schooling as reproducing this double standard.[17] In New Zealand, the double standard was reproduced in secondary school streaming practices. Academic stream girls were expected to delay sexual activity until they had completed their tertiary education; such girls frequently stereotyped girls in lower, or 'non-academic', streams, as more sexually active than academic girls.[18] Sexuality and intellectuality/professionality were socially constructed as contradictory.

During the 1960s and 1970s contradictions became evident in different constructions of female sexuality. According to Mary O'Brien,[19] improvements in contraceptive technology, such as 'the pill' removed the material and conceptual base of the sexual double standard. The ideas of the 'sexual revolution' urged women, as well as men, to explore their sexuality freely. Young women, brought up to conform to the sexual ideal of virginity followed by monogamous marriage, were now urged to conform to the alternative image of the 'swinging chick'. Feminist scholars such as Firestone, Mitchell and Rowbotham have analysed women's experiences of this contradiction as stressful and as out-comes largely of male fantasies as depicted in the capitalist-patriarchal mass media – the 'playmate', the 'pet', the 'page three girl'. Such images, they argued, served to alienate many women from their own bodies and created the pre-conditions for a feminist questioning of the basis of their construction.[20]

Post-war 'educated' women, then, including those training to become teachers, experienced contradictions between their femininity and their intellectuality/professionality and between conflicting constructions of their sexuality.

However, formal education does more than merely reproduce social inequalities and contradictions. Feminists have analysed education as also being important in their political radicaliza-tion.[21] One reason given has been that the increased availability of secondary and higher education in the post-war years offered many more women than ever before the possibility of 'careers' with financial independence and intellectual stimulation. The generous government financial assistance offered to school leavers willing to train as teachers during the 'teacher shortages' of the baby boom years made it possible for working-class, less-well-off middle-class and rural girls and boys to experience university and/or teachers' college. However, many such recruits, the first in their families to be so highly educated, have since written of strong feelings of alienation or marginality in bourgeois academic settings. These experiences have been described in fiction[22] in sociological studies[23] and in autobiographical accounts.[24] Such experiences of lacking what counts as academic cultural capital[25] are often painful. Education provided many such students with access to radical social theories which helped them to articulate this personal discomfort as a product of wider social oppression: racism and/or capitalism. Such 'left-wing' views were accessible through some academic subjects and through peer-group activities, such as the student protest movements on issues such as race-relations or the Vietnam War.

Many women who later became feminists were previously involved with these movements.[26] Having made theoretical/ political connections between their previously unnamed personal feelings of marginality or alienation (as working class, Black, etc.) in bourgeois white academic settings, many had little difficulty identifying with feminism, when in the early 1970s 'second wave' feminism named and analysed the contradictions specific to them as *women*. What was crucial in these women's politicization was coming across radical ideas at a time and in a form which enabled them to make theoretical connections between the personal and the political. Or, as C. Wright Mills expressed it, private (personal) troubles came to be seen as public (political) issues.[27]

In summary, these analyses suggest that people who develop radical (e.g. feminist) views of the social world have experienced in their lives contradictions and/or a sense of marginality and have access to radical social theories which articulate their private problems as outcomes of structural inequalities in society. The unpleasantness of experiences such as marginality, alienation, or irreconcilable contradictions, makes personal or social change seem desirable. Education helps to make such changes seem possible.

TOWARDS A HISTORY OF MY PRESENT

I shall begin, as Smith recommends, from 'where I am actually situated'. I started writing this chapter on 25 April 1988 – ANZAC Day, our national holiday to commemorate the actions, and mourn the deaths, of those who fought in wars. It was a warm and golden autumn afternoon. Our feet crackled against the fallen crisp leaves – maples and oaks. The trees glowed purple, red, orange and yellow.

By this time, you who are reading this in the northern hemisphere will be experiencing some degree of 'distancing' or 'alienation' from my text – a feeling similar to that experienced by my generation of children in New Zealand. The poems we read sang of April showers in spring. At Christmas we ate hot turkey and plum pudding, while sweltering in the December summer heat. The beach '*baches*'[28] we stayed in were festooned for the summer with Christmas cards depicting icicles and snow. While you northern readers may feel alienated by the geographical orientation of my account, there are other aspects of it which probably seem familiar, such as the deciduous maples and oaks. Here, however, these trees signify colonization. About a mile from the park I am describing here, is the city's last surviving stand of 'native bush' – the lush evergreen forest that once covered most of this land.

This ANZAC Day I went with George (my husband) and some university friends to the cenotaph to look at the wreaths laid in the ceremony earlier in the day. The sociologists among us joked about how we were there to do a semiotic analysis of the wreaths. We walked through the park on the banks of the Waikato River. At school, when she was 5, my daughter, Kate (now aged 11) learned a *waiata* (song) from her school's itinerant teacher of Maori language:

Tainui te waka	Tainui is the canoe (tribe)
Taupiri te maunga	Taupiri is the mountain
Waikato te awa	Waikato is the river
He piko he taniwha	At every bend a taniwha
Haere mai, haere mai	Welcome! Welcome![29]

We sang no such songs when I was at school.... As we walk through the park one of the small children with us points to a stone cairn and says, 'There's a World War Two memorial'. It stands beside the rusting hulk of the SS *Rangiriri* reputed to have been a gunboat during the nineteenth century in what are now known as the Land Wars. When I was at school, they were known as the Maori Wars. The SS *Rangiriri* has a new wooden deck with seats for weekend picnickers or strollers. The stone cairn, I tell the child, has nothing to do with World War Two, but is a 'monument to the first Pakeha (White) settlers'. We arrive at the cenotaph – a grey concrete erection. I walk slowly around the lower steps of the monument. I have never been so close to such a monument before. As a child I had learned to feel that walking on the steps of a monument was as taboo as playing in the sanctuary in the (Anglican) church. One of the wreaths is made from dense clusters of fiery bronze miniature chrysanthemums – similar to those remembered from my primary school days.

25

I attended two primary schools. The first was in a country town of about 2,000 people, about 10 miles from a provincial city (population around 20,000–30,000). When I was about 7, we moved – because of my father's job – to a smaller town (about 800 people) about 30 miles from the nearest small city. Here I attended the primary department of the local district high school. There were many 'bus children' – several hundred children in the school altogether. We had a religious service there each year the day before the ANZAC Day holiday. We stood solemnly in lines around the stone shaft of the monument in the school grounds. We sang 'Abide With Me'; someone played 'The Last Post' on a bugle – long and sad. Local men whom we knew well as friends' fathers, as local businessmen, or farmers, appeared at this time in unfamiliar dark suits – representing the unknown and invisible worlds of adult male power and authority: as 'members of the school committee', 'representing the Returned Servicemen's Association' (RSA), or 'from the town board'. Awed by the pomp and ceremony and embarrassed at the uncustomary expression of feeling in our normally tight-lipped Pakeha rural community, we children adopted freely the solemnity of the occasion. Sometimes we were also involved in the parades on the Day itself. I have vague memories of being there once in my Girls' Life Brigade uniform. There were a few women in the parade – WAAFS, WRNZNS, WAACS, nurses. The district nurse, a single woman and family friend, marched and, like the men, had medals. The men 'had a beer' together – the RSA wives baked and catered. The war widows were always remembered and cared for. Sometimes some Pakeha men would attend the *hangi* at a nearby *marae*,[30] for Maori soldiers – such as the Maori Battalion – had been heroes. This was the only such intercultural socializing I can remember.

At secondary school ANZAC Day was also important. I boarded in the hostel attached to the state girls' school in our nearest provincial city. I played the piano often for the school choirs and massed singing at assemblies. I sang in choirs. Our religious services were musically highly sophisticated: hymns in four – sometimes more – parts. The older teachers fought back their tears – we thought they cried for all the young men in their lives who had been killed or damaged; brothers, fathers, husbands, fiancés, lovers. We constructed elaborate myths around the lives of 'attractive but single' women teachers, whose celibate state, we presumed could have been caused by having a fiancé killed in the war. To be 'an old maid left on the shelf' for any other reason was, to our adolescent minds, an inexcusable failure. Our parents' lives were periodized by 'the war'. They spoke of 'before the war', 'during the war' and 'since the war'. My parents were engaged before the war, separated during it, married after it. During the war, my mother lived in Auckland, where she had spent much of her childhood. Her 'war work' was typing telegrams in the Post Office – news of death. My father drove a tank – spent time in Egypt, Italy, Palestine, India. He had photos of himself and his 'mates' standing on 'the pyramids'. I wanted to travel. At secondary school both World Wars loomed large in our curriculum-history lessons on their 'causes and effects', poems by the doomed young men who were the 'war poets'. There were other wars: the bloodiness of Shakespeare, and Latin translations which told of Cicero and his legions or Hannibal leading his troops (and elephants) over the mountains. We were recommended to read books about World War Two heroes, such as *The Wooden Horse*. In their spare time, many girls read of women spies – Odette, Violet Szabo, members of the French Resistance. There were women who were strong, brilliant and brave, but they remained largely invisible or marginal to the curriculum and our recreational reading. At Sunday School I had learned about courageous 'medical missionaries' – women were doctors but more commonly nurses. Nurses, however, could go to war, or work in 'the jungle'. In childhood reading I found only one New Zealand heroine – when I read Sylvia Ashton-Warner's novel, *Spinster*. This offered a critique of the rigidities of 'alien' curricula. She had worked to discover the 'natural language' of Maori children. She portrayed teaching as a glamorous art. If I taught, I would teach like that. She pre-dated Friere by many years.

It was always assumed that I would be a teacher. Both my parents had been bright, but unable to have tertiary education. My father was one of the younger children of a large family who had suffered financially during 'The Depression'. The two eldest sons, and only daughter, had 'passed their matric' then 'gone to training college' in Wellington. However, when my father's turn came to go, the government closed the college as a cost-cutting measure. My father took a job as junior with a stock and station agency firm. Eventually he was to work as a 'stock and station agent' – a person who liaises between farmers in the buying and selling of livestock. It involves a great deal of driving – taking farmers to sales, etc. As a child I accompanied my father and the farmers on many long drives. Unlike many city children, I came to understand a little of what was involved in my father's work. He was closely involved in the up-bringing of my brother and myself. His hours of work were long, involving late-night telephone conversations and a certain amount of entertaining. My mother was an excellent cook and a sociable person, who enjoyed these occasions. She was 'artistic': creative in her domestic work – original in the clothes she sewed, the meals she prepared. Her life too had been shaped by the Depression. Her own family life had been difficult and by her mid-teens she was 'orphaned'. Unlike my father, she had not completed high school or sat her 'matric', but instead had 'gone to tech' and taken a commercial course (shorthand and typing). During the war, however, she had attended evening courses run by the WEA (Workers' Educational Association) – music appreciation (classical), art appreciation, English literature. She loved ballet and other things of the city.

It was assumed that I would finish secondary school, then go to a city and train as a primary school teacher. Although my true vocation as a woman was to get married and have children, it was also seen as important for me to 'have a life' beforehand. My parents' generation had been cheated of their youth and wished their children to have the 'opportunities' they never had. Teaching would enable me to 'use my brain' and to experience city life. It was also seen as a 'secure' occupation – there was a 'teacher shortage' and teachers would always be able to find work. A woman should always be able to support herself – before marriage, or in case she didn't marry (seen as a great misfortune), or if she was widowed. As a means of employment teaching would always be 'something to fall back on' in times of need. For many of those who had experienced hard times during the Depression, these reasons were central to their encouragement of their daughters' education. I was provided in my family with academic 'cultural capital' – I was 'read to', taken to town for concerts and ballets, I learned classical piano from nuns at the local convent. And at great financial sacrifice, I was to be sent away at 13 to boarding school so that I could take Latin and French.

While my aspirations were 'urban', another part of me was oriented to the countryside and to the little town in which I grew up. Local farmers lent me ponies. We children commanded what now seem to me vast territories in our play. We rode our ponies, or our bikes, far into the countryside. We experienced the limits of such daily activities in terms of daylight hours and technology rather than parental restriction. The boys had secret 'huts' and we girls had our 'secret clubs', modelled on those in English Enid Blyton books. We searched for, but deep inside we knew that we would not find, crumbling stone secret passages beneath the rusty corrugated iron shed where we held our meetings. I knew a family who lived high on a hill farm up a narrow winding gravel road. Their house was old and dark inside, with oak panelling – the first I had seen – in the hallway. I tapped at the panels, and found one to be hollow – the sure test, in Enid Blyton books, of the existence of the entrance to a secret passage, which would almost inevitably lead to glories such as the discovery of stolen treasure, or the apprehension of 'crooks'. However, this hollow sound was explained to me as being 'where the old wardrobe had been'. I was told later that the wife of the house, a close friend of my mother, had thought of hiding a 'string of Woolworths pearls' there for me to find. I was told I had a very lively 'imagination'. In our early adolescence we girls read English comics and girls' annuals – *School Friend* and *Girls' Crystal*. Our books and comics told of dramas at English girls' boarding schools: we absorbed what Frith[31] has described as 'the ritualistic conventions of the school story narrative... the recurrent stereotypes (the snob, the sneak, the comically inadequate 'Mamselle', the heroine who succeeds at everything and ends up as head girl)'.

England was still seen by our parents' generation as the source of 'good things' – the best quality winter clothes, the best cars, our literary heritage, good manners and correct speech. To go there, for many Pakeha,[32] was a pilgrimage. Farmers' daughters and teachers from the district 'saved up' and 'went for a trip to England'. They travelled third class on huge passenger liners. I listened avidly when my mother had friends in for tea in the kitchen, as they read excerpts from letters sent by daughters in London: they worked as au pairs, or nurses, nannies, waitresses. They saved hard for tickets 'up in the gods' at West End theatres. I longed to do this. At secondary school many of our teachers were from England, had been there (and to Europe, which was referred to as 'the Continent'), or were 'saving up' to go there. Travel for single working women seemed both desirable and possible. I also had relatives – on my paternal grandmother's side (the only grandparent still alive in my lifetime), who had been to Denmark to meet relations there. I identified quite closely with my Danish and my Scottish, rather than my English, ancestry.

However, such dreams of Britain and Europe were of 'travel and adventure' for a few years only – never of permanent emigration. As a fourth-generation Pakeha New Zealander, I never thought of England as home – New Zealand was not like the England of the comics and the story books, and I longed for things 'of here'. I asked my parents for a greenstone *tiki*[33] one year for Christmas, and bought myself a book of 'Maori legends' with a book token given to me as a present. My skin was olive and tanned a deep chocolate brown in summer. Children teased me that I must have 'Maori blood'. I wished I had – it would make me a 'real' New Zealander. I was too dark to be the fairy in school plays. 'Beautiful' was blonde and petite. I was tall with big feet. I tripped when I ran in races. I was too 'dreamy' to be good at sport – too 'bookish' or 'arty'. I longed for town and boarding school, where I would fit perfectly into the culture of the school stories. At 11 I menstruated. I hated the subterfuge it entailed. One 'didn't discuss it with men' and this 'estranged' me from men who were important to me – my father, my brother, my male phys ed teacher. There was a lie, a 'secret' between us. I wore a brown cardigan buttoned up to hide my budding breasts all through one hot summer.

At 13 I left home permanently – to board at Girls' High School. It was a tremendous financial sacrifice on the part of my parents. Because I took Latin, I was awarded a government academic boarding bursary for children whose local schools could not provide academic subjects. To keep the bursary, I had to continue with Latin. I lived in terror of academic failure and worked excessively at all I undertook.

I remember that moment clearly. I was about 14, standing well-back in an orderly queue. It was the weekly shoe and badge inspection. I had polished my blue and gold enamelled badge with its gleaming motto, *ad astra*. I had polished my brown leather shoes to a burnished shine. The prefect waiting at the end of the queue 'passed' my efforts, and I gladly returned my shoes to the shoe-room. As I walked on the polished linoleum down the long oak-panelled passages, I decided, 'Some day, when I'm grown up, I'll write about how boarding school really is'.

At the time, I felt there was 'something wrong' with me. Everyone told me how lucky I was to have all my opportunities. But now, looking back, I think I was stifled by the constant surveillance, the rigorous discipline, the overcrowding, the lack of personal space (physical, emotional, intellectual) which can characterize 'total institutions' such as boarding schools.[34] In the boarding house, the time and the whereabouts of nearly 200 girls was continually surveyed and monitored. We got up at a set time and ate breakfast under the watchful eyes of teachers, matrons and prefects – at least one of these to every table of girls. The Headmistress of the day school also 'lived in' the boarding house. A single lady in her fifties, she took a deep interest in the lives and 'personalities' of the girls.

The hostel building had been the original school. It was two-storied and wooden, with wooden mock 'brick-work' at the corners to make it look like stone – Edwardian, drafty, and cold. Each storey had a row of tall sash windows. Beneath those on the second storey ran a narrow balcony, interrupted here and there by flimsy folding metal ladders – the fire escape. Regularly we would have fire drill, as fire was a serious worry in our old building. The fire escapes, however, presented the school with a security problem – girls getting out, and 'prowlers' getting in. Girls caught 'escaping' for the night to go partying with day-girl friends were expelled. For highly career-motivated girls like me, risking this was unthinkable.

I became in some ways a 'goody goody' in a desperate drive to achieve the necessary academic and musical hurdles which would make possible my escape to the freedom of the city. My French teacher introduced us to French intellectuals: existentialists – some of them women, like Simone de Beauvoir. I would live in a garret in Paris – painting, playing music, or writing. I would never marry – never surrender my independence. I might passionately 'live with' somebody. But such thoughts were so scandalous in my puritan childhood that I would have to run away as far as Paris to be able to do so. To get away with such a Bohemian lifestyle, however, a woman had to be extraordinarily talented. I worked hard at my piano – sat Royal Schools examinations, passed Grade Eight. Accompanied singers for their exams. Played 'pop by ear' for dancing. My 'pop', however, was never taken seriously. Some of the 'non-serious' music students learned 'modern' – I listened to them practise and copied their 'vamp'. But 'pop' or jazz were strictly limited to 'recreation'. I was also 'good at art'. However, I could not take it as an examination subject because it clashed in the timetable with some of the subjects seen as 'academic'. I loved to write and kept diaries. Everything I wrote could possibly be read by the prying matrons, who rifled through our drawers and peeked beneath loose dormitory floorboards. I could not, therefore, express my deepest feelings freely. Terrified of discovery, I burned my diaries shortly before leaving school. It was assumed by this time that I would become a secondary, rather than a primary, school teacher: I was considered 'too bright' for primary teachers' college. Since the post-primary teachers' studentships paid salaries to students prepared to 'bond' themselves to teaching, I could be self-supporting – independent – while undertaking full-time university studies. I was not confident about my ability to teach, but desperately wanted to go to university – like the women who taught me. It was also essential to be financially free of my parents. I felt guilty about the sacrifices they had made for the sake of my, and my brother's education. So that was what I did.

At the end of the fourth form (the second year at secondary school) I dropped science and mathematics. I had been 'good at' both, however failed to see the point of much of the teaching. Maths and science teachers were scarce, especially in girls' schools – such teachers were recruited from overseas or brought out of retirement. My imagination, however, was captured by other subjects. History I adored. My teachers were young, single women, who had travelled. They described their visits to castles and cathedrals – I learned of a relationship between architectural style and society and culture. English literature spoke of the great human passions – mainly male. But there was also the suppressed claustrophobia of Jane Austen's heroines – resonant of my boarding school life. I identified with Thomas Hardy's Grace in *The Woodlanders* – boarding-school educated, she was alienated from both her rural origins and the urban bourgeoisie to which her parents aspired. But, most of all I was inspired by an elderly Austrian man, who taught me geography: he was reputed to have fought for the Kaiser in World War One, and had motorbiked from Cairo to Capetown. He had made his own movies and photographed his adventures. Geography brought the outside world into my cloistered life. I learned of exotic cultures and of the mysteries of the earth: volcanoes, earthquakes, weather and soils. The subject matter connected with my childhood in the country and gave me theoretical explanations of life in my home town – farming patterns, the economic bases of country towns. I was later to major in geography at university, where it was to be one of the major sources in my life of 'radical ideas' with which to begin articulating my sense of marginality in terms of class.

We had been brought up to believe that we lived in a 'classless society'. However, from the time my family moved, when I was 7, from one country town to another smaller one, I had a knowledge of local class relations. My first day at school, I was teased because I 'talked la de dah – posh', and had learned ballet. Our family often listened to the non-commercial Wellington radio station (New Zealand's equivalent of the BBC) – my friends listened to commercial radio. We heard British comedy shows – 'The Goons', 'Hancock's Half Hour'; my friends didn't think them funny. We were considered strange. There were several 'important' farming families in the district. They were very wealthy, and sent their children away to board at private schools. Although they attended primary school with us, by secondary school, teenage friendships were becoming more stratified on class lines. The 'private school kids' had a social network which extended throughout rural New Zealand. They had a 'season' of private balls and dances. Some of us state school boarders would get the occasional 'invite' to one of these. The freezing-workers' and labourers' children from the small town remained there; those whose fathers owned shops or other small businesses sometimes, like me, boarded at state schools.[35]

Our secondary school occupied an ambivalent position in the class structure of its provincial city. Originally, it had been a private school, but for many years had been a state school. The old buildings were used as the hostel. Junior boarders walked the 2 miles from the hostel to the modern concrete school, with its 600 girl pupils. They walked in 'crocodile' – a prefect at the back. Our brother school, Boys' High School, had previously been the local co-educational 'tech'. Our school choir joined Boys' High for joint productions of Gilbert and Sullivan operas and we also went to dances there. There was another local boys' school – Boys' College – which was expensive and Church of England; it was modelled on the English public school. Selected girls would be invited to dances there. We also partnered the College boys at regular ballroom dancing classes – the waltz, the quick-step, 'old time' and Latin American. Those of us in the choir joined their choir for performances in their chapel of 'The Messiah'. Boys' College's 'sister school' was an Anglican boarding school in the country several hours' drive away. Many years later, I was told by an ex-College boy that they 'used to practise dancing with the Girls' High girls as preparation for the 'real dances' with the [private school] girls'. On my first night at the hostel, I was asked by a senior, 'Are you Tech or College?'. I wasn't then 'into boys' and said it was silly to have to choose – I was sure there were 'nice boys' at both. In this, as in many other things, I refused to choose, had friends at both, went to two lots of dances and sang both Handel and Gilbert and Sullivan. I resisted allowing myself to get interested in boys sexually – even then I associated 'sex' with loss of choice. In my first week, I wrote in an English essay that I wondered how I'd settle in at boarding school, as I disliked the 'three most popular things there: knitting, boys, and custard'.

Our sexuality was constantly regulated and monitored. In analysing the processes in which this takes place, Foucault's discussion of secondary schools is useful:

> On the whole one can have the impression that sex was hardly spoken of at all in these institutions. But one has only to glance at the architectural layout, the rules of discipline, and their whole internal organization: the question of sex was a constant preoccupation.... What one might call the internal discourse of the institution... was based largely on this assumption that this sexuality existed, that it was precocious, active, and ever present.[36]

For example, 'the architectural layout' became problematic in terms of how to make Edwardian buildings safe for girls – both easy to get out of in case of fire, and hard to get into, in the case of 'prowlers'. To this day I cannot sleep in a house with open windows. There was a 'panty snatcher' who stole our underwear from lines. It felt 'yucky' – we had no word for it. In crocodile we were whistled at, our legs jeered at, our uniforms mocked. Uniforms made us shapeless and drab. For dances we wore special dresses: most fashionable were bronze satins with bell shirts, gold stilettoes. Shoe-string straps were not allowed. Teachers searched the gardens with torches in search of couples 'pashing'. Love-bites were frowned upon. The music was local versions of The Shadows. Girls lined up alongside one side of the hall, boys the other. When the MC said 'Gentlemen take your partners' the boys charged across the 'no-one's land' in the centre, making a beeline for the girl in his line of sight. Girlfriends and boyfriends had previously positioned themselves in relation to each other. I was short-sighted and believed the myth of the time that 'Boys don't make passes at girls who wear glasses'. I was therefore dependent on friends to tell me who was where so that I could decide whether to duck behind a post, make myself visible, or flee to the 'ladies' – the refuge of the tearful.

Factual information about 'sex' was difficult to come by. There were a few girls who were reputed to have gone 'all the way', but few of us knew exactly what that entailed, except that it almost invariably led to pregnancy and 'shot-gun' marriages. We all knew of girls who 'had to' get married. There was no Domestic Purposes Benefit until 1972. At school we were taught about 'reproduction' in fourth form general science: the pollination of flowers, the reproductive cycle of the rabbit. There were the long-awaited lessons on 'human reproduction': we drew diagrams of our 'reproductive organs' – we learned why we got periods, about the growth of the foetus in the womb. We were never told about the act of intercourse: I read about that from a book we found secreted under the floorboards of the prefects' study. So generations of prefects subverted the silencing of sexuality by making available 'the secret' information.

Our school was stratified both intellectually and sexually by its streaming practices. I was in the 'top' third form – 3L – we took Latin and French. On my first day, I felt 'left out' – marginalized – as the form teacher identified individual town girls whose family connections made them already part of the elite of the school: 'The head girl's sister', 'R, whose mother is on the staff', 'P, whose mother's on the Board of Governors'. These girls had been to Intermediate[37] and had 'done some French and algebra'. I learned that girls from country schools were expected to be 'behind' academically. Riddled with anxiety at the possible collapse of my dreams, I 'swotted' and came second in the class. By my final (seventh form) year, I was head girl at the hostel and, in the day school, a prefect and a house captain. That year, to relieve our arduous academic studies, the headmistress introduced 'Cooking' for relaxation. However, we did not that year bake the scones and pikelets we had made in the junior classes or which the girls 'down in homecraft' streams produced. We did 'continental cooking' in preparation for adult status as bourgeois wives.

The seventh form also brought 'current events' with the head-mistress, who was deeply devoted to British royalty, traditions and the Empire. Already, because of my feelings of marginality in class hierarchies, I was becoming anti-royalist and devoted to the idea of meritocracy – no-one, I believed, should inherit privilege. But I knew no-one else with these 'funny ideas'. General Elections saw nearly all the hostel girls supporting the National Party – the traditional ally of the New Zealand farmer. After all, the farmers were the 'backbone of the nation' – economically, New Zealand was Britain's outlying farm. However, we saw the Empire disintegrate as one British colony after another won its independence. I read Joyce Cary's *Mr Johnson* in English that year. I was beginning to question the rightness of colonization, but did not have the theoretical tools with which to articulate this. The headmistress told my mother I had a 'thing' about Apartheid and did I have Maori blood?

Victoria University of Wellington brought the long-awaited 'freedom'. For two years I lived in a women's hall of residence, then 'went flatting'. During term-time I supplemented my studentship with odd babysitting jobs; during the long vacations I worked in shops and offices. In the Hall and at university I met 'overseas students' from Asia and the Pacific and New Zealand girls – daughters of diplomats or military officers – who had lived overseas. I majored in geography and was strongly influenced by a 'left-wing humanist' professor, Keith Buchanan,[38] who taught us about the 'Third World' as a product of capitalist imperialism – the works of Fanon and Marcuse influenced his lectures. I experienced then, in the mid-1960s, what today's anti-racist activists refer to as 'white guilt'. I marched against the Vietnam War. I took Maori studies, which helped me see connections between the position of Maoris in New Zealand and that of non-white peoples of the Third World. I decided I was a 'communist'. In the holidays I had loud arguments with my father and his friends about 'politics'. At university I was an ignorant, conservative 'country bumpkin'; in my home-town I seemed the 'hippy radical'. I was confused and insecure – marginal in both worlds.

I studied piano with a European woman, who despised New Zealanders because she saw us as 'English'; I scraped through my university examination in musical performance and never played again for twenty years. In French I had women lecturers who inspired in me a love of social theory – the Enlightenment thinkers and, once more, the exotic Parisian Existentialists – reviving teenage fantasies of artistic Bohemian cafés on the Left Bank. I somehow found and read Erich Fromm's *Art of Loving* and, later, his *Fear of Freedom* which explained for me many of my adolescent insecurities. I took 'Education I', but it involved tedious rote learning from American texts. Although I scored the only A pass in my BA in that subject, I did not continue it because in the second year one had to 'do statistics' and I 'couldn't do maths'. I avoided stats throughout my degree, which excluded most of the social sciences. Through my education tutor, I did voluntary work with 'special class' children.[39] In English, we studied some New Zealand literature. I did not enjoy it – I realize now that it spoke only of male experience. My own struggles and confusion in my 'private' life were barely visible in the curriculum – however, I identified closely with Dorothea in George Eliot's *Middlemarch*.

As young women, we were under great pressure sexually. Many such students became engaged to steady boyfriends. Regarding marriage as a trap, I avoided 'getting serious', while feeling desperately inadequate if I didn't have a date on Saturday night. Uncommonly for the times, 'the pill' was freely available to students on our campus and who was 'on it' was a matter of considerable interest in the Halls. I went to balls, sang and danced in the student capping review, helped with floats in the capping procession, fell in and out of love and completed my degree in the minimum three years, with steady B passes.

In 1969, I headed south to a one-year secondary teachers' course. The Teachers' College was a stone building designed a hundred years before by an English architect. The classrooms all faced south – the direction of the biting Antarctic winds. The northern sun poured into the corridors. I had gone to the South Island for my one-year 'grad' course so that I could see the South Island. Because of my radicalization in Keith Buchanan's human geography courses at university, at that time I saw geography as a means of radicalizing students. I also had an empathy for children with 'difficulties' and a strong sense of outrage at the colonial racist orientation of the curriculum. Teachers' College, however, worked on different assumptions. In pedagogy we learned about behavioural objectives (BOs) and topic analyses (TAs). To teach successfully, all one had to do was analyse one's 'topic' and present it in a form appropriate to the child's 'level of readiness'. Problems such as 'what should count as worthwhile knowledge' were not raised. Teaching was made out to be a set of scientific/techno-logical problems. We prepared our lesson plans according to a set formula: we had to design hierarchies of questions we would ask the children. If the lesson failed, we were told, it was because we hadn't prepared the topic or the questions correctly or had pitched it inappropriately to the pupils' level of readiness. I felt alienated from this approach, but could not yet articulate my reasons.

There were also some positive aspects to college: I learned classical guitar and taught myself folk and rock styles and in drama I played the role of a demented nun in *The Devils*. One of my flatmates brought home Betty Friedan's *The Feminine Mystique*. We all read it avidly – it was 1969. Not yet part of any visible women's movement, we agreed with its arguments: women should retain their autonomy. As someone who would 'never marry' and would always be financially self-supporting, I felt excited and validated by the book, although it seemed to speak for 'older women' rather than my 'liberated' generation.

My first teaching position was in the South Island. It was a large school in a country town about half an hour's drive from a major city. I lived in the city and commuted to the school. I was given a heavy teaching load: a class of fifth formers 'repeating' School Certificate for English, and another for geography; the 'Ag and Tech boys' for social studies, the fourth form 'Commercial girls' for English, the fifth stream third form for French, and miscellaneous one-off current events sessions. I taught guitar in the lunch hours and helped with the school musical, 'Wild Violets'. I worked late into the night on my TAs and BOs, but they couldn't help me deal adequately with Janice in 3D who slashed her wrists with broken glass, or Sally, the milk-bottle money thief. It snowed, I became ill with recurring infections, bronchitis and flu. The 'free periods' allowed me as a first-year teacher were taken for relieving – for example, I would find myself thrown in for two periods with 4G in the chemistry lab with no books. The elderly woman who came to 'inspect' me awarded me my 'Trained Teachers' Certificate' a few days before I ended up in hospital with a minor 'breakdown' – anxiety/depression and sheer exhaustion. She asked what she could do to help – she saw potential in me as a teacher. I asked for release from my 'two-year clause'.[40] From hospital I applied for a position in another co-educational school, this time in a dormitory suburb near Wellington. I had heard of the school's 'child-centred' English programme, where the children chose the themes to be studied. Remembering Sylvia Ashton-Warner, and repelled by the clinical 'technocratic rationality' of college days, this felt right to me. The principal flew to Dunedin to interview me. A woman who'd 'had a breakdown' (even one of only four weeks' duration) was seen as a risk. He gave me the job and thus helped my survival as a teacher. I completed my year's teaching in the south, then began my job at my new college.

There I spent a stimulating two years. That year, I became close friends with older women – who had lived exciting lives. They had travelled, they had had 'lovers', they had 'careers' and they were single by choice. One of them in particular guided my 'professional reading' and thus gave me a theoretical critique of 'technocratic rationality' as well as a rationale for the child-centred programme we were running in English and social studies – there were 'progressive' books on language, and the popular 'education' paperbacks of the time – I read books by John Holt and Herbert Kohl as well as Postman and Weingartner's *Teaching as a Subversive Activity*. I moved towards a more individualized approach so that not all children were necessarily studying the same theme. For the first time, my sense of personal discomfort with aspects of education was being validated, named, articulated theoretically. I taught the guitar in lunch hours and some evenings sang in a folk club and performed in a coffee bar; Joan Baez, Donovan, Dylan – 'protest' songs, which I also used as poems in my English and social studies classes. When Germaine Greer toured New Zealand in 1972, I did not hear her speak – but I read her book, *The Female Eunuch*. Its anarchistic 'do your own thing' message expressed a lot of what I felt – I was definitely a 'women's libber'. By the end of that year, I had taught the three years needed to pay off my bond. Now I could travel.

I went with two women friends – by sea up the coast of South-East Asia, youth hostelling in Japan, then across the Trans-Siberian railway. We hitch-hiked and youth hostelled our way round Scandinavia and continental Europe. I ate escargots on the Left Bank. In London I worked as a waitress, a clerk, an au pair. I was a digger on an archaeology site in Edinburgh. With my guitar I 'busked' in London tube stations. I sat 'in the gods' at West End shows. I also visited schools in several countries and helped with music and drama at a South London free school. My left-wing political leanings, my anti-racism and my 'free-school' or 'child-centred' educational philosophy were confirmed, deepened and developed during my year of travels.

I arrived back in New Zealand broke. I needed a job quickly. I had already decided not to return to secondary school teaching: I hated the constrictions public examinations imposed on the teaching of senior classes and preferred teaching the third or fourth formers. I decided to try an intermediate school. With no primary teacher training, I became a 'supernumerary' teacher[41] in an intermediate school in a working-class multicultural satellite city near Wellington. The principal informed me, as I outlined my views on 'child-centred' teaching, that 'These children have no background' and 'These children can't handle freedom'. 'These children,' I was told, 'needed discipline'. There were few women teaching in the classrooms. Tall, broad-shouldered rugby-playing men had with 'these children' a natural authority. Maori and Polynesian women teachers were culturally respected. As a white woman, I had to 'prove my toughness' – with the staff as well as the children.

As a supernumerary on the staff, I ran the stationery shop, and was then to take over the remedial reading programme. I began to prepare a child-centred programme for this. However, due to staff sicknesses I was used 'relieving'. In the first week, a 'special class' boy threw a knife at me; in other classes children were restless and noisy. I was told by the principal that I was 'too soft' and should be a social worker rather than a teacher. I was angry at this, applied for and won a permanent position on the staff. Gradually the children and I became used to one another and I was able to introduce 'themes' and 'individual or group choices' as central in the day's routines. We made movies and tape-slide sequences; we wrote books illustrated with photographs taken by the children. Music, art, poetry and drama were part of the children's 'academic' inquiries. The parents were enthusiastic because their children liked coming to school. The inspector who graded me was supportive. Previously, my support had come from a group of staff: Maori, Pacific Island, British and a few Pakeha teachers, all in our late twenties or early thirties. We gathered on Fridays in the pub, where the staffs of thirteen schools armed with guitars attempted to 'out-sing' each other. We could really sing – in four, even more, parts. We had a harmony too in our working relationships, despite the oppressive puritanism at the top. I met George – a Welshman – also on the staff. We lived together. The school had a now-famous Polynesian Club run by Maori and Pacific Island (mainly Rarotongan) teachers. Each year, they gave a concert. In my final year there, some Pakeha staff expressed concern at the under-valuing of 'Pakeha culture'. The principal, who 'took the choir', decided to put on a 'rock opera'. It was not until the dress rehearsal that we saw what he had done. It was the Bible story of Elijah. The choir children (mainly Pakeha) were cast as the followers of Yaweh, the One true God; the Polynesian Club children (in Maori costumes bought at great expense for the school by parents) were the worshippers of Baal, the heathen god.

I won my first senior position at a nearby primary school, teaching and administering the 'special class'. I wanted to prove that my approach would work with 'slow-learner' as well as 'bright or average' children. Drawing on Sylvia Ashton-Warner's 'key words' scheme for inspiration, I helped the children make their own readers; using the models and costumes they produced, we devised and captioned photo-sequences. We made science fiction movies, we photographed slide sequences. The children were 'succeeding' at what they undertook. For once, the 'special class' had something to show off in assemblies. The acting principal and other associates said I wasn't teaching properly – 'these children' needed 'structure'; I should persevere with the graded readers (with which they had been previously 'failed'). They called in 'the advisors'.

By this time I had also returned to university part-time to study education; higher qualifications would, I felt, give me theoretical ammunition. I drove to lectures after school for my Dip.Ed., even struggling with the dreaded statistics. I scored A+ passes. George 'coached' me through the stats. We decided to marry and to try for a baby. I left teaching towards the end of my pregnancy and returned to full-time study, always intending to return to primary school teaching.

How did I become a sociologist of women's education? I completed my Dip.Ed., then a B.Ed. studies – the equivalent of an Honours year in education. In 1979 I was working on my Masters thesis in the Education Department at Victoria University. I was also teaching an undergraduate course in the sociology of education and tutoring in a philosophy of education course. My 'funny ideas' about teaching were now being given names. In my diploma (completed, because of breast-feeding, extramurally through Massey University), I studied Maori education and curriculum theory. I had written a one-paper 'investigation' in which I recorded and theorized my school teaching practice using the liberal theories of the London School (Hirst and Peters). At last I had theories which enabled me to critique and reject the 'technocratic rationality' that had loomed so large at Teachers' College – I wrote a critique of Skinner's *Beyond Freedom and Dignity*. I read Freire, R.D. Laing and the 'anti-psychiatrists' (who also helped me to theorize my 'breakdown' as resulting from social contradictions rather than from personal weakness). I was strongly attracted to phenomenology, which articulated the importance of the 'personal' dimensions in teaching and I was exploring the possibilities of a phenomenological perspective as a part of teacher education. The thesis was to be called *A Phenomenological Perspective for the Classroom Teacher*. However, by the end of that year it had acquired a longer title, as I added the words ... *and Its Application to the Education of Women*.

For, although I had felt sympathy for 'women's lib' before this time, I had had little, if any, contact with feminists or feminist events. I became more actively involved through contacts at the university crèche. There I became close friends with other 'mature' women students, who had children the same age as Kate. We spent many afternoons in each others' houses, drinking tea or coffee, eating, attending to our children's intermittent demands: 'I'm hungry' ... 'She hit me' ... 'Read me a story' ... We talked at length of our experiences of child-birth, of children's illnesses, of how to 'cope' with all the work we had to do. That year (1979) I went with one of my 'crèche friends' (a lecturer in women's studies) to what was to be the last United Women's Convention in Hamilton – my first visit to this campus. There were over 3,000 women. I met 'lesbian separatists' who wore purple armbands and who confronted 'bourgeois heterosexism' with vigorous demonstration.[42] I heard my first feminist concert, saw my first feminist art. There were workshops at which women discussed 'unmentionable' things – experiences of sexuality, experiences as psychiatric patients. An 'overseas' speaker, Charlotte Bunch, spoke of the importance of 'feminist theory' – I had never heard the term before. I decided that that was what I wanted to do – to develop a feminist theory of education. I returned to my thesis re-charged. I read psychological studies of 'sex-roles'; studies of sex-differences in teacher-pupil classroom interaction. I had not yet discovered feminist 'grand theories'.

In 1980 I moved to Hamilton to take up a position as lecturer in the Education Department at the University of Waikato. I was the first woman lecturer in this department. I felt very isolated and apprehensive about my ability. I began collecting statistical data on the position of women staff in teachers' colleges and universities.[43] I became friendly with several feminist women in the Sociology Department and, through them, avidly 'devoured' volumes of feminist theory. I joined the Committee on Women's Studies and began contributing lectures to courses in its inter-departmental women's studies programme. In 1981 I offered this country's first university course on 'women and education'. My male colleagues at first were dubious about this course and I had to prove to them that there was indeed a 'body of feminist knowledge' to transmit. I found little New Zealand material, and poured much of my intellectual energy into 'maps of feminist educational knowledge': how did the different schools of feminist thought relate to those in educational theory? I read and critiqued from my feminist perspective the various neo-Marxist theories that had begun to dominate the sociology of education. I floated my typology at conferences and published it in journals[44] and then gradually came into contact with like-minded women in other universities within New Zealand and overseas. In my classes I tried to find ways of helping students to use these theories to articulate their own lives and teaching strategies; I theorized and wrote about my teaching practice.[45]

At the same time, I felt continually marginalized as an academic. The newness of my chosen field of study meant that I had to devise my own curriculum. The women's studies programme as a whole was marginal and vulnerable. With no guaranteed staffing of its own, it was maintained by a few women – most in untenured positions. My intellectual 'home base' was continually threatened. In addition, I was fighting for my own tenure at the university. Our university then had different contractual arrangements from those at other campuses – these affected those most recently appointed. Believing our tenure to depend on the maintenance of student numbers in our departments, many of us were alarmed by rumours that our contracts might not be renewed on grounds of financial expediency. We took collective action: thirty-three younger staff from a broad range of departments. Our coming together challenged the hierarchical compartmentalization of knowledge whereby junior staff are often insulated from one another – the pattern Bernstein termed the 'collection code'.[46] Collectively, we undertook research to assess the likely impact our removal as a group would have on the university. We used our statistical data in a position paper, which the union used in negotiations on our behalf. A colleague and I wrote a theoretical paper, which we presented at conferences.[47] We urged that our removal would dramatically affect the balance within departments, since 44 per cent of the women (14 per cent of the men), many of the theorists and radicals, were in the threatened group. At least partly as a result of this activity, most of us gained tenure.

In 1982 I was asked to take over the department's 'multicultural course' on a temporary basis – I ran it for six years. Feeling inadequate as a Pakeha, I sought the help of Maori speakers – school principals, teachers, researchers and community workers. I provided connecting lectures on racism. However, this arrange-ment was adding to the workloads of already over-committed Maori speakers. I wrote and published papers about the theories behind, and strategies developed in, teaching this and the 'women and education' courses. I encouraged the students to theorize their own, and others', experiences of education and their wider political strategies. For example, one student – a photographer – wrote a photo-essay on a street-theatre type protest she had been involved with on ANZAC Day: 'For all the women raped in war' – at the same cenotaph at which this account began.

In my doctoral thesis I wove together the various aspects of my university life and teaching experience: the maps of feminist knowledge, analyses of the compartmentalized and competitive structuring of academic knowledge and the resulting marginal-ization of women's studies, the development of radical teaching strategies. I wanted to know how and why so many post-war-born New Zealand women had become feminists and how their femin-ism influenced their educational practice. I undertook long life-history interviews with feminist teachers and developed collaborative strategies to enable them to participate in theorizing the interview material.[48] My doctorate was awarded in 1985. With this present paper I add my own story to its analysis.

Writing this autobiography has involved me in the process of connecting my personal biography with wider historical events and with the limitations imposed on my personal 'choice' by the 'social structure' of my time and place – the social relations of class, race, gender, town and country. This focus of biography, history and social structure is the central concern of my courses at the University of Waikato. For example, in my undergraduate 'women and education' course, students study women's educational life histories. They encounter these biographies throughout the course. They read about them in their set text (my own collection, *Women and Education in Aotearoa*) and in other set readings: autobiographical accounts, biographies and examples of oral history research. Throughout the course, students are asked to compare their own experiences with those they are reading about and to share these with other students in small-group discussions. Students' biographies thus become important subject matter in the course. A major course requirement is an assignment which requires students to conduct educational life-history interviews with two New Zealand women of different ages and to theorize their lives in terms of the historical events, educational provisions and ideologies, and race/class/gender relations of their time and place. All these activities are designed to help students recognize the constraints and limitations on women's lives in their historical specificity – to question the truth of today's dominant belief that we already have 'freedom of choice' while, at the same time, recognizing people as creative strategists who devise ways of dealing with the limitations and contradictions they experience. I do not require students to share with me their own personal biographies, although they have the option of doing this if they so choose. This is because I respect their right to privacy. Through writing this personal account I have made some formerly private aspects of my own life public and I hope that sharing it with students will give many of them the confidence to scrutinize, analyse and communicate their own.

The two dominant 'messages' I hope to get across in my classes is that change in women's lives (and education) is both desirable and possible. The question of desirability is strange to some of the younger students, who tend to come from privileged backgrounds. Some espouse fundamentalist and other conservative religious views. Contemporary feminism can appear both frightening and alienating to such students. However, women's educational history provides a gentle route to such awareness. They read about nineteenth century New Zealand feminist demands – fired by religious evangelicalism (and the desire for the moral reform of men) rather than liberalism, New Zealand women were the first in the world to achieve the universal franchise – in 1893.[49] They read of women's struggles for formal access to education – they learn how successful New Zealand women were in achieving this. The life-history focus enables them to come to grips with ordinary women's everyday struggles and choices in a restrictive world. Many students discuss these with their mothers and grandmothers. The wealthy learn about the lives of the poor, the Pakeha about the realities of Maori women's lives. We make New Zealand the centre of our academic universe and compare our experiences and decisions here with those of our sisters overseas. We thus break through the 'colonial' experience that academic (including feminist) theories are created 'over there' and take from these what we need to understand our lives – what will assist us to see ourselves with our own eyes.

The sense of change as 'possible' also comes about with our study of women's educational history and contemporary feminist movements in education. Women are not, never have been, and never will be, mere 'passive victims', but have struggled to resist sexism in all dimensions of personal and public life. Our education system has denied us this knowledge – alienated us from our own collective history, casting us adrift in alien seas of male knowledge which constitutes us as marginal, as 'other'.

My other educational strategies have included writing New Zealand feminist material for 'education' and 'sociology' textbooks. I have contributed 'the chapter on feminism' to several local books of readings and recently edited a text for New Zealand university 'women and education' courses (there are now five at undergraduate level and two at graduate level). This work has analysed educational policies and experiences of New Zealand women. In overseas publications I am above all concerned with making visible New Zealanders' ways of looking at the world. For, as I concluded in my book:

> To orient ourselves here in the South Pacific, we need to turn our knowledge map around. Orientation to the northern hemisphere colonises our thoughts, our language, our assumptions. We speak of Europe and North America as the 'west'; yet to the west of Aotearoa lies what Europeans termed 'the far east' and the nations of the 'eastern bloc'. We speak of Australasia as 'down under'. Our everyday reality is still

partly colonial. In international relations, trade and defence these assumptions are beginning to change. Our academic studies, too, require a similar reorientation.[50]

It is 15 May 1988. A few red-brown leaves still cling to denuded branches. They flap in the wind against a leaden sky. It is winter. It is also school holidays. Kate and her cousin are playing Madonna tapes in her bedroom. It is to this generation of girls that my research interests will now turn – to the daughters of feminists, born in times of economic crisis and social upheaval. Can we, the feminist educators nourished in times of hope and plenty, develop analyses and strategies which will help empower them as New Zealand women of the late twentieth and twenty-first centuries?

NOTES

1 I am assuming a knowledge of feminist theory. Liberal feminists aim for equal distribution of the sexes throughout the hierarchies of capitalist society. In contrast the radical theorists (i.e. radical feminists, Marxists and socialist feminists) see women as an oppressed class rather than as disadvantaged individuals. Radical feminism is a set of theories centred on the analysis of male power (patriarchy) as the cause of women's oppression. Marxist feminists see women's oppression as a product of class relations under capitalism. Socialist feminists see both patriarchy and capitalism as causing women's oppression – the elimination of one, but not both, will not liberate women. For discussion of the various positions, see Eisenstein, Z. (1981) *The Radical Future of Liberal Feminism*, New York: Longman; or Segal, L. (1987) *Is The Future Female?*, London: Virago.
2 Spender, D. (1981) 'Education: The patriarchal paradigm' in Spender, D. (ed.) *Men's Studies Modified*, London: Pergamon.
3 Bowles, G. and Klein, R. (eds) (1983) *Theories of Women's Studies*, London: Routledge and Kegan Paul.
4 Giroux, H. (1982) *Ideology, Culture and the Process of Schooling*, Philadelphia: Temple, p. 124.
5 Mills, C.W. (1959) *The Sociological Imagination*, Harmondsworth: Penguin. A useful introduction to life-history methodologies is Plummer, K. (1983) *Documents of Life*, London: Routledge and Kegan Paul.
6 See note 1. Socialist feminism is explained in more detail in the next section of the chapter.
7 The term 'sociology of women's education', now widely used, was first coined by Madeleine MacDonald (1980), who now writes as Madeleine Arnot. MacDonald, M. (1980) 'Sociocultural reproduction and women's education' in Deem, R. (ed.) *Schooling For Women's Work*, London: Routledge and Kegan Paul.

47

8 Giroux, *Ideology*, p. 158.
9 Walkerdine, V. (1984) 'Developmental psychology and the child-centred pedagogy: The insertion of Piaget into early childhood education' in Henriques, J., Holloway, W., Urwin, C., Venn, C. and Walkerdine, V., *Changing the Subject*, London: Methuen.
10 Poster, M. (1984) *Foucault, Marxism and History: Mode of Production Versus Mode of Information*, Cambridge: Polity, p. 114.
11 Smith, D. (1983) 'Women, class and family', *The Socialist Register*, London: Merlin, p. 135.
12 ibid., p. 5.
13 Smith, D. (1974) 'Women's perspective as a radical critique of sociology', *Sociological Inquiry*, Vol. 44, No. 1, pp. 7–13.
14 Mitchell, J. (1973) *Women's Estate*, Harmondsworth: Penguin, p. 28.
15 ibid.; Also Eisenstein, Z. (1982) 'The sexual politics of the new right: Understanding the "crisis of liberalism" for the 1980s' in Keohane, N. *et al.* (eds) *Feminist Theory: A Critique of Ideology*, Chicago: Harvester.
16 This analysis has been developed more fully in Middleton, S. (1986) 'Workers and homemakers: Contradictions in the education of the New Zealand "Post-War Woman"', *N.Z. Journal of Educational Studies*, Vol. 8, No. 2, pp. 13–28. (Also reprinted as Chapter 6, 'A short adventure between school and marriage?' in Middleton, S. (ed.) (1988) *Women and Education in Aotearoa*, Wellington: Allen and Unwin/Port Nicholson.)
17 The origins of the sexual double standard were discussed by Engels, F. (1944 edition) *The Origin of The Family, Private Property and the State*, Sydney: Current Books (originally published in 1891). Recent studies of the reproduction of the sexual double standard in schools include: McRobbie, A. (1978) 'Working class girls and the culture of femininity', Women's Studies Group (ed.) *Women Take Issue*, Birmingham: Centre For Contemporary Cultural Studies/Hutchinson; and Willis, P. (1977) *Learning To Labour*, Westmead: Saxon House.
18 Middleton, S. (1987) 'Schooling and radicalization: Life histories of New Zealand feminist teachers', *British Journal of Sociology of Education*, Vol. 8, No. 2, pp. 169–189.
19 O'Brien, M. (1981) *The Politics of Reproduction*, London: Routledge and Kegan Paul.
20 Firestone, S. (1979) *Dialectic of Sex*, London: Women's Press; Mitchell, *Women's Estate*; Rowbotham, S. (1973) *Women's Consciousness: Man's World*, Harmondsworth: Penguin.
21 Heron, L. (ed.) (1985) *Truth, Dare or Promise: Girls Growing Up in the Fifties*, London: Virago; Steedman, C. (1985) *Landscape For a Good Woman*, London: Virago.
22 Alther, L. (1976) *Kinflicks*, Harmondsworth: Penguin; Piercy, M. (1983) *Braided Lives*, Harmondsworth: Penguin.
23 Ingham, M. (1982) *Now We Are Thirty*, London: Methuen; Middleton, S. (1985) 'Feminism and Education in Post-War New Zealand: A Sociological Analysis', D.Phil. thesis, University of Waikato, Hamilton.
24 Heron *et al. Truth, Dare or Promise*; Steedman, *Landscape*.

25 Bourdieu, P. (1971) 'Intellectual field and creative project' in Young, M. (ed.) *Knowledge and Control*, London: Croom Helm.

26 Mitchell, *Women's Estate.*

27 Mills, *Sociological Imagination.*

28 *Bach*: a holiday cottage.

29 Taniwha: mythical creature. This *waiata* acknowledges the local tribes as *tangata whenua* (the people of the land).

30 *Hangi*: feast cooked in an earth oven. *Marae*: a tribal meeting place.

31 Frith, G. (1987) 'The time of your life: The meaning of the school story' in Weiner, G. and Arnot, M. (eds) *Gender Under Scrutiny*, London: Hutchinson, p. 119.

32 Pakeha: white New Zealander.

33 *Tiki*: a pendant in stylized human form.

34 Okely, J. (1987) 'Privileged, schooled & finished: Boarding education for girls' in Arnot, M. and Weiner, G. (eds) (1987) *Gender and The Politics of Schooling*, London: Hutchinson.

35 The 'urban' orientation and educational aspirations of the New Zealand rural petit bourgeoisie have been discussed by Nash, R. (1982) 'The NZ District High Schools: A study in the selective function of rural education', *New Zealand Journal of Educational Studies*, Vol. 16, No. 2, pp. 150–160.

36 Foucault, M. (1980) *A History of Sexuality, Volume 1*, New York: Vintage, p. 28.

37 Intermediate schools are junior high schools and exist in the larger towns. Small country schools include 'forms one and two' in their primary schools.

38 Author of several texts on China and South-East Asia, he also wrote and taught about education as an artifact of cultural imperialism. Buchanan, K. (1967) 'Letter to a New Zealand University Student' in Buchanan, K., *Map of Love*, Australia: Pergamon.

39 'Special class': for 'slow learners'.

40 Secondary teaching appointments were for a minimum of two years.

41 Extra staffing given to 'problem' schools.

42 Dominy, M. (1986) '1979: A cultural analysis', *N.Z. Women's Studies Journal*, Vol. 2, No. 2, pp. 25–40.

43 Middleton, S. (1980) 'The covert curriculum as a source of inequality for women in schools and higher education', *Delta*, Vol. 27, p. 29–37.

44 Middleton, S. (1984) 'The sociology of women's education as a field of academic study', *Discourse*, Vol. 5, No. 1, pp. 42–62. (Reprinted in Arnot and Weiner, *Gender and the Politics*.)

45 Middleton, S. (1987) 'Feminist academics in a university setting: a study in the politics of educational knowledge', *Discourse*, Vol. 8, No. 1, pp. 25–47.

46 Bernstein, B. (1971) 'On the classification and framing of educational knowledge' in Young, M. (ed.) *Knowledge and Control*, London: Croom Helm.

47 Middleton, S. and Moss, L. (1982) 'The politics of educational research: A case study', NZARE Conference paper, Christchurch.

48 Middleton, S. (1988) 'Researching feminist educational life histories' in Middleton, S. (ed.) *Women and Education in Aotearoa*, Wellington: Allen and Unwin/Port Nicholson.
49 Bunkle, P. (1980) 'The origins of the women's movement in New Zealand: The Women's Christian Temperance Union 1885-1895' in Bunkle, P. and Hughes, B. (eds) *Women in N.Z. Society*, Auckland: Allen and Unwin.
50 Middleton, S. (ed) (1988) *Women and Education in Aotearoa*, Wellington: Allen and Unwin/Port Nicholson, p. 198.

3

COLLABORATIVE AUTOBIOGRAPHY AND THE TEACHER'S VOICE[1]

Richard Butt, Danielle Raymond,
G. McCue and L. Yamagishi

INTRODUCTION

This chapter presents a personal and a theoretical rationale for using an autobiographical approach in understanding how teachers think and act and how they have come to think and act in the way they do. This approach is seen as providing a fundamental understanding of the teacher's perspective which has been missing from efforts at research, development, reform, curriculum implementation and change during the last twenty-five or more years. We think that understanding how teachers, individually and collectively, think, act, develop professionally and change during their careers might provide new insights as to how one might approach the reform, change and improvements in education that are necessary to equip our students for a desirable future within a context that is rapidly altering the nature of teachers' work.

Following an attempt to conceptualize teachers' knowledge, the main part of the chapter attempts to illuminate, for the reader, the potential of this approach through interpretations of two teachers' autobiographies. The collaborative interpretation of these teachers' autobiographies identifies the nature, sources and manner of evolution of the special kind of thinking, action and knowledge that pertains to their teaching. A brief comparative analysis is included to reveal similarities and differences and illustrate themes that might characterize many other teachers' lives. We should point out at the outset that even though our focus in this chapter is on *individual* teachers' lives, therefore on their uniqueness, we have also begun to identify collective themes that run across many teachers' lives which reflect the social structure in which individual lives are embedded.

A CONCEPTUALIZATION OF SUBSTANCE AND METHOD

Theoretical perspectives

Elsewhere we have identified three major interrelated crises that have plagued education. They are: a crisis of scholarly inquiry, a crisis of professional knowledge and a crisis of reform.[2] We see the crisis in scholarly inquiry, caused basically by an over-reliance on logical positivism, as currently being overcome by a return to the neglected ground of educational reality through the complementary use of both quantitative and qualitative approaches that focus on the phenomena of education in a direct and holistic way. In this way, the dynamic complex interrelatedness of classroom activities and human interactions and the situation-specific nature of teaching are better respected. As well, we think these approaches permit both the uniqueness within and commonalities across classrooms to be reflected.

The crisis in professional knowledge, related to the foregoing problems of scholarship, finds its root cause within a preoccupation with the discovery or invention of sure-fired models which would guarantee generalizable problem solutions. This preoccupation with prescription has led to the formation of bodies of professional knowledge which have been largely ignored by professionals-in-action since they have found that little of this prescriptive technology is appropriate to specific situations whose nature is uniquely personal, instinctive, intuitive, reflective and practical. The solution of practical problems derives more from reflection-on-action, reflection-in-action, professional intuition, craft and art, and the special knowledge held by the teacher.[3] The nature, then, of professional action, especially teaching, requires us to focus primarily and initially on the qualitative rather than quantitative nature of practice, in order to derive professional knowledge useful to both scholars and practitioners.

Given this background, it is not surprising that we have experienced a crisis of reform. Firstly, most attempts at educational reform in the last several decades have relied on prescriptive science and technology. Secondly, the hidden relationship

52

between theory and practice in prescriptive science, that theory is superior to practice and must be directly applied to the practical in order to improve practice, became embodied in the human interactions between reformers and teachers. The relationship of outsiders (reformers) to insiders (teachers) was a vertical and unequal one.[4] Teachers were not able to participate in determining the changes that were thrust upon them. Reformers did not work with teachers in understanding classroom reality. In general they were ignorant of the culture of the school and classroom.[5]

It is within this broader context of crises in scholarly inquiry, professional knowledge, and educational reform that we locate three interrelated concerns that fuelled our interest in the study of teachers' knowledge. First, and foremost, critical assessments of the reasons for the limited impact of curriculum innovations on classroom practice have pointed to the reformer's neglect of the central role of teachers' intentions and pedagogical expertise in effecting significant classroom change.[6] The development of more adequate views of curriculum development and implementation thus calls for a shift of focus and of approach in the study of classroom change; instead of adopting an outsider's perspective whereby researcher-, reformer- or innovator-generated criteria are used to make judgements about change, we need to ask the teachers themselves what classroom change means for them, from their own perspective and criteria. In so doing, we need to develop research approaches that allow the teacher's knowledge of classroom realities to emerge.

Studies of implementation that attempt to take the teacher's point of view more seriously suggest that implementation be envisaged as staff development[7] and that traditional professional development models should undergo important revisions. This second area of concern has indeed for some time been the object of vituperative comments from both practitioners and researchers. Teacher professional development efforts, the key to school improvement, have been 'so frustratingly wasteful as the thousands of workshops and conferences... led to no significant change in practice when the teachers returned to their classrooms.'[8] In-service education has disregarded the teacher as an active learner and has based its interventions on less than adequate, if any, conceptions of how learning occurs throughout her/his career:

teachers expressed the feeling that there is no continuity in teacher development, they usually added that there was simply a smorgasbord of workshops. Workshops were often characterized as '101 tricks for Monday morning' and while there may be some value to learning some tricks early in your teaching career, you rapidly outgrow that stage.[9]

More recent points of view on classroom change thus think of implementation as a learning process in which teachers are seen as adult learners. For instance, Fullan and Guskey suggest that teachers do not learn when staff development efforts focus first on initiating changes in beliefs, attitudes and perceptions.[10] Cognitive and attitudinal changes would occur only after modifications in classroom practices have led to significant and desirable changes in classroom-related events (e.g. student learning outcomes, involvement in activities, attitudes towards school). However valuable, these suggestions are still tainted with a preoccupation for the 'effectiveness' of implementation efforts; the changes in teacher beliefs, attitudes, practices and behaviours are those deemed desirable by programme developers. Seeing the teacher as an adult learner entails acknowledging that she holds an articulate and elaborated practical knowledge of classroom practice that, if examined on its own grounds, might not be organized in terms of 'beliefs', 'attitudes', 'instructional practices'. Seeing the teacher as an adult learner implies that teachers will seek a kind of knowledge that can, in some way, be incorporated in the structure of knowledge they have developed; it also means that they will learn in several ways, from several sources and in various manners at different moments in their careers. Evidence from studies of teachers' professional life cycles illustrates important changes in teachers' concerns,[11] relationships with pupils,[12] and relationships with colleagues[13] that suggest differentiated learning interests and processes throughout their careers. Huberman's (1984, 1988) interviews with 150 teachers indeed indicate that most teachers see themselves as achieving mastery of different pedagogical competencies at various moments in their careers, while, even late in mid-career, still lacking proficiency in certain areas (teaching children with learning problems, individualization of instruction, working with heterogeneous groups of students). Huberman also observes that at various moments of their professional lives, teachers will seek for different sources of knowledge, with a preference for informal discussions with selected and available colleagues.[14]

Although these data present some important limitations, such as the use of researcher-generated categories in order to create general patterns and minimize individual configurations, they are useful to broaden the scope of questions asked about teachers by innovation-minded curricularists. A thorough acknowledgement of the teacher as learner and of classroom change as a learning process calls then for an understanding of the phenomenology of teachers' professional development, of the genesis of her personal knowledge.

Our third concern is political in its nature as well as in its implications. All their lives teachers have to confront the negative stereotypes – 'teacher as robot, devil, angel, nervous Nellie' – foisted upon them by the American culture. Descriptions of teaching as a 'flat occupation with no career structure, low pay, salary increments unrelated to merit' have been paralleled with portrayals of teaching as 'one great plateau' where 'it appears that the annual cycle of the school year lulls teachers into a repetitious professional cycle of their own'.[15]

Within the educational community, the image of teachers as semi-professionals who lack control and autonomy over their own work and as persons who do not contribute to the creation of knowledge has permeated and congealed the whole educational enterprise. Researchers have torn the teacher out of the context of the classroom, plagued her with various insidious effects (Hawthorne, novelty, Rosenthal, halo), parcelled out into discrete skills the unity of intention and action present in teaching practices. Researchers who view knowledge solely as empirical or analytic preclude the acknowledgement of and responsive inquiry into the nature of *the teacher's personal* professional knowledge.

Pre-service teacher education has served to prepare the ground for such a view to take hold in the teachers themselves. Plagued by the 'lack of an agreed upon knowledge base that creates a vacuum into which marches technological neutrality',[16] the pre-service curriculum, often attacked as intellectually empty and pedagogically unsound, extols the 'corrected method' over freedom of thought, the authority of 'science' over critical examination of established models of inquiry and 'reduces the intrinsic ambiguity of teaching through a technological mindset that deintellectualizes teachers and depoliticizes the inherently ideological activity of teaching'.[17] Shaped by their training to look outside of themselves for truths about their own reality and further 'deskilled' by the bureaucratization of teaching that isolates them into the classroom, experienced teachers find themselves at mid-career in a state of burn-out that: 'does not come from overtaxing one's intellectual and mental capacities... but from not being able to use those abilities to handle difficult emotional and managerial problems'.[18]

The view of teachers implicit in the social context of education thus contributes to their disempowerment by limiting their opportunities to develop and exhibit the knowledge and intelligence that are necessary in working effectively with groups of students.

More positive outlooks on the teacher in alternative models of curriculum development, studies of curriculum practice[19] and conceptions of teaching[20] have recently contributed to the elaboration of studies depicting teachers as active holders of knowledge, as well as agents in the reality of the classroom. These studies provide a foundation for the emergent evolution of the *notion* of personal knowledge. In our view, they might also do more than that: the conceptualization of practical knowledge from the teacher's perspective, while possibly contributing to the enhancement the teacher's 'professional' status, or the fuller use of the human resources teachers bring to their work can be seen as an eminently political endeavour. The study of experiential knowledge, where an understanding of the search for individual meaning is critical, will expose the teacher's voice, in both its alienated and unadulterated modes, to the researcher and the teacher herself.

The potential of the collaborative study of personal professional knowledge for providing teachers with the power to transcend their present situation and take control of their own lives and for bringing researchers to liberate themselves from stultifying conceptions of scientific inquiry locates it within an emancipatory epistemological and practical approach to curriculum inquiry. From the personal vantage point of individual teachers the placing of teaching at the centre of practice, reform and research is an *existential* issue. From the perspective of teachers in general, representing the collective knowledge of teachers as a legitimate and worthwhile body of knowledge is a *political* issue. Making relationships between insiders and outsiders in a horizontal and *collaborative* learning enterprise is an issue of power. Moving from existing alienating practices to teacher- and school-based approaches must be regarded as an issue of teacher empowerment and emancipation.

Teacher thinking, action and knowledge are of vital importance in the endeavour to understand how classrooms are the way they are. How teachers' thoughts, actions and knowledge have evolved and changed throughout their personal and professional lives will help us to understand how classrooms have come to be the way they are and how they might become otherwise. In considering how to approach understanding these issues it was essential to ask what methodology could carry, in the most authentic way, the *teacher's voice*.[21] The notion of the teacher's voice is important in that it carries the tone, the language, the quality, the feelings, that are conveyed by the way a teacher speaks or writes. In a political sense the notion of the teacher's voice addresses the right to speak and be represented. It can represent both the unique individual and the collective voice; one that is characteristic of teachers as compared to other groups.

From this background we hope that the reader can understand our interest in the special type of knowledge that teachers possess, its potential nature, sources and development. One way of exploring these issues that combines the advantages of collective and individual learning with the notion of empowerment is a form of collaborative autobiography practised by university and teacher researchers. In evolving our approach to biography which reflects our interest in the personal and emancipatory research, we have been influenced by, and have drawn from, reconceptualist literature, particularly the works of Pinar, Grumet and Berk.[22]

The biographic character of teachers' knowledge

In order to understand the knowledge that teachers possess it is imperative that we know it in the way that the *individual teacher* does. More importantly, as outsiders and researchers, we need to understand how teachers evolve, develop and change their practical knowledge in the way that they perceive their experience of it. These arguments bring with them a regard for and interest in the teacher as a unique *person*, and the teacher as a *learner* who possesses a special type of knowledge. We see ones' architecture of self[23] – the private person – as significantly influenced and shaped by experiences of context and situation. In turn, in cyclic fashion, how a person acts in a situation and context may shape and influence it. Given this background and our interest in the teacher as person and adult learner, we choose to conceptualize the cyclic relationship between person and context in terms of Dewey's theories, as interpreted and adapted from a conceptual theory of informal education[24] and a biographic conception of education.[25] Dewey[26] saw *personal* experience as the prime source of education, and saw the values, interests and abstractions of individuals *other than the learner* as a potential source of distortion if they obstructed individual learners in making their own sense of their world. Dewey's criteria for the worth of a particular experience for learning were interaction, continuity and wholeness. The more deeply a learner interacts with objects and others in a situation, the better the experience and learning; also, the more continuous and whole a sequence of activities is, the better the experience.[27] If successive experiences are well integrated with one another, the learning and knowledge that results are equally well integrated. But from whose perspective do we judge the quality of interaction, wholeness, continuity and integration of experience? Obviously the interests of the learner are paramount here. Despite Dewey's interest in socialization for democracy he did say

> There is, I think, no point in the philosophy of progressive education which is sounder, than its emphasis upon the importance of the participation of the learner in the formation of the purposes which direct his activities in the learning process.[28]

Here we encounter, then, unique personal intentionality.[29] The form of education that stays with us and informs our subsequent choices and actions is that which results from experiences which have a telling impact on our person. In a similar vein, Rogers[30] argues that only experiences that involve the learners' genuine self result in any learning of lasting significance. Learning which is of importance can only be self-discovered and self-appropriated; it is most telling when experiences emphasize the self, personal relevance, interest, involvement, activity and feelings, as well as cognition.[31] As well, Dearden[32] extrapolates from Dewey to emphasize intentionality and the value of reflection in and on experience to state that 'nothing is of value to us unless it can enter our experience in such a way which enables us to realize what is valuable in it.' The knowledge that results from those personal experiences, and reflection in and on them, is what we see as *personal knowledge*. We apply these notions of significant learning through experience resulting in personal knowledge to the teacher as a person and the teacher as adult learner. We gain personal knowledge throughout our lives. Experiences prior to teaching shape what Pinar calls the architecture of self, which consists of the contribution of the many elements of the private existential person, such as beliefs, values, dispositions, feelings, guiding images, principles whether explicit, implicit, tacit or intuitive. Of specific interest to us, as well, is the personal, practical and professional knowledge that evolves through the teachers' interaction with, and experience of the classroom, school and broader educational context. We think that the above experiential conceptualization of learning is an appropriate framework through which to view how teachers evolve their own special ways of thinking and acting in the classroom, how they continue to learn to be teachers and evolve their own particular knowledge.

We wish to emphasize the biographic nature of teachers' knowledge in one final way that is drawn out of the Deweyan sense of experiential learning and personal knowledge by Berk. Berk[33] quotes John Dewey's definition of education which 'is the reconstruction or reorganization of experience which adds to the meaning of experience, which increases ability to direct the course of subsequent experience.' Berk[34] contends that this definition of education and the nature of Dewey's other major concepts of experience, interaction, continuity and wholeness make his conception of education *biographic.*

Studying teachers' knowledge: autobiographic praxis

Berk[35] suggests that if we were *to study* the nature of quality of the education of particular learners that we should properly use biographic means of inquiry. We have transposed Berk's suggestion as to how one can discern what is educative in students' lives and applied it to our interest in teachers' learning to become, and in being, teachers. How teachers, through experience, both in their private lives and in professional contexts, have educated themselves, and been educated, as teachers, can be answered through biographical inquiry. It permits us to make sense of individual experience, to discover the educational significance of a teachers' experiences; and to discover the quality of experience through its relation to previous and later experiences.[36]

A person interacting with situations in particular contexts gives rise to experience and the evolution of personal knowledge. In order to understand how a person thinks, acts, feels and intends, and how a person knows what they know, it is necessary to understand the relationship and tensions among context and individual lives[37] not only as related to the present but the past, as well. To understand one's present situation one needs to bring forward prior related experience.[38] In order to understand a teacher's knowledge with respect to classrooms we need to understand the contexts within which they currently work – that is their working realities, both in the collective sense and in the existential sense. Seeing the pressure of the formal situation and the force of the inner private definition of the situation[39] enables us to see relationships and tensions that contribute to thoughts, actions and the shape and shaping of a teacher's knowledge. Of equal importance are *past experiences*

> which will give us the details of that process whose character we would otherwise only be able to speculate about, and the process to which our data must ultimately be referred if they are to have theoretical and not just operational and predictive significance. It will describe those crucial interactive episodes in which new lines of individual and collective activity are forged, in which new aspects of the self are brought into being.[40]

Teachers' knowledge reconsidered

Our work is characterized by: the deeply personal notion of the architecture of self created through interaction of person and context that the private person brings to the public act of teaching; the integration of this personal knowledge with the professional knowledge that evolves out of personal interaction with professional contexts; and how the *teacher* perceives and holds this knowledge. Besides substance, we are interested in how this knowledge is evolved and formed. Our particular interests are in the biographic formation of teachers' knowledge both in the sense of process, and in the sense of substance and structure. A third important interest which relates both to the ongoing biographical process of formation of teachers' knowledge and its practical manifestation or expression – is the relationship among knowledge held, expressed and context. The final interest is in creating unity between the foregoing three foci and methodology through the practice of autobiographical inquiry both outside and inside the classroom.

We have a phrase that names and integrates these four lived interests of biographic substance, process, the relationship between knowledge held and expressed, and methodology. It contains the potentially synergistic, dialectic and problematic interactions between person and context, thought and action, experience and reflection. It reflects the relationship between past, present and future. The term 'praxis' better reflects those interactions than the word knowledge. It also reflects the dynamic nature of teachers' professional craft as well as its ongoing evolutionary nature better than the somewhat static or fixed connotation of knowledge. Praxis, as substance and process, includes action, reflection-on-action, reflection-in-action, thought, thought-guided-action and action-guided-thought in a cyclic unity which occurs both inside a teacher's personhood and in action. The term 'autobiography' reflects how we think a teacher's knowledge is held, formed, and how it can be studied or understood. 'Autobiographic praxis', then, is the term we use for our conceptualization of teachers' knowledge. Moving from praxis to 'praxeology' brings with it the meanings of studying and understanding, and the theory of human action. So that the phrase 'autobiographic praxeology', refers to our methodology. It means the study of teachers' knowledge, the process of how it has been and is being elaborated, how it is expressed through autobiographical inquiry.

QUESTIONS, METHODS, AND STORIES

The following major questions are the focus of our research into the nature of teachers' knowledge as revealed by their autobiographies.

Questions of substance

1 What might the central aspects of a teacher's knowledge be interpreted to be at the present stage of professional personal life and in the present context? What forms do they take?

2 What are the major elements of a teacher's present professional personal context?

3 What are the major elements of a teacher's past personal and professional life that are relevant to a teacher's knowledge?

Questions of formation

4 How do elements of *current* context interact with and shape a teacher's knowledge and its expression?

5. What are the major sources of or influences on a teacher's knowledge from the past?

6 How have elements of a teacher's perceived past influenced the formation of a teacher's knowledge? How are antecedents related to subsequent elements?

7 What crucial life episodes occurred in which new lines of activity were found or new aspects of the self brought into being? How and why?

With respect to the dynamic interplay between person and context over time, we have speculated that a framework of particular contexts are pertinent to autobiographic praxis in teachers. They include: intrapersonal (existential), interpersonal, cultural (collective), practical, professional, institutional and societal contexts. These contexts might be from either the private or professional domains of a person's life. A final set of questions might be addressed that relate to current interactions of person and context. Which interactions contain issues that are not resolved – that is, which interactions are problematic? How does a teacher live with these? Which interactions contain issues that require continuing resolution – that is they are dialogical or dialectical in nature? In which interactions is there a significant degree of congruence between person and context – that is the interaction is synergistic?

Evolving and interpreting teachers' stories

We have been enabling teachers to construct personal and professional autobiographies through a graduate course which is described in detail elsewhere.[41] We work through four phases of activity and writing: a depiction of the context of their current working reality, a description of their current pedagogy and curriculum-in-use, an account of their reflections on their past personal and professional lives insofar as they might relate to an under-standing of present professional thoughts and actions and, finally, a projection into their preferred personal/professional futures as related to a personal critical appraisal of the previous three accounts. The process of the course is based on a collaborative social learning approach.

A significant proportion of what can be interpreted from a person's autobiography with respect to the nature of events, relationship between events, thinking, action and meaning lies within what is written by the author. In this sense each auto-biographer has the major role in the process of interpretation. The first two authors of this chapter, in attempting to further elaborate interpretative accounts, have taken measures to represent the teacher's perspective and voice in several ways. The first author participated in the course process as the facilitator and so was exposed to the social education that provides a context from which to interpret autobiographies. As well, the first author engaged in an exercise of 'rewriting' the autobiographies used as illustrations in this chapter in the form of summaries in the third person, using, as far as possible the language, words and concepts of the teacher. This exercise was thought to enable a deeper appreciation of the text in a verbatim sense and also was thought to discourage interpretive conceptualization which was premature – prior to a thorough understanding of the text.

These summaries were shared with our autobiographical co-investigators who validated the accounts. There were no major disagreements as to text. Some suggestions were made with respect to confidentiality of certain aspects of the accounts. Visits were made to the field to compare the images held by the first author of the teachers and their classrooms to actual realities. There was a high degree of congruence – sufficient to attest to the basic validity of the accounts. Participant-observation is now ongoing in order to examine how the teacher's knowledge is expressed in action. The second author interpreted the autobiographies independently as a second reader of the text. The second author also wrote a descriptive summary of the autobiography. This summary carried the concepts, categories, phrases and expressions used by the teachers. Then, the second author used a form of charting, in order to highlight important elements in the accounts as well as relationships identified by the teachers in their own renditions. Interpretive ideas were noted as they pertained to the nature, sources of influences, change and evolution of the teacher's personal practical knowledge. It was then possible to see potential relationship among specific elements of the teacher's current pedagogy and biographical influences and, at the same time, to identify the most potent influences from the past. Following this process a joint description and interpretive summaries were constructed. This account was subjected to validity checks by the researchers and our teachers co-investigators.

LLOYD'S STORY

Lloyd is a 38-year-old teacher with twelve years of teaching experience. He currently teaches grade six pupils, most of whom are of average or below average ability. He has been teaching in his current school for the past eleven years. Four years ago he was made administrative assistant. Lloyd is a Japanese Canadian whose family was interned during the war and resettled in Southern Alberta. He is the third youngest in a family of ten children. He is married with three children.

Working reality

Lloyd experiences pressure from several sources: covering the curriculum at the upper elementary level, dealing with the many non-curricular tasks and interruptions that significantly diminish curriculum time, dealing with intercollegial relations, coping with the pressure of being scrutinized 'in the fishbowl', and dealing with perceived expectations of being an administrator.

The most predominant theme relating to working reality for Lloyd and most other teachers is intercollegial relations. To understand this more fully for Lloyd, however, we need to go back to his early years of teaching when he encountered Mrs S, an elderly teacher who was two years away from retirement.

> This elderly teacher...was very set in her ways, having taught a great number of years. As she always like to put it, 'I'm very experienced, you know.' During our initial meetings, Mrs S., Joan (the other third grade teacher) and I got along quite amicably. However, one thing was wrong – Mrs S. seemed to be dominating the meetings and my suggestions counted for very little. In fact, whenever I suggested a new or interesting

(in my opinion) way to handle problems or impending situations, she would cross her arms and state emphatically and in a condescending tone of voice, one of her patented retorts – 'I've tried that before and it doesn't work...too much time and energy required... no way!'...and finally the ultimate putdown – 'You're just a pup... I guess you'll just have to learn the hard way!' I assumed the other teacher had locked horns with her a few years earlier, as she kept very quiet during these skirmishes and just nodded in agreement regardless of who was on the floor at the time. In a very short time, these supposedly constructive sessions became increasingly less productive and longer silent periods became more the rule than the exception. It was surely a classic case of 'new' vs. 'old' and no party could ever lay claim to victory.

Lloyd was disappointed that these grade level meetings were not focused on professional growth. He became more frustrated and very aggressive in attempting to sway Mrs S, but it was like tackling an immovable object. This experience left a scar that was to last for a long time. When Lloyd moved schools, though not by choice, he changed.

I became a 'closet teacher', in that I would listen to suggestions, not offering any suggestions, and then 'do my own thing'. I found great success with this mode of operating and up to a few years ago, I hesitated to share any of my strategies/worksheets/lessons I developed on my own. Becoming an administrator forced me into sharing, for I wanted to provide teachers with access to as many resources as possible – the better the programmes they had, the better it was for the school. It also started to make me feel worthwhile and proud when teachers tried some of my ideas and they actually worked for them as well.

Social development of students

The description opens with a vignette wherein a colleague of Lloyd's angrily requests to talk with him about the behaviour of his class.

As she stormed away, my innocent-looking children stared at me with disbelief. 'Boy, is she ever mad at you,' volunteered

Sara sympathetically. 'At me?' I questioned. 'I'd say she was quite upset with you students,' I added.

I guess it was lecture time again. My students' overall work habits, attitude, and general conduct had not been up to par since the Christmas break and a gentle reminder during the first week back must have been ineffective...

When I dispense my responsibility lecture, I deal with key concepts such as self-respect, self-discipline, maturity, pride, teamwork, commitment and responsibility.

Lloyd prides himself in having one of the classes that is the most responsible, trustworthy and disciplined in the school. He also feels part of the reason for this, besides his disciplinary skill, is that he has good rapport with his students due to his personality. He shows warmth through talking to them, not at them, through joking around, through physical contact, and feels his small stature lessens the physical distance between them. Having a well-disciplined class also brings pressure. At times he fears that his classroom has become a dumping ground for students with every conceivable weakness... academic, social, disciplinary, and emotional. The principal and parents request placements. He wonders whether he is a social worker or a teacher – whether to go into counselling full-time, therefore not having to plan lessons and teach curriculum! He worries about burn-out, especially when some classes don't catch on quickly and require repeated reminders like his current class.

In making sense of how he came to think and act this way in terms of what he calls social development in the classroom, Lloyd posits several shaping influences.

Family

Lloyd sees his parents and family as having a major effect on his teaching. Throughout his life, his parents have repeatedly stressed the concepts of respect, responsibility, commitment, self-discipline, teamwork, trust, and right and wrong. They had the ability to ingrain these values without spanking or verbal abuse. They were good role models and used the identical lectures that Lloyd uses now with his own children and his class. Lloyd sees himself using the same concepts in the classroom and, as a professional, insists on the same high level organization, efficiency, commitment and standards of work that his parents exemplified in their community work for himself and his students.

For Lloyd, when he was growing up, the focus at home and elsewhere was collective family life, whether working hard as a team to 'pull and top' sugar beets to get out of old shacks and beet farms to a better life, or other 'doing' projects. The notion of family and teamwork also comes through from Lloyd's background due to being the third youngest of ten siblings. A rough early life required them to care for, stick up for and help each other. Rules and organization, including not speaking when others were, were a necessary part of such a large group of siblings!

This feeling of family has also filtered down into my classroom. I stress to all my students that everyone is important in the classroom and no one student is the most important. I make sure that everyone has equal opportunity over the course of a week to assist in the daily routines, such as passing out books, being messengers, getting the fluoride rinse, etc. I also like to stress the notion that each member of the class is responsible to the class as well as to himself.

Developing a feeling of sticking together, helping and caring for each other – a feeling I had in my family – is also promoted in my classroom. I always stress in my lectures to my students on the subject of family, that they may not appreciate their parents/siblings right now, but sooner or later, they come to realize their value. Their family make up their true 'best friends' who are there when needed – blood is thicker than water.

Cultural deprivation

My parents, like all others of Japanese ancestry, were relocated and placed in internment camps during the Second World War. Allowed to take only as many personal possessions as they were able to carry, they lost virtually everything they had worked for in this 'Land of Opportunity', except their dignity. From living in nice, clean homes, they were corralled into prison-type camps and later shipped to farms in Southern Alberta where they lived in 'beet shacks' with few of life's amenities. Through all this, my parents were able to maintain their sense of objectivity to channel all their

67

energies into gaining acceptance and the respectability that they desired.

Lloyd's family successfully worked and earned its way out of the beet farm shacks and into the city.

> Our quest for respectability was not an easy one. At that time, there were very few Japanese Canadians willing to reside in Lethbridge for they were like 'bananas' – yellow on the outside and white on the inside – and were not able to hide from the glaring eyes and sharp tongues of some bigoted people. I am certain that my sensitivity towards students of visible minority groups – like Native Indians, Vietnamese, Japanese, Chinese and Pakistanis – is a direct result of the many instances of discrimination I personally faced some 20 years ago.

Lloyd's own experience of cultural deprivation enables him to relate to the children in his class, most of whom could be described in similar terms or, at least, socio-economically deprived. He can empathize with their lot and feels that 'with a joint effort we will have a smooth-running operation with a common goal – *to move upward*'. The common goal obviously includes Lloyd himself. Becoming an administrative assistant was very important. Lloyd also is highly motivated to do a good job, to be the best teacher, a good administrator and also to be seen to be doing a good job so that he might become a principal of his own school.

Academic development

I am a stickler for mandated curriculum for the following reasons:
1 I have made a habit from my earliest teaching days to refer to the curriculum guide and follow it like the Gospel.
2 I want to avoid criticism from my students' subsequent teachers.
3 I want my students to have an easy transition from grade to grade.
4 I want to have the black and white data to justify my programs to administrators, parents, students and other outside groups (safety measure).

5 I have made a commitment – however covert – to superiors that I would teach the curriculum guide and having a well-developed sense of right and wrong, I just do not want to eliminate any areas.

Earlier Lloyd had also written that he didn't want authority figures to come down on him for failing to cover the curricula, that nothing should be left out in a system of progression, and that he found it challenging to learn and cover all curriculum areas since it gave him a sense of knowledgeability.

However, I must admit that I do deviate from the curriculum guide, in that my practical knowledge influences how much time and detail I will use in covering certain areas. For example, I will spend much more time than recommended with numeration, operation and problem-solving concepts than the areas of measurement and geometry. In essence, I am making a decision for the students, saying that the former is much more important and useful than the latter.

Lloyd has a plethora of language arts materials which he has used throughout the last five years. He had gradually grown away from using the teacher's guide so closely, tending to pick and choose on the basis of relevance and suitability.

The recommended math textbook lacks sufficient practice examples and also seems to make too many presuppositions as to previous experience and therefore creates a lack of sequence or a sense of progression....

However, whenever I am teaching a subject for the first time, I follow a prescribed text, providing me with a vehicle to learn the subject matter. I may or may not leave the text, depending on its value and whether or not I am able to find and develop my own materials....

As in most of my subjects, I use the text as only a guide and add a lot of supplementary activities of my own. Generally speaking, I place stock in my own materials more so than a prescribed text.

Lloyd uses his own and other tests quite frequently, including pre- and post-tests since: growth can be measured from start to finish; problem areas can be diagnosed; any concept worth teaching is worth testing; children need to write tests so as to do well in external assessment; also Lloyd does not want his teaching to be labelled by unfavourable test scores.

Lloyd's description of his approach to various subjects illuminates his teaching style which is characterized by structure, organization, flexibility, sequential order and progression. Lloyd finds he prefers teaching in a block approach rather than a spiral method, with sequential order and progression starting from the basics then proceeding in increasing levels of difficulty to more complex concepts.

Influences of the past

Lloyd locates his general attitude towards mandated curriculum in his parents' emphasis on right and wrong (you are required by law to teach the curriculum), commitment (complete the curriculum as prescribed), and survival (if you teach what you are supposed to you don't get into trouble), and in his striving to gain acceptance and respectability. The theme of upward mobility can be picked up again, here, from the previous section. The necessary striving for success as a member of a minority group combined with the strong work ethic of the Japanese culture contributed to what Lloyd calls his great obsession. This relates not only to his attitude to curriculum but the total teaching job, including thorough preparation and very detailed plans.

Lloyd arrived at his first full-time job with 'an inner drive and gusto to become the best damn teacher in the world!' He was obsessed with being the best using all his energy and time, even at the expense of his family and friends. Everything revolved around the realm of education. It became more than just a preoccupation.

> Each day, for the first seven years of my teaching career was like a ritual. I would arrive at school an hour before the first bell and leave about an hour and one half at the close. This made it a solid 7½ hours of productive and instructional time at school, not including noon hour extra-curricular supervision which occurred at different intervals during the year. After my evening meal at home, I would then settle down in my den and fly through yet another five or six hours of marking, creating worksheets and drawing up new and innovative lesson plans. I also studied the Alberta Program of Studies and the Alberta Curriculum Guides like a monk would study his Bible. I was ready.

Even though he felt emotionally and physically drained at each day's end, the many instant rewards from the students plus requests from parents to have their children in his class, made it rewarding and provided motivation for Lloyd to pursue 'being the best'.

Lloyd's emphasis on language skills can be related to his experience as a child in school for whom English was a second language. Lloyd floundered for the first few years of schooling due to language difficulties and lack of a person to direct him at school. In fact he can hardly recall any teachings during that first few years. He went through a period where he was embarrassed when his parents came to school or when, with his parents, he accidentally encountered friends, and also, he didn't bring friends home, due to his parents' inability to speak English fluently. The teaching of language skills in his class is influenced by his parents' lack of English and Lloyd learning it as a second language; its importance is deeply ingrained.

Lloyd's beliefs and practices regarding the provision of a carefully and logically sequenced set of concepts with clear structure and organization, and the use of rote memory types of activity on occasion, relate to his own first four years of school, as well as to a particular teacher whom he calls his 'white mother'. These historical events, as well as his personal involvement in a project on Objective Based Education in Mathematics, contributed to evolving such beliefs that some content must have priority – the basics must be taught and mastered first, and skills must be presented according to difficulty level.

Understandably, with Lloyd's language problem, his first years of school were very difficult. He remembers having to struggle and agonize over simple concepts himself. But this changed significantly in the fifth grade with Mrs Hunt.

> My struggles as a student were nearly at an end after the fifth grade, thanks to a kind, young, energetic lady who brought everything all together for me and made me into a conscientious student. Mrs Hunt taught in a very structured manner, was sensitive to our needs as students, and always had interesting lessons, however basic. She had many motivating techniques and was probably the single most important factor in my appreciation for handwriting, reading, neatness and order. To this day, I attempt to influence my students to do likewise. Since I learned most of my skills, it seems, from

71

Mrs Hunt, I still can remember some of her strategies, many of which were of the rote memory type of activities. This has led me to believe that with students who are unable to conceptualize data (such as I was in those days), the use of a similar approach is effective. I try to use it with my modified students and it seems to be working.

His own suffering – culturally and economically – has made him try to be a patient, understanding, and humanistic teacher. At the same time as being humanistic and remembering to teach basic knowledge through logical, sequential order, he illuminates this with life experiences through discussions, pictures, role playing and drama.

Interpretation: the nature, sources and evolution of Lloyd's knowledge

Lloyd's personal knowledge seems to be embodied by the notion of the basics for the three Ss – survival, safety and success. These three aims relate simultaneously to Lloyd himself, his personal and cultural history, his career progression, and to his socio-economically disadvantaged pupils. These are perceived by Lloyd as very strong mutual interests which he translates into a common goal – to move upward. Lloyd, in order to pursue this goal of upward mobility with his pupils, has a strong image of family in his personal practical knowledge. It embodies and generates a significant amount of the content and process of curriculum and pedagogy for his classroom.

The notions of safety, survival and success include acceptance. Positive feedback is necessary to indicate both acceptance and success. We can see how Lloyd feels quite secure and successful with his students from their feedback; they love him actually. When we move to a second potential source of acceptance and success – colleagues – we hear the story of Mrs S and apathetic colleagues – negative feedback. Lloyd withdraws for a number of years until his colleagues on the Objective Based Education give him very positive feedback and acceptance. Lloyd also feels a lot more comfortable sharing his ideas now that he is an administrator. By now, success as a teacher has given him the confidence that his ideas are worth sharing with his colleagues, combined with the fact that success in becoming an administrator gives him legitimizing authority.

Lloyd's personal and cultural background, and his striving for the three Ss, underpin his obsession with hard work, and constant pursuit of acceptance and competence for both himself and his pupils. Lloyd's craft knowledge integrates three main themes in order to provide for pupil acceptance, safety, survival and success. Firstly, social development derives directly from his personal background and family life. He examines this first; it is considered at least as important as, if not more important than, academic development which relates to the mandated curriculum. The values and ideals that Lloyd identifies as the fundamental content of his social development curriculum provide personal anchorage points of which Lloyd is certain. They relate to Lloyd's personal and cultural identity; they have also provided Lloyd, himself, with safety, survival and success. They bring Lloyd as a person into the classroom and provide for authenticity and continuity as they are applied to his pupils. The words used to describe his pedagogy in the social development aspect of his curriculum should also be noticed. He enforces, reinforces, trains, repeats, ingrains, stresses and emphasizes. A pedagogy that seems to be oriented towards long-term goals (personal growth objectives) would, therefore, be characterized by repetition, emphasis, training and reinforcement. Lloyd wonders if he is a teacher or a social worker. Yet, if he gave up this aspect of his practical knowledge, he would be giving up the part of himself that represents an appeal to the authentic part of his culture and his experience that gave survival, safety and success, and that binds him to his students' lives.

The second theme that is integrated into Lloyd's craft knowledge evolves out of academic development. This knowledge and practice evolves from family values, his experience as a learner, and through complying, for safety and survival reasons, to curriculum guidelines. He covers the curriculum, but interprets what *he* thinks are the basics, in a logical, well-planned, sequenced, structured and organized fashion. His sort of kids, from his experience, need to know this material to make sure they move up; they also learn it better if it is formulated in the above manner.

The third theme is what one might characterize as the transformational medium of Lloyd's practical knowledge. The first two themes involving 'ingrainment' of acceptable social values and learning the basics through a structured and sequential approach, on their own, make Lloyd's pedagogy seem dry, boring and traditional. This, however, is not the case. The third theme can be called the human side of his personal knowledge, which appears to derive both from the image of family and Lloyd's background as well as being acceptable ways of teaching according to the modern theories of learning implicit in his curriculum guidelines, and the nature of children. Lloyd and his class, together as a team in an active way, provide the experience necessary for skill development. Through this approach there are opportunities for interaction and concrete experiences. He emphasizes establishing warm and friendly relationships with children as individuals and provides opportunities for expression of self and emotion through various means. Lloyd, through his past suffering, is able to identify and empathize in a very human way with his students. In the end, this human side is the predominant flavour of his pedagogy that they experience. They are part of a nurturing family which has the necessary structure and direction.

Lloyd's early life (persons, experiences, family) are the major sources of Lloyd's thoughts and actions. Later professional influences and experiences serve mainly to elaborate or refine his personal knowledge from the early years into his form of professional knowledge. His experience with socio-economically deprived children, and his upward mobility within teaching (Mrs S – withdrawal, administrative experience) and the Objective Based Education project served to reinforce the interest in the basic fundamentals, structure, sequence and organization. Other sources of professional development have served more immediate instrumental, technical and acceptance needs.

Lloyd's knowledge was evolved in a professional sense very early in his career through his hard work at becoming a combination of what external sources and internal cultures and familial values might say 'the best possible teacher' would be. Following this early development of teaching competence, Lloyd claims he has changed very little. If he has changed he has done so in response to mandated policies, changes in roles, or through technical elaboration of existing skills such as determining, structuring and sequencing curriculum content, and designing effective tests through the Objective Based Education project. Experiences such as these allow Lloyd to become more explicitly what he already is. Following, then, the relatively rapid initial formation of his practical knowledge which combines the personal with the mandated through practical experience, Lloyd's professional development mainly involves incremental elaboration of original patterns.

GLENDA'S STORY

Glenda is a 44-year-old teacher with nine years of experience, two of which were in an International School in Pakistan. She comes from a white lower middle-class background and was the eldest of four children in her family. She teaches in a multi-grade English-as-a-second-language classroom in a school within a low socio-economic area. Children from a wide range of cultural back-grounds attend the school. Immigrant and refugee children constitute her class. Glenda works with her children on a pull-out resource room model basis. Besides working with ESL children in her classroom, she works in a supportive role with other teachers in the school assisting them in looking after the needs of children of different cultural and linguistic backgrounds.

Working reality

Glenda describes herself as being comfortable with her assignment since she has developed an approach, through training and experience, which works for her and her pupils. While she is comfortable within the working reality of her classroom, she experiences significant problems as a result of influences from outside the classroom.

> Issues that are outside my mandate and extend beyond the walls of my classroom frustrate me. I have little control over the attitudes and actions of others, but because they affect my students and their families as well as native students and non-white minorities, I have become committed to an inter-cultural education model that develops understanding and respect for diversity.

Glenda uses illustrative experiences which show how she is frustrated. Vignettes included: how a Vietnamese boy, after one and one half years in Canada, was disturbed that he didn't know whether he was Canadian or Vietnamese; how Chinese students, in order to be seen as similar, insisted that Chinese New Year was Chinese Christmas; how Vietnamese parents refused to allow their children to attend camp because they could see no educational value in it; and how a native student hung his head and quit working when singled out for praise.

I have been saddened for these students who are caught in situations over which they have no control and who valiantly try to find their identity in an often conflicting environment. In order to succeed they often turn their backs on their culture and even then find that they still are not accepted.

Glenda seems to convert these feelings of frustration and inadequacy into energy for commitment to implement her dream of what intercultural education might be.

Schools would acknowledge, respect and encourage the diversity in its citizens. Schools would encourage students to retain their language and customs... the multicultural nature of the classroom and community... would be more than dress, diet and dance.... Students would be educated about the history, language, religion, politics, values and customs of students in the school community in a way that would not value one culture over another. They could be eager to share experiences and participate together to broaden their understanding and develop respect for each other.

Glenda sees a number of constraints that impede progress towards this dream. They include problems within the social context of the community, colleagues in education, educational policy and funding, and her own lack of time. Glenda feels that since the dominant societal group does not live a multicultural life, the value of multiculturalism is not seen and appreciated. The attitude of the majority is implicitly superordinate in that they assume that immigrants should 'become like me'. Differences are viewed as strange in comparison to the dominant culture. Strange practices, if they persist, are experiences as threats. 'They still speak Chinese at home!' 'There are six adults in that apartment.' These tendencies, Glenda feels, can lead to fear and prejudice. Members of the dominant group develop stereotypes to cope with their fears. 'Native students are lazy', 'Chinese kids are good at math'.

By labelling groups, the uniqueness of individuals is lost. Stereotyping also closes minds for further understanding; that is all there is to know about a particular minority group. Therefore, there is no need to take time out of an already full curriculum for multicultural activities.

76

A second major set of constraints is related to Glenda's colleagues, who, apart from prejudices they might have themselves, are ill-prepared for multicultural education. Some of Glenda's colleagues who are sensitive to the issues, and who would like to meet multicultural needs, do not have much time to devote to it. A number of teachers who were sympathetic to multicultural education transferred out of the school due to frustration with relationships with the administration of the school. This significantly diminished Glenda's support group. An innovative project that these teachers normally would support was resisted because it was pushed by the administration. Finally, Glenda felt that some teachers envied her class size, preparation and release time, lack of curriculum pressure, and her enthusiasm. They also did not want to be part of anything that meant extra work.

Glenda also feels that local and provincial policies do not sufficiently support multicultural and intercultural education – a reflection perhaps of community attitude described earlier. The lack of public support – a strong voice – also means a lack of funding.

The last constraint that Glenda describes is lack of time to do all that has to be done. Her own words can graphically paint the picture.

> The greatest constraint I feel is that on my time. A look at last week's diary showed, in addition to my full-time teaching responsibilities, the preparation of a proposal for a multicultural lighthouse grant, a meeting with my director for funding to attend a week-long multicultural training program, orienting the native tutor to work with native students at... school, a meeting with the Native Liaison Officer to discuss a cultural awareness workshop for classroom teachers with native students, a Board of Directors meeting for Immigrant Settlement Agency, a graduate course, a computer writing workshop, and a call from the superintendent inviting me to speak to a local service club on ways they might assist immigrant and refugee children in this community. In addition, I serve on an Alberta Education Committee for English as a Second Language and am a member of the writing team for a grade three Social Studies unit. I am also a single parent with three children and sometimes I feel really stretched to try and give them 'quality' time.

In reflecting on her working reality, Glenda notes that there is a wide gap between the ideal and the real which creates a paradox for her. Her ideal of intercultural education she likens to a hearty country vegetable soup. Each ingredient is distinctive and each contributes to the broth that binds them together. Intercultural education would allow students to savour the richness of that soup in the way that a gourmet would – not the way that a hungry child might gulp it down in his eagerness to be outside. She sees the 'Festival' approach as gulping down the soup; it provides stereotyping through accentuating the three Ds – diet, dress and dance. Since, however, this is where the school is at, she will use the Festival to promote looking at similarities and values, and move on next year to something better.

Pedagogy

Glenda started teaching ESL four years ago at the elementary level. Her previous experience had been at the secondary or adult level. When she commenced teaching ESL in a mainstreamed context she both taught and advised teachers as to how to teach her students in the regular classroom. She soon realized, however, that

> My linguistics oriented ESL training, though useful for describing language for me, had no direct practical application in the classroom... I realized quickly that I was in deep trouble with this linguistics oriented approach... I was able to hide my instructional inadequacies in the cubby-holes where I was assigned to teach in the various schools I travelled to. However, I was unable to disguise my lack of knowledge when questioned by teachers on what they could do to assist my students... I felt totally inadequate and incompetent and a failure because I was unable to assist them.

Glenda felt a serious sense of responsibility to her students and their teachers. This, combined with her highly developed desire to succeed impelled her to develop a plan to solve the problem, maintain some pride and save face. Her plan involved:

1 Observing classrooms that seemed successful to find out what elementary students were capable of doing.

2 Asking lots of questions about reading programmes which allowed her to evolve more of a language-oriented programme as opposed to the skill-oriented ESL training she had received.

3 Taking a reading theory course at university during the summer which provided a psycholinguistic framework from which to respond to teachers' questions.

4 Using experience, observation, selected courses and workshops to evolve ways for practical application through appropriate classroom strategies and resources.

'Four years later I feel I have made progress and am comfortable with my personal pedagogy because it works! It is enjoyable for my students and me.'

Glenda's classroom, only 14 feet square, is lined with bookcases and bulletin boards which reflect current themes. Most activities occur at a hexagonal table in the centre of the room. To one side, piled high with files, correspondence, things to do and ignore, sits Glenda's desk. She never works there. The environment encourages conversation and activity to which all students are expected to contribute as far as they are able within class rules to which they have contributed. Within a language development approach, Glenda uses themes that capture the pupils' interest around which to organize a variety of activities that encourage and integrate communication through viewing, listening, reading, speaking and writing. Errors are considered developmental, which, as proficiency increases, students correct themselves. Students develop language at their own rate as they become ready for the next natural step.

Glenda uses singing, chanting, realia, audio-visual experiences, repetitive and predictable stories.

The beginning group has been learning about farms. I introduced the *Little Red Hen* with a filmstrip and then used a rhebus story on large chart papers which I read and encouraged the students to chime in when they felt ready. Because the story is highly predictable they were all reading parts by the third page....

A trip to the Agricultural Exposition produced a group story. I used this language experience story as an evaluation instrument to assess their grasp of concepts and vocabulary and, although there are a few syntax errors, I am delighted with the product. The students are as well as they love reading their own stories.

Glenda does not use phonics, grammar drills, worksheets, as they are irrelevant to the students and boring to her; besides they are not consistent with her philosophy of language development. She does not write behavioural objectives which she finds too prescriptive and restrictive. She plans a general direction from a theme. Student responses and interests influence specific directions which experience has shown her to be 'beyond written objectives'. Her long range plans 'go as far as Friday'.

Glenda feels she has an advantage over other teachers in that she has no mandated curriculum. Whereas the daily challenge of developing resources and activities to interest and motivate students was exhausting for the first two or three years, her current level of experience and teaching enables her to quickly select those resources which are appropriate. She still, however, develops activities in an ongoing way as she responds to children's readiness and interests within each theme. A second advantage Glenda feels she has is that she is not pressured by provincial or local examinations – she is accountable to her students, her administrators, and to herself.

Glenda feels that two major factors influence her current pedagogy. The first is the cultural heritages and needs of her students. She feels that they are already proficient communicators in one language and she just provides them with the opportunity to use their communication skills in another through a supportive environment relevant to their interests which provides confidence, comfort and proficiency. She feels that it is the students who have enabled her to create a unique learning environment. The second factor that influences her pedagogy is Glenda as a person. Such characteristics as a desire to succeed, a fear of failure, and a highly developed sense of responsibility towards herself and others are sources of motivation for the self-initiated way she evolves her expertise and particular philosophy in ESL. She has not stopped this process. This year she has identified the provision for creative writing for advanced students as an observable weakness in her teaching. She has already attended several workshops and intends to pursue more. Glenda also realizes that not having a mandated curriculum and tests has provided her with the freedom and challenge to do what she has done in terms of curriculum and pedagogy. She surmises that maybe she would not have evolved her pedagogy the way she did had she had to function within curriculum guidelines and the provincial tests. She also asserts, however, that if they were introduced now she would not change her pedagogy and curriculum in any major way!

> In spite of the time, energy, and commitment as well as the constraints mentioned earlier, I enjoy my work. It is satisfying to work with students who are highly motivated to learn, who are responsive and appreciative, and who hold the teacher in high esteem.

Tales from the past

How did Glenda's past life history influence who she is as a teacher? How did she come to think and act the way she does in the classroom? In reflecting on her past and these questions, Glenda reconstructed her memories using the metaphor of a 'slow motion film of a seed developing and growing into a blossom', since 'the awareness of and respect for the values and traditions of cultural groups has been a gradual process for me.' She relates significant events that represented crossroads in her life and identifies key people who influenced her within phases called 'Planting the Seed', 'Nurturing', 'The Bud Begins to Open', 'Full Bloom', and 'Planting Again'.

Planting the seed

Glenda's parents, through their teaching and own example, planted the seed of respect for others who were 'different' for whatever reason – particularly her father.

> I remember the night before starting grade 1. My father sat me on his knee and talked to me about the importance of education and doing my best. He also told me that I would meet other children who might have a different colour skin, different shaped eyes or different kind of hair, but in spite of these differences all boys and girls were like me because we all have feelings and we all want to be happy.... That discussion had an enormous impact on me.

Nurturing

The impact of her father's words was strong enough to enable Glenda to respect children of different races, although she did not make any overt gestures of friendship towards any minority students during her schooling. Her schooling years, however, did provide for the development of 'a strong root system and a stem' in nurturing Glenda's seed of interest in other cultures in two particular ways. Firstly, she sought out as much information as she could about other cultures throughout elementary school. She can even remember the names of particular books she took out from the public library which focused on children from other lands. This search for information continued unabated and evolved into a very strong interest in social studies.

Secondly, a social studies teacher in high school had a tremendous influence on Glenda's attitude towards people of other cultures. Ted Aoki, a Japanese Canadian, university professor and curriculum scholar of note, was Glenda's high school social studies teacher. He spent the first few weeks of grade nine relating how the internment of Japanese Canadians and the 'resettlement' in Southern Alberta had affected his family and his life. Her class examined the event from historical, social and moral perspectives.

> It was in his class that I realized that all the interesting bits of information that I had read about other cultures was personal and human. I became aware that lives were structured around Islamic laws; that people suffered and grieved after Hiroshima; that the Renaissance was pain and anguish for those great artists. I learned that all events affected me because I was a member of humanity. It seemed everything that was taught in Ted Aoki's class had meaning in my life....
>
> Ted Aoki was able to inspire me with his knowledge and ideals because he was sincere and caring that we learned and understood. He was more than a model for me of what a teacher should be, he has often been my conscience.

For Glenda a bud appeared on the stem at this time but it remained closed for a number of years. A planned university major did not work out, some teaching (home economics), marriage, children and suburbia took care of her time and interests for a number of years.

The bud begins to open

It was when Glenda's husband joined External Affairs and was
posted to Pakistan that she resumed her interest in other cultures.
It allowed her 'to catch a glimpse of the blossom that had been
dormant for so many years.' This glimpse, however, was only
apparent after a number of traumatic and paradoxical experiences.

The realities of life in Pakistan did not match the expectations
she had created in her mind. As well the social and heady whirl of
diplomatic life, of mingling with ambassadors, diplomats, and
other VIPs from around the world was her major lived experience
– not participation within the host culture. 'It has been just lately
that I have been able to put in perspective the years with External
Affairs and to realize that we all suffered from a severe case of
cultural superiority.'

One negative experience Glenda identifies as culture shock,
whereby firstly there is initial euphoria at the novelty of experience
of the new culture, secondly, frustration is experienced as the
individual attempts to deal with conflicting sets of rules, thirdly,
dysfunction occurs, and lastly, there is resolution of cultural
conflicts. Glenda did not experience the first stage upon arriving
in Pakistan. A second stage of irritation was characterized by her in
terms of servants unable to perform their tasks during Ramadan,
driving on the 'wrong' side of the road, and the unavailability of
bacon.

In her third phase Glenda rejected the Pakistani culture and
refused to understand or accept what appeared to her to be
meaningless behaviours and traditions. 'I was angry with External
Affairs for sending me to such a God-forsaken hole. Small things
bothered me a great deal.' Glenda vividly remembers the emotion
associated with a regulation that did not allow her to have a lamp
on the hall table because her husband's professional status did not
entitle her to have one. She was miserable, unhappy and felt
betrayed by everyone and everything. Glenda, however, decided
that she was responsible for solving her own problems (fourth
stage) and making the most of her experience.

> And my thoughts turned to Ted Aoki. I asked myself what
> would he suggest for me to do and I realized that I had to find
> the personal, human element in Pakistan which was not at
> the receptions, tea parties, and dinners I attended. I took an

interest in the lives of my servants, found out about their families, their villages, their beliefs and their dreams. Artisans and shopkeepers also shared experiences with me. Finally I was getting better.

Glenda talks of the curing process that continued while she was teaching English at the International School of Islamabad: this is where the bud began to open.

With some previous experience, an anthology, a teachers' guide and student workbooks, she felt she could survive teaching twenty grade ten students from fourteen different countries. She was pleased with the discussion of one of the first stories of a woman from New England at the beginning of the century who renounced her husband's authority, but then she noticed that only the Western students were participating.

> A student from Thailand seemed upset so I invited his comments which were startling to most of the class.... 'Women are very special' he said, 'and should not be bothered by unimportant details. A woman has an important job to help her husband and children become great and good. The husband should take care of things that are not important.'

At this point Glenda bit her lip and resisted the urge to argue the point. Other non-Western students began to share the role of women in their cultures as the class engaged the issue with great fascination. 'The teachers' guide was closed and the students' workbooks were returned to the bookroom. The culture and knowledge within the classroom was infinitely more exciting.'

Glenda and her class explored the feminist movement in the West as well as attempting to understand women's roles from many different cultural perspectives. The teaching of English had served a dual purpose; it had also been a stepping stone to intercultural understanding.

Full bloom

Teaching English as a second language has provided Glenda with the opportunity to continue her involvement with people from other cultures in a personal way. This phase was described in the previous sections of this chapter. Glenda also talked of 'planting again', whereby the focus of her efforts will take her beyond the classroom into the examination of the development of quality intercultural education throughout the school system.

Looking ahead

Glenda uses insights gleaned from examining her own personal professional biography and from the social learning of others' life histories in order to project herself into the future. She plans to focus on engaging those constraints from outside her classroom that made her feel helpless. She intends to use her personal strengths and new knowledge to initiate a major school-based project in intercultural education at the school. In doing so she will not impose her personal agenda on others but will participate with her colleagues in evolving what they want out of it. She will take the position that each teacher has a unique understanding of his/her classroom and therefore can determine how best to incorporate project activities therein. At the same time, however, she realizes that when teachers feel inadequately prepared her support should always be felt. She will try to create a sharing and collegial atmosphere wherein she will be a learner who does not have all the answers as well as a resource person. She will also bring in community resource people. She feels and has the aim that, a project like this will create an open and cohesive school climate.

Glenda's longer range plans include: providing for educational programming needs for minority students; providing professional support for classroom teachers in cultural awareness, programmes and instruction; implementing cultural components within the curriculum; creating activities for the classroom and outside that are cross-cultural in nature. She thinks that the best position from which to promote these activities would be as a consultant in intercultural education for a school board. She notes that she needs to continue her work as a catalyst for this thrust within the school board to gain administrative commitment and support.

Interpretations: the nature, sources, and evolution of Glenda's knowledge

The content of Glenda's personal knowledge of teaching is based on children of minority cultures and intercultural education. We can understand this interest from the perspective of her early romantic fascination with far off lands, later made a more human and personally experienced phenomenon, both in the sense of how minorities might experience oppression, but most important how Glenda felt when in the same position. Her experience in becoming a self-determined person out of the foreign and oppressive cultures of Pakistan, the diplomatic service, and the traditional woman's role provides a core experience and image in her personal, practical knowledge that brings her to her work with her students and their lives.

In her work, there is a structural continuum from the real to the ideal. Though the gap presents a dilemma, Glenda appears to use the tension created as energy to move gradually from the real to the ideal. There are three terrains within which she has real–ideal continuums, along which she aims to progress. One concerns the primitive dress, diet and dance approach to multicultural education and the ideal 'vegetable soup' form of intercultural education. Another is her own professional competence which ranges in the past from inadequacy and incompetence towards a future whereby she will have evolved her skills to be able to work effectively within an intercultural notion of education. The third is the broader context of the school, school board and society. This framework, regardless of the *content* of Glenda's personal, practical knowledge, characterizes it as much as a process as anything else. We see her moving along a developmental continuum in an open and dynamic way. Her knowledge is self formed out of personal and professional experience, moved along by a strong sense of responsibility to herself and to others as well as a desire to succeed. As a result of this process the content of her practical knowledge, so far, is undergirded by several key factors. Emotionally, Glenda is able to understand and empathize with her students. She is able not only to accept but value them as individual humans with personal stories but also their cultural and linguistic backgrounds as well. This is manifested in a central way in her curriculum and pedagogy.

Glenda claims that her pupils have taught her what her curriculum and pedagogy should be. In that sense she lives the notion of teacher as learner, not only in her personal but also in her pedagogical life. The relationship in the classroom then is horizontal in the sense that everyone participates in some sense in discerning where to go and what to do next – important ingredients in reducing alienation and increasing the opportunity for self-determination. Glenda hastens to add, however, that this hasn't been easy. She still has difficulty leaving 'the teacher as dispenser of wisdom and knowledge' to trust in her students.

Her father and the romantic fascination with other lands contributed an important predispositional interest on Glenda's part. Ted Aoki, as teacher, and a mentor image, served as an important transitional catalyst in moving Glenda from a distant other focused/directed framework of multiculturalism to a personal, human and authentic view of minority persons and herself. These incidents and persons, though significant, only presage the major source of Glenda's knowledge, which is herself. The key, for Glenda, and in her view, for her pupils, is self-directedness. This involved putting significant others in facilitative relationship to self as opposed to a source of self. The major sources, then, of Glenda's knowledge are rooted in personal and professional experiences that gave rise to her self-directedness. These occurred at the nadir of her anomie. Following the 'stagnant period' of being a suburban wife, having children, teaching what she didn't want to teach (home economics) she was alienated further by being immersed in a foreign culture, the artificial diplomatic life, being still a traditional wife and woman. Many conflicting sets of rules, none of them hers, governed her life leaving her powerless and inauthentic. In a sense, the symbol of the hall table lamp encapsulates and represents, at once, the depths of other-directedness, the decision to liberate and author herself and to begin to understand other people (minorities) in their own terms too. Her personal development intertwined with that of others through her explorations of the people and culture of Pakistan, as well as through her explorations of the role of women in different cultures while teaching. She returned the texts of others in a literal and metaphorical sense to the storeroom and proceeded, with her students, to examine and create texts of her own and their own. She no longer rubbed and polished Aladdin's lamp in the hope of magic or treasure, but created her own.

The foregoing discussion of the nature and sources of Glenda's personal practical knowledge has also characterized, in a general sense, its change and evolution. The watershed experiences which enabled Glenda to become self-initiated and self-determined constitute a revolution of her disposition and activities with respect to her own life. This facilitated the commitment and energy for the evolution of a curriculum and pedagogy in intercultural education over an exhausting but satisfying three or four-year period. She acknowledged her inadequacy, lack of competence and the uselessness of particular theories and set about a process of practical self-education and professional development in the three terrains of her professional life. She did this through observation, questioning, experience, reflection on experience, and the careful selection of courses, workshops and conferences that met her needs providing a coherent curriculum for professional development. This evolutionary and developmental process continues in all three terrains. Glenda has already embarked on activities involving a school-based approach whereby she, with her colleagues in a cooperative team, are evolving their own version of intercultural education.

A COMPARATIVE ANALYSIS OF LLOYD'S AND GLENDA'S PERSONAL PRACTICAL KNOWLEDGE

As a way of beginning to approach a consideration of both the uniqueness and the potentially collectively held aspects of teachers' knowledge we will compare Glenda's and Lloyd's biographies. As well, in a spirit of exploratory speculation we will relate this discussion to preliminary interpretations of sixty other teacher biographies.

Before sketching some comparisons between the nature, sources and evolution of the two teachers' personal practical knowledge, we find it important to draw attention to significant features of their working contexts. Indeed, 'changes' in the financing of education, in the degree of political intervention in school matters, and in the views of, and general level of, esteem for teachers held within the public at large, have, and are having profound effects upon the ways that teachers experience their jobs.

Thus, both Glenda and Lloyd work in situations that are somewhat demanding; Lloyd with his lower socio-economic group who have a variety of problems, Glenda with ESL children. They are both well-respected and effective at their jobs. They have to work hard, having worked particularly hard, as do most teachers, at the beginning of their teaching careers to be able to build up the professional expertise necessary for effective teaching. They both relate how their jobs are stressful and constrained in several common and several different ways. Firstly, despite the stress of teaching in the classroom, they both see the major sources of stress as emanating from outside the classroom or from sources over which they have less control. Perhaps that is why they are perceived as more stressful or alienating. Most teachers appear to feel this way. The details of these external stresses are different in several ways for each as a result of both situation and personal disposition. Lloyd cites interruptions, the fishbowl and external testing as problems, whereas Glenda cites the educational system, political, and societal attitudes and commitments. One particular source of stress that both Glenda and Lloyd identify is intercollegial relations, both with peers and administrators. Glenda's and Lloyd's responses to intercollegial problems are quite different perhaps due, primarily, to their personal dispositions and motivations, although their situations might contribute as well. Lloyd withdraws and becomes a 'closet teacher'; Glenda does not. She continues to work in a collegial way. It could be argued that Glenda's job requires her to collaborate more than Lloyd, and indeed this might be part of the reason why Glenda does not withdraw, but Lloyd's grade level meetings did provide some pressure to collaborate. We argue this way because Lloyd's personal dispositions, the three Ss and upward mobility are likely to lead to withdrawal. As well, in other biographies we have noticed other male teachers practising the same tactic when faced with intercollegial problems. This example is one potential instance of gender differences that are beginning to emerge in our interpretive work.

A third element, common to both working contexts, is curriculum guidelines. Even if they mean different things to each one of them – Lloyd respects them and Glenda is relieved she does not have to follow them – they seem to be a part of the working environment that cannot be ignored. In our future work with other biographies it will be interesting to investigate the role of curriculum guidelines in the worklife of teachers.

The nature, of course, of Lloyd's and Glenda's personal, practical knowledge, though having similar aims for pupils, with respect to acquisition of communications skills, are quite different in the sense of means, illuminating the distinct uniqueness that the interaction of person, task and situation bring. Lloyd's three Ss and upward mobility contrast with Glenda's self-determination and real–ideal continuums. There is, however, one strong common factor between Lloyd and Glenda. In each case the nature of their practical knowledge enables both to be able to identify with the situations of their students. This provides a bridge between teacher and students that binds them together in a common effort. This is a form of mutualism that can maximize congruence of teacher and pupil intentions and, therefore, learning. We suspect that many successful classrooms exhibit this phenomenon. Glenda emphasizes (assisted by no mandated curriculum or tests) the child and teacher as selves negotiating curriculum and pedagogy, as compared to Lloyd, who combines ingrainment with structure. These appear quite different. In the end, however, both pedagogies are active, concrete, expressive, personal and varied with a distinct emphasis on empathy, warmth and humanness. This, regardless of other differences, leaves a similar experienced flavour with the students. One difference in experienced flavour, however, might be with respect to student choice. Lloyd's students do make choices and are able to be expressive but the spectrum is constrained by their being subjected more to the mandated curriculum and external tests. The context of mandated curriculum and external tests, combined with personal disposition gives rise to Lloyd being, not a puppet, but a carefully planned negotiator, an arbitrator, a mediator, on behalf of his students, within the social structures in which the students, and Lloyd, find themselves. The aim is success within the existing system. Glenda, on the other hand, is able to plan and negotiate with her students as, and for, self-determination. She thinks in terms of them and her transcending and/or transforming school-based and societal constraints to 'interculturalism'.

The influences on, or sources of, both Glenda's and Lloyd's knowledge include experiences as children, parents, teachers, their cultural background, personal and professional experiences, and peers. This spectrum of possible influences is relatively common across the teachers in our biographies, although the unique patterns and emphases do differ. Some teachers, but not all, have current mentors, past mentors who remain with them in spirit, or images that guide their thoughts and actions. Teacher education is seldom mentioned; when it is, it mostly relates to an outstanding professor or teacher associate. There are sometimes, but rarely, references to outstanding teacher education programmes. Though they differ as to pattern and emphasis of influences, with Glenda's being more personal and later than Lloyd's early and familial pattern, they cluster around when they had their most significant life experiences, traumas and transformations. This attests to the links between life history and professional thought and action.

The evolution of their personal knowledge, their attitude and approaches to professional change, improvement and development are quite different and distinct. If this variety is sustained over a large number of teachers one can appreciate the necessity of teacher-initiated approaches to participating in and interpreting large-scale changes that are deemed necessary for our pupils' futures.

DISCUSSION

Recently, qualitative paradigms have regained respectability in educational research. Autobiographical research, however, even within the qualitative field, remains controversial since its data are subject to incompleteness, personal bias and selective recall in the process by which the narrative is constructed. The fallibility of memory, selective recall, repression, the shaping of stories according to dispositions, internal idealization and nostalgia all present the possibility of biased data. The inward-looking nature of autobiography, the making sense of ourselves in our own terms, can also be seen as narcissistic and solipsistic, lacking the contrasting 'countersubjective' view of others. Our methodology, however, has been designed with these concerns in mind. With respect to memory lapses and selective recall, both the collaborative nature of the exercise and the process of starting from the present and following leads back into the past to stimulate recall. Focusing initially on feelings enables us to think back to events associated with them. Being exposed to other's stories helps memory, as do the questions we ask of one another. As well, significant events in a person's life and career are most easily remembered. Being surrounded by persons telling their own stories related to a shared context of teaching prods the edges and blank spaces of our selective recall and repression of certain areas. That we ground our stories in current reality, illustrated by vignettes, provides a measure of reality testing, within and across our stories, to hold in check over-fictionalized accounts or rationalizations. Other's stories do, as well, act as counter-biographies of, or alternative interpretations of, similar contexts. We ourselves have acted as participant-observers in our autobiographer co-researchers' classrooms and been impressed by the face validity of their accounts, the congruence between the story and our observations. This can, perhaps, be understood because the trust that is built up within the conditions of narrative interaction, and the authentic examples of others, encourage us to unmask ourselves, to disclose underlying problems. Participants do reveal personal flaws, discontinuities and concerns, as well as taking responsibility for their own stories. In a more formal sense we can borrow from the criteria within the field of ethnobiography[42] to speak to phenomenological validity. Here, the 'counter-biographies' of the various participants represent a horizontal cross-checking of accounts. The fact that individuals make multiple drafts, over time, of portions of their autobiographies represents a type of longitudinal or vertical cross-checking. The interaction of these two forms of validity checks provide for further, intersubjective checks of accounts, as the collaborative autobiographical process evolves.

One fundamental issue related to the development and understanding of teachers' knowledge that we face is that it should be known by others as teachers know it. This presents a challenge to the customary relationship of researchers to their subjects, where researchers frame the research, analyse the data, create categories and generate or apply interpretive concepts. In our research, we address this problem by working with the teacher as co-researcher in finding and expressing her own voice in the understanding of her knowledge. We need ways, however, of helping our teachers to deepen their own interpretation, perhaps by responding to 'framing' questions generated collaboratively. This point reflects our concern about the degree to which we, the researchers, still shape the interpretation of teachers' knowledge. We are also concerned about the collegiality of relationships: Despite our efforts, to what degree are the issues of asymmetric power, education and status still problematic? This is of concern especially within the context of the graduate course from which teachers' stories originate.

We have also been wrestling with whether to use various critical frameworks through which to interpret the autobiographies; especially if it deepens teachers' interpretations. Many of our colleagues see potential in applying adult developmental, linguistic, literary, psychoanalytic, feminist, or neo-Marxist frameworks, for example. Using these interpretative frameworks is thought to give the data meaning beyond individual stories; not using them would run the risk of solipsism. These frameworks can be used in two ways. First, they can be brought into the class and integrated into the autobiographical process, particularly during the interpretive phase, to aid understanding of our own lives. Secondly, they can be used for a more 'external' yet collaborative interpretation of individual stories or groups of stories. Until now, we have deliberately chosen to do neither. We would prefer that our teacher colleagues make sense of their realities in terms that are meaningful to them – invent their own frameworks. After all, we are interested in teachers' self-construed knowledge. Looking at other frameworks might be a next stage for teacher autobiographers, but only after they have had the chance to evolve their own. Our disposition, then, could be construed as reflecting an 'existential frame'. As for meta-interpretive frames, we prefer to investigate the stories inductively, to see which internal frames might exist, especially those guided by our research questions. Having done this for individual and collective stories, we may then examine other frameworks for commonalities. We might also invite a variety of scholars to interpret a particular set of stories from different perspectives and have teachers respond to these interpretations in some kind of interchange where the insider–outsider issue could be addressed. An eclectic framework might then be evolved for understanding teachers' knowledge and lives.

Autobiographical research of this sort brings with it a need to encourage disclosure yet also to assure ethical handling of personal data. In the course from which our autobiographers start their writing, each has ultimate control over what is disclosed and whether or how their stories are to be used for research purposes. For some critics, the course is an invasion of privacy. This may have been the case for three teachers out of some 120, with whom alternative ways of pursuing the course were negotiated. The climate of the class is not geared to 'probing' and groups working collaboratively on autobiographies appear to have an in-built sensitivity about where not to tread; individuals have a sense as to personal readiness for self-disclosure regarding particularly personal topics.[43]

For understandable reasons, those who work in an autobiographical mode are also prone to the criticism of 'practising therapy without a licence'. Our position, very simply, is that we do not see ourselves as practising therapy. Nevertheless, some forms of self-reflection or self-education, including this type of course, *may* prove therapeutic. There is, however, one issue that does concern us: When teachers' autobiographies are made public, anonymously or not, they are vulnerable to the judgements about their practices and lives that come with the cut and thrust of scholarship and politics. This can include abuse of qualitative data. When asked about this issue, our autobiographers usually respond that, having found their own voice and released their own stories, they are prepared for this eventuality, enjoying, for example, participating with us in conference presentations.

Another major issue for us is moving from understanding individual teachers' professional lives to understanding teachers collectively. How can we simultaneously represent commonality and uniqueness? Even though each teacher's story, knowledge and development is unique, there are commonalities: One teacher's story can be seen as representative of a particular group[44].

We can simultaneously represent both commonality and uniqueness by comparing and contrasting small collections of teachers' stories, as we have attempted to do in this chapter with two teachers. Through accumulations of these comparisons, perhaps we can build an image of what is common and unique. A third possible approach draws on methods in collective biography, specifically prosopography[45] and ethnobiography[46] whereby we might attempt to identify groups of teachers who, on the basis of criterion variables related to context and person, are experiencing similar professional realities. In prosopography, these criteria are set up as tests that will indicate whether a teacher qualifies as a member of a particular group. Membership, while facilitating comparison and generalizations within the group, also provides for generalization to other potential members in the teaching force at large.

CONCLUSION

We have outlined examples of an evolving approach to collaborative autobiography as a means for understanding the nature, development and function of teachers' professional knowledge. We wish to note, however, that the effect of any aberration, in the way that teachers see their own knowledge, is less important if one recalls that teachers think and behave *as if it were true*. The important question in the nature of teachers' knowledge is what generates thoughts and actions, not whether it is 'true'. The same, however, cannot be said with respect to understanding the development of teachers' knowledge. Here, limitations in the data require us to make every effort to minimize their effect.

For the immediate future, we will continue to refine our methodology, interpret more individual stories, and gradually try to discern commonalities that might exist across teachers' lives. We have also begun more participant-observation in classrooms, to examine how teachers can express the professional knowledge they hold in particular contexts. Also, in order to evolve a conceptualization of teachers' knowledge that is grounded in classroom reality, we have recently combined ethnographic and biographical approaches in exploring one teacher's knowledge and development. This approach seems to address further some of the validity issues that were raised earlier. In this approach, discourse on practice and practices themselves are understood dialectically; the 'philosophy of teaching' is seen as a practice.[47] The validity issues raised by the remoteness of written discourse from action can then be at least partially addressed.

ACKNOWLEDGEMENTS

This research was supported in part by a grant from the Social Sciences and Humanities Research Council (Canada).

We wish to acknowledge Pat Panchmatia, Joyce Ito, Shari Platt, Karen Karbashewski and Pam Attwell for typing many drafts of this manuscript.

NOTES

1 This chapter is based on extracts from three papers: Butt, R.L., Raymond, D., McCue, G. and Yamagishi, L. (April 1986) 'Individual and collective interpretations of teacher biographies'. Paper presented at AERA, San Francisco; Butt, R.L., Raymond, D. and Yamagishi, L. (1988) 'Autobiographic praxis: studying the formation of teachers' knowledge', *Journal of Curriculum Theorizing*, Vol. 7, No. 4; and Butt, R.L. and Raymond, D. (1989) 'Studying the nature and development of teachers knowledge using collaborative autobiography', *International Journal of Educational Research*, Vol. 13, No. 4, pp. 403–419.

2 Butt, R.L. and Raymond, D. (1987) 'Arguments for using qualitative approaches in understanding teacher thinking: The case of biography', *Journal of Curriculum Theorizing*, Vol. 7, No. 1, pp. 62–93.

3 Clandinin, D.J. (1985) 'Personal practical knowledge: A study of teachers' classroom images', *Curriculum Inquiry*, Vol. 15, No. 4, pp. 361–385.

4 Butt, R.L. (1982) 'Curriculum: Metatheoretical horizons and emancipatory action', *Journal of Curriculum Theorizing*, Vol. 6, No. 2, pp. 7–23.

5 Sarason, B. (1971) *The Culture of the School and the Problem of change*, Boston: Allyn and Bacon.

6 Aoki, T. (1983) 'Curriculum implementation as instrumental action and as interpretive praxis' in Butt, R.L., Olson, J. and Daignault, J. (eds) *Insiders' Realities, Outsiders' Dreams: Prospects for Curriculum Change, Curriculum Canada IV*, Vancouver: Centre for the Study of Curriculum and Instruction, University of British Columbia; Clandinin 'Personal practical knowledge'; Elbaz, F. (1983) *Teacher Thinking: A Study of Practical Knowledge*, London: Croom Helm; Werner, W. (1982) 'An interpretative approach to curriculum implementation' in Leithwood, K. and Hughes, A. (eds) *Curriculum Research and Development, Curriculum Canada III*, Vancouver: Centre for the Study of Curriculum and Instruction, University of British Columbia.

7 Fullan, M. (1982) *The Meaning of Educational Change*, Toronto: OISE Press; Fullan, M. (1985) 'Change processes and strategies at the local level', *The Elementary School Journal*, Vol. 85, No. 3, pp. 391–422; Guskey, T.R. (1985) 'Staff development and teacher change', *Educational Leadership*, Vol. 42, No. 7, pp. 57–60.

8 Fullan, *Educational Change*, p. 263.

9 Flanders, T. (1983) 'Teacher realities, needs and professional development' in Butt, R.L., Olson, J., and Daignault, J. (eds) *Insiders' Realities, Outsiders' Dreams: Prospects for Curriculum Change, Curriculum Canada IV*, Vancouver: Centre for the Study of Curriculum and Instruction, University of British Columbia, p. 148.

10 Fullan, *Educational Change;* Fullan, *'Change processes'*; Ingvarson, L. and Greenway, P.A. (1982) *Portrayals of Teacher Development*, ED 200600, p. 28; Guskey, 'Staff development'.

11 Adams, R.D. (1982) 'Teacher development: a look at changes in teacher perceptions and behaviour across time', *Journal of Teacher Education*, Vol. XXIII, No. 4, pp. 40–43; Fuller, F. and Brown, O. (1975) 'Becoming a teacher' in Ryan, K. (ed.) *Teacher Education*, The 74th Yearbook of the National Society for the Study of Education, Chicago: The University of Chicago Press; Newman, K.K., Burden, P.R., and Applegate, J.H. (1980) 'Helping teachers examine their long range development'. Paper presented at the National Convention of the Association of Teacher Educators, Washington, DC, ED 204321; Newman, K.K., Dornburg, B., Dubois, D., and Kranz, E. (1980) *Stress in Teachers' Mid-career Transitions: A Role for Teacher Education*, ED 196868, p. 23; Ball, S. and Goodson, I.F. (1989) (eds) *Teachers' Lives and Careers*, London: Falmer.

12 Huberman, M. and Shapira, A.L. (1979) 'Cycle de vie et enseignment: changements dans les relations enseignant-eleves au cours de la carriere', *Gymnasium Helvetium*, Vol. 34, No. 2, pp. 113–129; Newman, K.K. (1979) 'Middle-aged experienced teachers' perceptions of their career development'. Paper presented at the Annual Meeting of the American Educational Research Association, San Francisco, ED

171697; Newman *et al.*, 'Helping teachers'; Newman *et al.*, *Stress*, p. 23.

13 Gherke, N.J. (1981) 'A grounded–theory study of beginning teachers' role personalization through reference group relations', *Journal of Teacher Education*, Vol. XXXII, No. 6, pp. 33–38; Huberman, M. and Shapira, A.L. (1983) 'Evolution des relations entre enseignants', *Gymnasium Helvetium*, Vol. 37, No. 5, pp. 285–305; Newman *et al.*, 'Helping teachers'; Newman *et al.*, *Stress*, p. 23.

14 Huberman, M. (1984) 'Vers une biographe pedagogique de l'enseignant', *Education permanente*, Vol. 7, No. 73, pp. 183–193; Huberman.

15 Newman *et al.*, 'Helping teachers'; Newman *et al.*, *Stress*, p. 23.

16 Lather, P. (1984) 'Gender and the shaping of public school teaching: do good girls make good teachers'. Paper presented at the Annual Meeting of the National Women's Studies Association, Douglass College, NJ, p. 2.

17 ibid., p. 6.

18 Freedman, S. (1983) 'Master teacher/merit pay – Weeding out women from women's true profession: A critique of the commissions on education', *Radical Teacher*, Vol. 25, p. 27.

19 Reid and Walker (1975) in Elbaz, F. (1983) *Teacher Thinking: A Study of Practical Knowledge*, London: Croom Helm.

20 Hunt, D.E. and Gow, J. (1984) 'How to be your own best theorist II', *Theory into Practice*, Vol. 23, pp. 64–71; Bussis, A.M., Chittenden, E.A., and Amarel, M. (1976) *Beyond Surface Curriculum*, Boulder: Westview.

21 Butt and Raymond, 'Arguments for using qualitative approaches'.

22 Pinar, W. (September 1978) 'Notes on the curriculum field, 1978', *Educational Researcher*, Vol. 7, No. 8, pp. 5–12; Pinar, W. (1980) 'Life history and educational experience. Part I', *Journal of Curriculum Theorizing*, Vol. 2, No. 2, pp. 59–212; Pinar, W. (1981) 'Life history and educational experience. Part II', *Journal of Curriculum Theorizing*, Vol. 3, No. 1, pp. 259–286.

23 Pinar, W. (1988) 'Autobiography and the architecture of self', *Journal of Curriculum Theorizing*, Vol. 8, No. 1, pp. 7–36.

24 Butt, R.L. (1978) 'The development of a conceptual system for the open classroom', PhD dissertation, University of Ottawa.

25 Berk, L. (1980) 'Education in lives: Biographic narrative in the study of educational outcomes', *Journal of Curriculum Theorizing*, Vol. 2, No. 2, pp. 88–155.

26 Dewey, J. (1963) *Experience and Education*, New York: Macmillan.

27 ibid., p. 40.

28 ibid., p. 67.

29 Butt, 'The development of a conceptual system'.

30 Rogers, C.R. (1969) *Freedom to Learn*, Columbus, Ohio: Merrill.

31 ibid., pp. 151–157.

32 Dearden, K.F. (1968) *The Philosophy of Primary Education*, New York: Routledge and Kegan Paul, p. 38.

33 Berk, 'Education in lives', p. 88.

34 ibid., p. 89.

35 ibid.

97

36 ibid., p. 93.
37 Goodson, I. (1980/1981) 'Life histories and the study of schooling', *Interchange*, Vol II, No. 4, p. 63.
38 Pinar, 'Notes on the curriculum'.
39 Goodson, 'Life histories', p. 63.
40 Becker, H.S. (1970) 'The career of a Chicago schoolmaster' in Becker, H.S. (ed.) *Sociological Work: Method and Substance*, Chicago: Aldine. Goodson, 'Life histories'.
41 Butt, R.L. (1989) 'An integrative function for teachers' biographies'in Milburn, G. *et al.* (eds) *Reinterpreting Curriculum Research: Images and Arguments*, London, Ontario: Althouse.
42 Abbs, P. (1974) *Autobiography and Education*, London: Heinemann.
43 Clapier-Valadon, S. and Poirer, J. (1980) 'Le concept d'ethnobiographie et les recits de vie croises', *Cahiers internationaux de sociologie*, Vol. 69, pp. 351–358.
44 Pineau, G. and Marie-Michele (1983) *Produire sa Vie: Autofomation et Autobiographie*, Montreal: Editions St Martin.
45 Raymond, D. and Surprenant, M. (April 1988) 'Investigating teachers' knowledge through ethnographic and biographic approaches: A case study'. Paper presented at AERA, New Orleans.
46 Clapier-Valadon and Poirer, 'Le concept'.
47 Raymond and Surprenant, 'Investigating teachers' knowledge'.

4

MODELS FOR UNDERSTANDING PRE-SERVICE AND BEGINNING TEACHERS' BIOGRAPHIES

Illustrations from case studies

J. Gary Knowles

Biography is increasingly believed to have a significant bearing on the classroom behaviours and practices of teachers.[1] In particular, biography seems to play a major role in how student and beginning teachers approach their early experiences in the classroom.[2] The focus of this chapter and of my investigations into biographies rests on the assumption that pre-service teachers' thinking about teaching and their classroom practice is partially shaped by their prior experiences.[3]

In the context of this chapter, biography refers to those formative experiences of pre-service and beginning teachers which have influenced the ways in which they think about teaching and, subsequently, their actions in the classroom. Biography especially refers to those experiences that become the basis for teacher role identity suggested by Crow[4] and, simply put, teacher role identity is the way in which individuals think about themselves as teachers – the images they have of self-as-teacher.

This chapter presents the composite conclusions from five separate case studies of pre-service secondary teachers.[5] It provides explanations, be they partial and in the process of refinement, as to the connections between biographies and how student teachers and beginning teachers think about teaching, the education process and their practices in the classroom.

Within the context of the literature on teacher socialization, as it is interrelated with knowledge about teachers' biographies, the purpose of this chapter is to present consolidated findings from several pre-service and beginning teacher case studies, make some sense of the origins of their teacher role models and present initial theoretical models to explain how biography is related to teaching practice. There are two major sections to this chapter: (1) a survey of foundational teacher socialization literature and a summary of recent case studies; and (2) some theoretical views of how biography impacts practice. Implications for pre-service teacher education are imbedded in the discussion.

FOUNDATIONAL LITERATURE AND CASE STUDIES

It is not the purpose of the chapter to provide the reader with a thorough review of the relevant research. Crow, for example, provides a comprehensive literature review on biography within the context of pre-service teachers, and others have dealt with broader issues of biography and teaching, and teachers' lives and career experiences.[6] This section has three components: (1) biography in the socialization literature as emphasized by researchers who have speculated about the place of biography in the practices of teachers; (2) several research efforts that have had an explicit objective of understanding some aspect about the impact of biography on teaching; and (3) a summary of five individual case studies that I have conducted.

Biography in the socialization literature and research

There are two major viewpoints which attempt to explain the socialization of beginning teachers.[7] One view places the role of the student teaching experience, along with the latter years of pre-service teacher education and early inservice teaching, as the major socializing influence.[8] Contextual influences that seem to be important, from this perspective, include: the structure of schools;[9] cooperating teachers;[10] and the powerful ecological force of the classroom,[11] of which miseducative results are possible for the pre-service and student teacher.[12]

The other major view of the teacher socialization process asserts that formal pre-service education and student teaching has little effect on the beliefs and practices of student teachers and beginning teachers. As Zeichner and Grant acknowledge, 'this position emphasizes the primacy of *biography* in the socialization of student teachers and locates the major sources of socializing influence at a point prior to the advent of formal training.'[13] The genesis of this viewpoint is the recognition that, unlike future physicians or lawyers who come to their formal professional preparation relatively ignorant and unskilled about their future professional duties and places of work, future teachers do not come to teacher education and beginning teaching ignorant and unskilled as to the mechanics, processes and rules of their place of work – they already know classrooms.

Such is Lortie's claim: that countless hours spent in classrooms as students and the personal predispositions of prospective teachers formulate the basis of a beginning teacher's thoughts and actions. Early perceptions of teachers' work are importantly formative:

> Socialization into teaching is largely self-socialization; one's personal predispositions are not only relevant but, in fact, stand at the core of becoming a teacher.
>
> Years of unformulated experience as a student precede formal socialization; teachers themselves emphasize the importance of the private experiences they have as beginning teachers.
>
> The lessons taught by early yet persisting models rest on chance and personal preference; training in pedagogy does not seem to fundamentally alter earlier ideas about teaching.[14]

Zeichner and Grant concur with Lortie's position, that the impact of student teaching and pre-service training is minimal, and they suggest:

> Future research on student teacher socialization should give more attention to the influence of biography on socialization outcomes. Although it is probably incorrect to assume that biography is the sole determiner of socialization outcomes. . . it is clear. . . that what students bring into the experience cannot be ignored in attempts to illuminate socialization mechanisms and that social structural influences have probably been greatly overemphasized in many earlier studies.[15]

Zeichner and Grant believe that research on the development of student teacher perspectives and the ecological and psychological contexts that predispose students to think and act in particular ways offers considerable potential for understanding 'the existential reality of becoming a teacher'.[16] In other words, understanding the origins of student teacher perspectives is largely a product of understanding the impact of biography – those experiences that have directly influenced an individual's thinking about teaching and schools.

Woods maintained that research on 'teacher identities, their interests and biographies', is urgently needed because 'we have little knowledge of how teachers' early experiences affect their careers and strategies'. He believed that ethnographic research efforts can uncover the meanings behind the actions of teachers.[17] Woods' assessment of the need for research on teacher biographies has been largely derived from observations about the manner in which teachers develop strategies for survival in the classroom – a phenomenon something akin to Pollard's coping strategies.[18]

Benyon observed that interactionist viewpoints on the work of teachers, that is, views which place emphasis on situations and strategies of the classroom, have obscured the importance of previous experiences in formulating actions and reactions to classroom difficulties because those prior experiences are not held to be importantly formative because they do not appear to be usefully substantive.[19] He noted that researchers such as Goodson argue that the actions of teachers cannot be separated from their personal socio-historical past.[20]

Research on biography: understanding teaching behaviours

As a first-year teacher in a small, urban, community, secondary school in New Zealand I was initially unaware of the effects that my biography had on my teaching. Yet, in retrospect, the manner in which I went about teaching in those early years was a reflection of my environment as a young learner in public, primary and secondary schools in New Zealand – not upon the substance of professional teacher preparation.

Intuitively, and apart from the literature, the study of personal biography as it impacts the beginning teacher makes good sense. Despite the case for there being some effect of biography – among many other conditions and contextual influences – upon the teaching of neophytes, there is relatively little empirical evidence generated which pertains to the subject.

The example of personal biography afforded by Sue Middleton (Chapter 2) illustrates the value of considering the forces and experiences which shape one's orientation to teaching. Indeed her collection of feminist educational life histories gives further credence to the value of considering biography's role in shaping the reactionary forces and actions of the classroom.[21]

While the empirical literature which relates teaching practice to biography is rather scant, there are a number of studies which highlight the angles from which biography have been viewed. Several examples follow: Some work merely points to it as an important key to understanding behaviours and treats the issue of biography in peripheral ways.[22] Other studies explicitly seek to understand the direct links between biography and practice.[23]

Barone made an in-depth examination of one student's biography with the express purpose of understanding how and why she became a pre-service teacher. Barone recognized the impact of significant life experiences on the classroom practices of teachers and advocated a teacher selection process that considers components of biography.[24] The study by Eddy shed light on the transitions from pupil to teacher that beginning elementary and secondary teachers made within the context of teaching in East Coast, inner-city American schools. Eddy examined the transition teachers experienced as they moved from student teacher to beginning teacher. Eddy likened the transition to rites of passage as experienced in primitive cultures, and recognized teachers' difficulties in overcoming their own socialization as pupils, particularly since there are definite limitations in the transfer of socialization skills and knowledge between being a pupil and being a teacher. Those beginning teachers assigned to school environments which were vastly different than their experiences as pupils found adjustments difficult to cope with.[25]

Although not directly concerned with pre-service teachers, Woods examined one classroom teacher's view of self and became involved in investigating the 'teacher's total life and career. [He tried] . . . to identify some of the major strands of the development of self' and the important life and career influences that affect it. Self was defined as the expression of the individual teacher in the school and classroom which revealed the varying and complex personal, environmental and experiential influences, personal dispositions, attitudes and beliefs of the teacher. From this, Woods concluded: 'Elements of that self have been formulated in early life.'[26] Woods purposely tried to link the present elements of the teacher's life with the past and derived two major sources of the teacher's self: the 'macro self' and the 'micro self'. The micro self relates to a number of early and formative pre-service experiences: home and parents; literature and art; teachers and coaches; and those of one's adult family from marriage. The macro self of the teacher is derived from certain broader environmental factors: the teacher's social class origins; religious experiences; and the social, political and economic climate. Woods concluded:

> Our data have suggested how the formulation of self in the early years may relate to later teaching. . ., and the part played in the formulation of that self by such factors as home environment, parents, teachers, marriage and socio-economic and political factors. We need to give more consideration to this whole life perspective. . . .[27]

Woods underscored not only the importance of viewing teachers within the context of their ongoing careers but also within the influence that early life experiences have on the teaching self.[28]

Britzman's ethnographic case study of two student teachers specifically set out to describe and analyse 'the interaction between each student teacher's biography and the social structure of the school'.[29] One of the questions that was addressed relates to the life experiences that student teachers use in their teaching to help construct meanings and actions in the classroom. Britzman concluded that the student teacher's conceptions of the roles of students and the roles of teachers were 'familiar and firmly rooted in his or her biography.'[30] The student teachers' biographies had many examples of previous and observed teaching models which profoundly affected their actions in the classroom. Student teachers have both positive and negative impressions of teachers and images of teachers they do not want to become. Britzman suggested that biography and socialization links be further explored:

> Prospective teachers participate in long-term radical thera-peutic relationships where life experience is articulated and analyzed in relation to how individuals affect and are affected by the social setting, people and personal experience.[31]

Britzman also urged greater consideration of the impact that student teachers' biographies have on the context of teacher education because student teachers bring with them their 'institutional biographies – the cumulative experience of school lives – which in turn, inform their knowledge of the student's world, of school structure and of curriculum'.[32] One of Britzman's arguments against the apprenticeship model of teacher preparation is that it does not address the 'over dependence on one's institutional biography' in becoming a teacher,[33] and it is her view that student and beginning teachers need to uncover the elements of their biographies which hinder and assist in their becoming an empowered or autonomous teacher.[34]

The purpose of Martinez's ethnographic study of four beginning teachers was to understand the personal perspectives, and origins of those perspectives, that new and beginning teachers bring with them to the classroom. Perspectives were examined within the institutional and systemic contexts of teaching. For some of the beginning teachers, the long period of classroom apprenticeship as a student was a major influence on their teaching perspectives. Martinez hypothesized that the effects of prolonged classroom apprenticeship may be greatest when the decision to become a teacher is made at an early age. The results also suggested it is not so much the educational theories presented at the pre-service preparation that impact beginning teachers as it is the teaching styles of the university teachers. Foundations for understanding the general regulation of schools and institutions also had bases in the experiences of the teachers when they were school students.[35]

In a case study of four pre-service teachers, Munro observed the effect of personal biography:

> That what the [pre-service] trainees bring with them into training may well have more significant effects on their teaching behaviour than the training experience itself. In particular, [pre-service] trainees' dispositions towards teaching, relationship with pupils, and classroom management would appear to owe much to factors embedded in personal biography.[36]

Munro noted that the personal biography is a rich source of information which not only helps clarify pre-service teachers' dispositions and behaviours, but also accounts for their readiness to accept institutional socialization. There were a number of ways in which biography influenced the in-classroom practice: confidence displayed in the classroom; relationship with students; and personal work habits, planning and organizational skills.[37]

A case study on socialization of pre-service teachers by Crow provided evidence of the influence biography has on individual's beliefs about teaching, education and practice in the classroom. The formation of the 'teacher role identity' was found to be strongly related to biography. Definable characteristics of teacher role identities included a number of beliefs held by the pre-service teachers regarding: (1) the life and the character of classrooms and, in particular, average and mediocre classrooms. Pre-service teachers believed they would not duplicate such classrooms but would provide heightened environments for learning; in other words, (2) providing resistance to the status quo; (3) envisioning themselves as the ideal teacher; and (4) confidence in creating classrooms and learning environments that were different from the average. The sources of their views of themselves as teachers, their teacher role identity, included: (1) role models, especially positive ones, provided by 'remembrances of previous teachers'; (2) previous teaching experiences; (3) significantly positive or negative university and pre-service educational theory classes; and (4) remembered childhood experiences about learning and family activities and family role models.[38]

The pre-service teachers' teacher role identities appeared to be used as 'interpretive lenses through [which] they viewed the [university] program, their teaching practice, and the teaching profession'.[39] Conflict between an individual's teacher role identity and the perceived programmatic ideals and curriculum may produce extreme discontinuities. Classroom behaviour of cooperating teachers and the pre-service teachers' own teaching practice are viewed through the lens of their teacher role identities. Such images of what it means to be a teacher endure and remain intact through the end of student teaching. The many difficulties that student teachers experience are often a reflection of the incongruities between their own perceptions of teachers' work and the specific directives of the cooperating teacher or the policy and organizational structure of the school.[40] Crow concluded that individual pre-service teachers significantly and consciously influence the condition of their own socialization into schools and, while their teacher role identities may be modified during the course of pre-service experiences, they remain an important frame of reference from which classroom actions of self and others are evaluated.[41]

Problem-solving and coping strategies

Problem-solving and coping strategies are one way to access and link classroom practices with biography. There is, however, a difficulty in fusing the literature on coping strategies because there is little consensus as to what it means to cope. In the literature, differences between problem-solving strategies and coping strategies are difficult to distinguish and, for the most part, represent nuances in assigned definitions where coping strategies are classroom derivatives of individuals' problem-solving strategies.

Woods' assessment of the need for research on teacher biographies has been largely derived from observations about the manner in which teachers develop strategies for survival in the classroom. He claims that the concept of teacher strategies can help understand the influence of biography on practice: 'This [research focus on teacher strategies] . . . allows for the consideration of the influence of both structurally generated constraints and of individual biography.'[42]

Understanding the problems that student teachers and beginning teachers experience provides an appropriate backdrop for comprehending the approaches and the origins of those approaches that neophytes use to solve problems in the classroom. As Zeichner perceives:

> The response of beginning teachers depends upon a number of individual factors such as a teacher's unique biographical history, the strength with which teaching perspectives are held, the level of a teacher's 'coping skills', cognitive-developmental maturity and the degree of sensitivity to the organizational dynamics of the school.[43]

Problem-solving strategies

Lacey identified a number of periods in the actions of student teachers that were oriented to their changing problem-solving strategies.[44] Lacey recognized changes in the manner in which student teachers arrive at solutions to problems and the periods are somewhat analogous to the teacher developmental stages suggested by Veenman[45] and Ryan[46]. First, the 'honeymoon period' was a time of 'euphoria and heightened awareness'[47] which occurred early in student teaching. The second period was one in which the student teachers sought materials and strategies of teaching, particularly in an effort to overcome inadequacies in classroom control and discipline approaches. Third, a 'crisis period' followed where they felt they were not in control of the classroom learning environment and were unable to 'get through to their pupils'.[48] To some degree they felt like failures and blamed the system and the students. A fourth period followed. They overcame the problems by one or more of a variety of strategies beginning with sharing the problems with peers – 'collectivization'. Yet another category of action was labelled 'privatization' where they refused to talk about the issues. Another way in which problems were handled was by 'upward and downward displacement of blame'[49] where student teachers blamed either the school and the system, or the pupils.

Lacey also recognized three theoretical types of social strategy for dealing with difficulties: 'strategic compliance', 'internalized adjustment', and 'strategic redefinition'. The value in thinking about the three theoretical categories is that they provide an overlay explanation of the way in which neophytes deal with problems. Strategic compliance refers to a situation where an individual merely complies with the demands of the situation in order to survive. This alternative may be resorted to in situations where there are tensions, say between the university and the public school, where internalized adjustment can not be implemented. Internalized adjustment, then, is evidenced when an individual makes a change in his or her thinking about a particular situation or difficulty in order to deal with the external demands of the situation. In particular, a modification of orientation or beliefs about aspects of teaching may be evident. Strategic redefinition refers to a case when an individual redefines or interprets the dynamics and conditions of a situation so that the problem is perceived as being something that can be dealt with at an appropriate level. By linking biography to teacher actions, Lacey summed up his concern for the implications of neophytes' social strategies and the usefulness of his developmental scheme for describing 'some of the common experiences of students as they take up a teacher perspective':

> The implication [of social strategy is] that the individual actor, who is at the intersection of 'biography' and the 'social situation' has some freedom to manipulate and change the

situation while at the same time being constrained to adjust to it.[50]

Coping Strategies

While Lacey attends to the social aspects of student teacher problem-solving (according to his definition of the strategies), others' viewpoints provide different yet supporting perspectives. Woods' analysis of 'survival strategies' paralleled Lacey's work and was completed independently about the time Hargreaves and Pollard were investigating 'coping strategies' from two very different perspectives.[51] Hargreaves focused on the 'macro' components of coping which were related to the broad and encompassing issues and circumstances in which individuals had to cope. Conversely, Pollard examined the subjective meaning of teachers' coping strategies. In particular, Pollard emphasized the importance of biography in fathoming the classroom coping actions of teachers. Pollard's theoretical model for understanding coping strategies is complex. Together, Woods and Pollard have had an ongoing discussion of Hargreaves' and their own ideas about the interrelated concepts of 'survival' and 'coping'.[52] As a result, they are largely responsible for the theoretical literature on the topic.

Woods' view is that 'survival strategies' represent the concessions or accommodations that teachers make in order to neutralize discomforting situations that arise in the classroom. To this end, teachers engage in activities such as domination, socialization, fraternization, routinization, morale boosting, and others, in an effort to provide for comfort in the classroom.[53]

Hargreaves suggested that coping strategies are generalized definitions of teaching; a result of creative, constructive and adaptive approaches used by teachers which allow them to successfully deal with constraints placed upon them and the situation at hand. While much of Hargreaves' effort was placed on identifying the kinds of constraints that teachers experience in schools and classrooms, he observed that the extent to which coping strategies become institutionalized or routinized depended to a degree on the responses of the students in the classroom. In turn, the teachers' experiences of the situations in which the coping strategies were used either validated or refuted their use.[54]

Pollard's view of how teachers cope was linked to their biographies and to notions of 'self' and 'interests-at-hand' where he concentrated on uncovering the subjective meaning of coping.[55] According to Pollard's model, coping strategies represent responses by teachers to situations caused by the contexts of the classroom and school but which are based on the influences from the larger society and cultural environment:

> Teachers do not act alone. Rather they act within a cultural context, often using cultural resources as a basis for decisions and adaptations. These resources are drawn on in addition to the understandings which have been negotiated with the children of their class.[56]

Pollard's revised model resulted from the critique of Hargreaves' work and the extension of his own previous work. Specifically, the model suggests that there are multiple 'analytical layers' for understanding the interactive process of teachers' coping strategies. Two of the three analytical layers, that of 'social structure' and organizational leadership ('hegemony'), and that of 'institutional bias', are concerned with macro-layers, while the third, that of the classroom social structure, is a micro-layer concern. Besides analytical layers, there are a number of factors that are important for understanding the context of coping strategies: 'the physical and material structure of the classroom setting, the biography and the self of both the children and teachers, and the role or decision-making problems with which they face'.[57] The biographical factors were seen by Pollard as referring to a number of influences on the teachers (and students). Social status and cultural perspectives were seen to provide the 'context of early socialization' and therefore 'influencing self and more general perspectives, knowledge and attitudes'. Other influences included 'class positions, likely social interests and cultural resources'.[58] Pollard also recognized the importance of analysing specific biographical influences for understanding coping strategies.

The concept of 'accommodation' is important for understanding Pollard's model and suggests that the classroom provides the negotiation context for teachers and students within which they each establish a 'set of understandings which allow for mutual survival':

> The children and teachers will approach any interactive situation in the light of particular perspectives and interests-at-hand. When they act they will each adapt their strategies to

cope with the specific situation in which they find themselves and by so doing will create new situations to be experienced sequentially.[59]

While recognizing the many facets of the origins of teachers' coping strategies, the complexity of Pollard's model makes it difficult to utilize. Woods also observed that the model may prove to be 'too complex to be of any theoretical use' as there may be 'too many factors operating on teacher biography to hold them all in a meaningful way'.[60]

While the previous discussions of coping revolve around experienced teachers, the descriptive researches of McDonald and Bullough are pertinent.[61] The work of Calderhead is also relevant since he discussed coping strategies within the context of beginning teachers' classroom decision-making.[62] Calderhead noted that the overwhelming anxieties many beginning teachers experience often 'emerge from an uncertainty of how to cope with particular classroom situations, and a fear of being unable to deal with crises when they arise'.[63]

McDonald's study revealed the importance of the learned coping strategies that beginning teachers bring with them to the classroom. Those skills for dealing with problems either help or hinder the individual's socialization into the teaching profession. The isolation in which teachers have to solve problems was also emphasized and the dependence that beginning teachers have on their past experience and personal resources was recognized.

> Individual teachers are more or less autonomous in coping with problems. Some seem to be able to generate their own resources for help in such matters, others seem to be very dependent on being led to solutions. Some are more adaptive and flexible, others are more rigid.[64]

In Bullough's case study of one beginning teacher, the individual's biography figured prominently in the story of her first year of teaching. The teacher was strongly guided by her prior experiences in dealing with the problems of the classroom. In particular, her experiences of motherhood and her perceptions about children were significant in the early stages of teaching as she tended to view students through the interpretive lens of her children and through her own experience as a junior high school student. When confronted with challenging discipline problems, she resorted to behaviours that were contrary to her beliefs but which were highly custodial, a result of extensive personal and public negotiation.[65] In addition, early problems that the teacher experienced were much in line with those suggested by Veenman.[66]

Solutions to problems the beginning teacher faced were largely derived from the immediacy of the situation and patterns of past actions. As time progressed, the teacher was increasingly able to adequately deal with problems that were beyond her prior experiences. Movement through the 'survival stage' into the 'mastery stage', as labelled by Ryan, brought about a new approach to problem-solving. Difficulties were reworked into problems that were amenable to solutions. By framing difficulties in ways that suggest solutions and with an increasing ability to implement alternatives, she was able to more successfully deal with classroom problems.[67]

The beginning teacher had several coping strategies and they were directly related to her personal dispositions and previous experiences. 'Environmental simplification' was one strategy that was adopted where she conformed to role expectations and reduced, by simplification, the many demands that were placed upon her. Some demands were forgotten; others were systematized. Another way in which she made life bearable was to seek support from friends, family and others by seeking 'strokes'. Alternatively, she simplified by compartmentalizing her life responsibilities. 'Context restructuring' refers to a third approach that was used. The teacher specifically sought to alter either the physical environment of the classroom, the instructional activity, or the curriculum content to fit her needs. 'Compromise' was used as a fourth strategy. The tension between personal and institutional requirements resulted in compromises of values and approaches so that she could feel more at ease in the school setting. An orientation to 'skill improvement' represents a fifth coping strategy. As a means of enhancing the learning environment, the teacher focused on developing both her own professional skills and those of students. 'Problem disownment' was also employed, as was 'laughter and emotional release'.[68]

As mentioned, there is considerable difficulty in synthesizing the literature on problem-solving and coping strategies. This is because of the inconsistencies of definition and the broad range of contexts within which both problems, problem-solving and coping strategies are discussed. While many of the researchers cited in this section (e.g. those dealing with theoretical aspects of strategies, such as Hargreaves, Lacey, Pollard, Woods, and those focusing on descriptive studies such as Bullough and McDonald[69]) imply or make direct reference to the biographical connections and relevance in viewing the ways in which teachers' problem-solve or cope, none have made biography a central reference point or variable in their investigations. The recognition that biography plays a role in understanding teaching practices is clear and it was from this perspective of the context of problem-solving strategies and coping strategies that the following case studies were made.

Summary of case studies of five student and beginning teachers

In the five individual case studies, I focus on the importance of prior experience for understanding classroom practices. One investigation centred on the experiences of three student teachers. Two individuals became successful beginning teachers; the other failed in student teaching. An important part of the analyses was to determine the sources of their teacher role identities and, subsequently, to theorize about the connections between their biographies and practices. The 'Biographical Transformation Model'[70] and refinement of the constructs of teacher role identity were previously presented in an analysis of two of the teachers. Two other previously reported cases focus primarily on the pre-service teacher who failed.[71] The other evidence comes from individual case studies.

The theoretical perspective of the case studies was based on Crow's work.[72] I extended her research to include student and beginning teachers. The exploratory investigations centre on uncovering significant prior experiences and linking them to classroom practices.

As opposed to the relatively large quantitative research base on teacher socialization, the use of the qualitative paradigm allowed different understandings about how student and beginning teachers think because it centres attention on the human elements of the teacher[73] and, besides, critics of teacher socialization findings have argued that we can only begin to uncover knowledge about socialization issues when observations are made in appropriate settings such as classrooms.[74]

Objectives of the case studies

The primary objective in each of the case studies was the exploration of the links between beginning teachers' biographies and practices in the classroom, especially as those practices relate to coping strategies – ways in which the teachers sought to make life comfortable in the classroom when faced with difficult situations. Two questions provided focus for each of the case studies: How do pre-service teachers and beginning teachers go about solving problems in the classroom and, when they adopt problem-solving and coping strategies, to what extent are those strategies related to their biographies? How does biography impact beginning teachers' strategies for coping with problems?

Several definitions help clarify the questions: 'Coping strategies' refer to the various ways in which student and beginning teachers manage difficult situations in the classroom. A coping strategy does not necessarily solve problems but leads to a reasonably comfortable working environment. 'Problem-solving strategies' have to do with the ways in which individuals think about a problem, the subsequent alternatives they consider, and finally what they judge to be the actions most likely to resolve the particular difficulty.

The Case Studies

In the exploratory ethnographic case studies, an express purpose was to generate theory rather than to merely describe the actions of the individuals in relation to their biographies.[75] In all cases, I was either co-instructor or principal instructor in the certification component of the pre-service teacher education programme in which the individuals were involved.

The participants and the settings

Three of the individual case studies use data initially taken from the evaluation of a pilot, graduate, secondary, pre-service teacher education programme of an accredited university during a recent academic school year.[76] The three pre-service teachers, Elizabeth, Cynthia and Mona, each entered the graduate programme with an undergraduate degree a major teaching area. The programme was intensive. Pre-service teachers took courses that related to curriculum, teaching methods, research on teaching, and critical

114

perspectives of education, besides the certification courses from which the data and context for the study were obtained.

Another case study centred on Dwayne, a participant in a year-long, pilot, undergraduate, secondary, internship, certification programme. This programme was a cooperative venture with a local school district. The first quarter of the programme was spent at the university where the focus of the state certification require-ments was on secondary school curriculum concerns, much like that in the graduate programme. After the summer, Dwayne began his internship. Workshops and seminars on discipline, classroom management, curriculum planning and other topics provided further preparation for teaching. Under the mentorship of an experienced teacher Dwayne began full-time teaching.

Kristen's experience was portrayed in the fifth case study. She participated in an undergraduate, pre-service, secondary, teacher education programme with similar components to the graduate programme in which Elizabeth, Cynthia and Mona participated.

Data collection strategies

One of the requirements in each of the programmes was to keep a reflective journal. The pre-service teachers (three were later begin-ning teachers) were asked to write from their experiences in the school classrooms, to reflect upon their observations, and attempt to make links between theory and practice. As reader of the journals I wrote responses to their entries and together these activities provided much of the data.

Weekly unstructured interviews and observations were used during student teaching. For those cases where the student tea-chers accepted a contract position and became beginning teachers, the process continued throughout the first semester of beginning teaching.[77] Biographical information was obtained through both structured and unstructured interviews and the journals.[78] In the case of the beginning teachers and the intern teacher, interviews were conducted at least biweekly over the duration of the first semester of the beginning teaching year. In one case, the parents and husband of the pre-service teacher and beginning teacher were also interviewed. In another case only the husband was interviewed. Personal letters from one of the pre-service teacher's parents provided an additional source of data.[79] The parents of the teacher intern wrote extensive replies to their son in response to my questions about his early experiences of family and school. In addition, papers which focused on their experiences in the school and classroom were required of all but the intern teacher.

Analyses

The journals, field notes, observations, interviews and term papers were subjected to standard procedures for ethnographic analyses where patterns and themes in the text were recognized. Anecdotal references were removed from the data that best represented positions, descriptions of events, perspectives and perceptions of situations.[80] Triangulation of methods enhanced the reliability and validity of the studies. Verification of outcomes and conclusions was achieved by having the pre-service teachers check ascribed accounts and meanings during the analyses and writing of the report. The names presented in all of the cases are pseudonyms, and some circumstances surrounding their experiences are changed to protect their identities.

Findings

A summary of the major results from the case studies is presented in Table 1 (pp. 118–19). Table 2 (pp. 120–1) relates the origins of teacher role identity to teaching attitudes, coping strategies and classroom practices of select cases. Together, these provide substance to the following discussions.

The influence of biography on teaching practice

The case study data as presented in Table 2 provide samples of explicit links between biography and practice in the classroom. Extensive evidence is impossible to present because of confines of space. Select, brief examples from three of the case studies provide insights into the data obtained and highlight some of the ways in which biography impacts practice in the classroom. Later in the chapter, references are made to all five individuals.

Impacts of Elizabeth's biography on her classroom practices The pre-service teacher preparation and early formative experiences laid the groundwork for Elizabeth's attitudes and values about teaching. Completing the teacher certification programme, she said, provided only a thin layer of 'useful experience'.

116

Elizabeth 'breezed through' her student teaching but, in the third week after beginning teaching, she had severe difficulties. There was a direct link between an earlier 'mission experience' in Germany and her practice as a beginning teacher. For a variety of reasons, the students became disrespectful and disorderly. In an endeavour to remove the complexities of teaching, she became increasingly structured and engaged less in behaviours utilized during her successful student teaching practice. Increasingly, she adopted coping strategies that allowed her to simply make it through the day. The eighteen-month-long period of teaching for her church in Germany had subliminal implications and effects on the manner of her teaching in the senior high school. As she had been taught in Germany when proselytizing, Elizabeth did not want to continue teaching people who actively stated they were not interested in her 'message'. For a time, she actually stopped teaching. Later she refrained from teaching in the ways in which she believed she should teach. Initially, the practice of her prior teaching experience seemed to hold more value than even the images of good teaching that she obtained at the hand of family and exemplary teaching models. But, eventually, it was the impressions of traditional teaching that were utilized in her classroom.

Another factor that made it very difficult for Elizabeth to deal with the perceived student disorder was the question of failure. Elizabeth's kindergarten through grade twelve experience was not only stable, but it was very successful. She was a straight 'A' student. Towards the end of the first month of teaching, she perceived herself as a failure – as many beginning teachers do[81] – and, for the first time in her life, not only was failure a reality, it was public knowledge. Besides, she 'was very vulnerable to [student] opinions' and sought verification for her success in the classroom as she had done when teaching in her local church. When the students were not forthcoming in their praise, Elizabeth became very depressed about her teaching performance.

Her mother recollected a comment that one of Elizabeth's junior high English teachers made at a parent-teacher conference. It reinforced the notion of the young Elizabeth's influential character. The teacher told the parents: 'I don't know why I bother to come to class. Kids don't pay attention to me. They watch Elizabeth, and what Elizabeth tells them to do, that's what they do.' When her senior high school students were not willing to accept

Table 1 Summary of case study findings

Name and programme	Age	Education	Student teaching setting	Beginning teaching setting	Teacher role identity (TRI) components	Family experiences	Early school experiences	Previous teaching	Other experiences	Strength of TRI	Teacher classroom behaviours
1. Elizabeth graduate	26	BA	Urban junior and senior high school, multicultural, succeeded	Urban senior high school, multicultural, provisional certificate	Parent teacher, positive teacher role models, family role models, viewed as leader, influence of church, teaching experience	Stable, supportive, warm, parent role models, intellectual, professional, respectful	Positive role models, leader, popular, liked school, good student	Church, Sunday school and mission teaching	Minimal: university, friends, travel, reading	Strong	Relied on methods used in church mission teaching, mother a filter for understanding students, respect, innovative
2. Mona graduate	28	BA	Urban junior high school, monocultural, succeeded	Rural junior high school, monocultural, provisional certificate	Influence of early teacher in different cultural settings, values of childhood, sense of 'mission', previous teaching experiences important, strong interpersonal relations, self-reliant	Stable, supportive, warm large family, intellectual, professional, sibling support, freedom	Positive role models, popular, liked school, good student, composite role models, firm discipline, varied settings for education	Some small group	Minimal: university, travel, experience of cultures	Strong	Organized, effort, strong discipline, innovative and varied instruction, respects students, consistent, strong interpersonal communication skills and subject preparation
3. Cynthia graduate	37	BA, BS	Urban junior high school, monocultural, failed	did not teach	Strong negative family influence on behaviour and personal relationships, negative teacher role models, dislike school, small group teaching, theory	Part stable, critical, taught to be unassertive, creative, poor social skills	Negative role models, average student, many schools, social problems minimal study, discovery learning	Some small group	Minimal: university work and life experiences, interest in theory	Weak	Individual student focus, unassertive, inappropriate management, innovative and creative, good planning and hands-on activities

4. Dwayne intern	39	BA, MA	Urban junior high school, multicultural, succeeding	Educated in Africa as child, family separated, boarding school, poor student, negative role models, traditional teaching, hated school, no teaching experience or relationships with children, university	Unstable, separated, distance, difficult disappointed with family, alienated, professional, intellectual	Negative role models, varied schools, home school, harsh boarding school, failed, discipline problem, very poor teaching	None	Minimal: university, no experience with children, various cultures	Weak	Organized, hard working, repetitive in instructional strategies, difficulty with discipline and management, strong communication skills
5. Kirsten under-graduate	22	BA at end of student teach-ing	Urban senior high school multicultural, school closing, succeeding	Urban junior high school, homo-geneous, provisional certificate	Positive family and neighbour role models, traditional & negative teacher role models, influence of others and university, disliked social aspects of school	Stable, supportive, distant, usually positive family role models	Mostly negative role models, traditional, excellent student, alone, organized, excited learning	Peer tutoring	Moderate: university, reading	Moder-ate to strong	High expectations of students, creative and intellectual, organized, caring, insecure, reflective actions, varied instruction

Table 2 Role identity and teaching attitudes, coping and instructional strategies

Examples of major components of *teacher role identity* (early experiences)	→ *Evidenced in* →	Examples of attitudes, classroom coping and/or instructional strategies (teacher behaviours)

Elizabeth (strength of component in brackets)
Family: (strong)

- Parents views about teaching → views and attitudes compatible with those of parents
- Methods of teacher mother → strategies compatible with those of mother
- 'Intellectual climate' of the home → emphasis on discussion and questioning
- Talking through problems → Problem-solving with mother and friends

Teachers and school: (strong)

- Success as student → unable to deal with potential failure
- Personal approaches of teachers → used same approaches of positive role models
- Popular student and leader → expected to be centre of attention in class
- Teaching methods of teacher role models → used exact methods of positive role models
- Experience of formal traditional classrooms → reverts room to traditional modes

Prior teaching experience: (strong)

- Dealing with disinterested people on 'mission' → used same method, stop teaching
- Individual differences are important → respect for students
- Intellectual discussion important → discussion used to advantage

Cynthia (strength of component in brackets)
Family: (strong)

- Taught to be unassertive → unable to assert herself in the classroom

Inadequate social skills ————————————→ social skills were uninviting to students

Creative parents and creative experiences ————→ creative and innovative lesson plans

Better able to relate to one individual at a time ———→ focused on individual

Teachers and school: (strong)

Traditional role models ——————→ could not use traditionl methods that she despises

Hated school ————————————————————→ did not like being in school

Positive role models used experiential methods ———→ emphasis on hands on activities

Negative role models did not respect individuals ——→ respect for individuals

Negative role models ——→ not able to implement satisfactory discipline or management

Prior teaching experience: (weak)

Small group ——→ not able to extend focus from individual to whole class

Dwayne (strength of component in brackets)

Family: (strong)

Weak parent role model ——————→ few skills in interacting with school students

Separation from parents and family ——→ reliance on self for problem-solving

Strong work ethic ——————————→ hard working and organization

Teachers and school: (strong)

'Traditional' role models ————————————→ adoption of teaching methods

Harsh disciplinary methods ——→ adoption of disciplinary methods contrary to ideals

No variation of methods ————————→ planning lacks variation and innovation

No relationship with teachers ——————→ not readily approachable to students

Elizabeth as being at the centre of the classroom arena she had severe discipline difficulties.

The difficulties of the first month also had an unexpected effect on my research project. At the end of the fourth week she admitted she was 'suffering from overload', and stated emphatically: 'I can only deal with a few issues at a time and one more thing for me to deal with is too much.' Elizabeth removed herself from the study as she sought verification of her worth and eradication of the pressures of the classroom observations and regular interviews. Her coping strategy of withdrawal was similar to that which she had used in the classroom with the students.

The outstanding finding from the analyses of data associated with Elizabeth was the high level of congruence between her educational views and values and the perspectives of her parents. It was as though the university programme had little effect on her beliefs about teaching. While she appeared to be open and accepting of the viewpoints of others, that acceptance did not seem to translate into actions that were markedly different from the advice and perspectives of her mother.

Impacts of Cynthia's biography on her classroom experiences
Cynthia failed her student teaching. Later, she came to realize that 'personality was crucial to successful teaching' and that her teacher role-related biography had negatively affected her. At first, she believed that learning to teach was a matter of mastering skills, and that she was lacking some essential ones relating to classroom management and discipline. Later, over a number of months, she became more aware of how personality and management skills were related. Her background had not prepared her for the kind of leadership or problem-solving strategies needed in a classroom.

The failure was difficult for Cynthia to deal with. But, as she admitted nine months later: 'It was in some ways easier for me to handle than success or potential success', since on some prior occasions she had even been 'blamed for success'. Her view was a reflection of her early upbringing.

In an attempt to explain her failure, Cynthia described negative aspects of her family upbringing: 'insecure parents who were unable to relate to children' and who had 'inconsistent child-rearing practices'. Cynthia was also insecure. Besides, there were traumatic family events she had to deal with. Her insecurity was evident on the first day she entered the school. Cynthia never developed the confidence that was necessary to deal with junior high school students but, rather, was hesitant about most of her actions. Cynthia had also learned 'to devalue [her] abilities, ideas, capabilities and. . . successes'.

A number of learned behaviours, important for childhood survival at home, were also important in explaining her classroom failure. She learned to keep a 'low-profile' by maintaining an unassertive manner. Behaviours thought to be socially correct, such as being quiet-spoken, unassertive and unassuming, were not effective for teaching in a public school with 30 to 40 students in a classroom. Despite the fact that she was intellectually aware of more appropriate actions, and could talk about their usage by other pre-service teachers, she was unable to engage in them.

Cynthia also had a number of negative school influences to deal with. As a student in kindergarten through grade five, she attended a private school, where social propriety was placed above achievement and where '*who* you were was more important than *what* you were'. During grades six through ten Cynthia experienced a new school every year. She had never really felt comfortable in schools. The last three years of her schooling were at one school. Cynthia became bored and frustrated with schoolwork. She could not see the larger scheme of things and was 'confused about the relative' value of learning and of the fragmentation of knowledge. More importantly, Cynthia had been socially inept as a student. She also felt 'awkward and different' as a young student because of family attitudes and her intellectual and creative abilities; attitudes that may help explain Cynthia's inability to relate to large groups as in the classroom. Junior high school, in particular, had not been an enjoyable experience for her as she recorded in her journal at the time of her student teaching.

The unequivocal message she got as a school student, she recollected, was that 'teachers are not interested in individual students, especially ones that don't fit'. She had other negative feelings about teachers: They were 'not fair'; were 'fault finding and very critical'; 'impatient'; 'insistent upon conformity and rewarded [people] for quietness and unassertiveness'.

The data suggest that Cynthia's teacher role identity was never clearly established in her mind, a factor that may explain her failure in the classroom. Cynthia's views of schools and teachers were not conducive to becoming a teacher: 'I did not like teachers.

(I liked learning.) School work was boring, lacked meaning and had no connection with [the] end result. It was too fragmented and too much busy work.' In the junior high school classroom, Cynthia was encumbered by her early behavioural patterns. At the same time, she did not want to replicate the sorts of teacher actions she remembered as having a negative effect upon her. Her coping strategies were direct reflections of much earlier patterns of behaviour and interaction with others.

Conversely, Cynthia fondly remembered her experience as a child in an adult art class she attended with a parent. The 'well structured art teacher' provided 'experiential education opportunities with simple yet unobtrusive instruction' and 'ample wait time'. Another teacher was warmly recollected for being 'appreciative of nonconformity, innovation and creativity'. It was this side of Cynthia's background that was evidenced in the innovative ways she thought about lessons and science experiments.

Dwayne's biography: The significance of some early and later experiences A child of expatriate American parents, Dwayne grew up in Angola and South Africa. He was educated in a 'one room Canadian mission school in the highland'; by his mother using the 'Calvert Correspondence Courses'; and eventually enrolled in a 'boarding school in Cape Town'. He recollected: 'at the age of 12 [I experienced] my first real school.' Dwayne's school experiences were difficult scholastically and were in settings vastly different from classrooms in the United States. Years later he recollected: 'It took a Masters [degree] to overcome the stigma of my early [school] failures.' His reasons for becoming a teacher revolved around his love of history and his abilities: 'I'm articulate and enjoy ideas'. But, in the classroom, Dwayne had the imprint of his own educational experiences to overcome.

In an American classroom Dwayne was immediately disadvantaged. At 39 years of age he had never taught before. But, he had an ability to solve problems, which was, according to him, largely a product of his being left to his own devices as a child. Dwayne's strategy centred on carefully analysing the difficulties he was faced with, presenting many alternatives for consideration, then selecting those strategies that seemed appropriate. Through evaluation of resulting outcomes, Dwayne further refined his approaches.

Dwayne's experience at the South African boarding school was not memorable and he prefers to forget that period of his life.

'The cold formality of the place, the rupture with family. . . and my scholastic retardedness, all send me into an emotional tailspin', was the way in which he remembered it. Dwayne saw himself as a 'very successful failure'. But, as he recollected, there was one bright spot in his early years at the boarding school: 'One year I nearly won the school history prize, but got straight F's in all other subjects'.

Many years later, Dwayne completed a Master's degree in African history, and it was not until then that he became clear about his accomplishments. Reflection on the successful educational experiences caused Dwayne to consider teaching as a career: 'During my years in graduate school, learning came alive for me. There was a personable one-on-one quality with my teachers that I enjoyed. . . . Nothing motivates like success.'

Dwayne was asked why he decided to become a teacher. There were a number of facets to his response, but essentially they revolved around the subject matter – history – and his abilities: 'I've been told by others that I'd do well as a teacher'. But Dwayne confided further, that there was the imprint of his own educational experiences to overcome: 'For years I'd rejected the idea of teaching', and it took 'a decade of footloose, blue-jeaned living to overcome my own regimented schooling'. Yet, despite his participation in a relatively progressive teacher preparation programme, when he taught in the classroom as an intern teacher, he found it very difficult to break loose from the structure of his early experiences.

GENERATING THEORY ABOUT BIOGRAPHY

This section consolidates conclusions from the case studies and is organized around discussions of: (1) teacher role identities; (2) the 'Biographical Transformation Model'; and (3) the 'Interaction between Biography and School Environment' model which explains the influence of biography on teaching practice within the context of the school.

The data from the five case studies provide evidence of life-long patterns of reasoning about teaching, education and schools that had evolved in the thinking of the individuals. Past experiences impacted their early classroom behaviours to a high level. Subsequent changes, induced by the teacher education programmes, regarding the ways in which the pre-service teachers thought about teaching and education, seemed to occur to a minimal degree over the duration of the pre-service year. That is not to say that there were not changes in their perceptions of teaching. In the case of the graduate pre-service teachers, at least, there were changes, but these were not visibly evident in their classroom teaching practices.[82] There is not merely a cause and effect relationship; instead, biography interacts with context and experiences of teaching in a variety of ways, some of which may be extremely difficult to determine.

All the case study findings support the notion that biography is important for understanding the formation of a teacher role identity and thinking about classroom practice. Student teachers, and subsequently beginning teachers, do not enter pre-service education programmes like empty vessels waiting to be filled with the skills, aptitudes and experiences appropriate for a first year teacher. Neither do they begin full-time teaching with only the experience of student teaching and the university. Rather, they have been subjected to a lifetime of 'teacher education'. Many come to university classrooms, early school placements and student teaching, not only with their own agenda, but with definite views as to the knowledge and experiences which they will accept as valuable for them as future classroom teachers. The fact that university programmes often appear to have little effect is, in itself, evidence that the images of teaching created in the teacher preparation environment are probably incompatible with long-held views and perspectives. These conclusions are generally compatible with Lortie's hypothesis and the inferences of others.[83] Personal biography seems to have profound effects on what occurs in the individual's classroom and the concept of teacher role identity is central for understanding the process by which prior experiences are transformed into classroom practice.

Teacher role identities

These studies provide evidence about teacher role identities that are congruent with the findings of Crow.[84] The results suggest that early childhood experiences, early teacher role models, and previous teaching experiences are most important in the formation of an 'image of self as teacher'.[85] Contrary to Crow's findings, the five case studies indicate that the university experience was not a very strong component of teacher role identity. Apart from the experience of Kristen (see Table 1), the other individuals were not influenced greatly by their participation in formal teacher education. While, on the one hand, Dwayne could recite progressive educational theories and intellectualize about more appropriate ways of acting in his classroom, he invariably was unable to choose, or chose not to utilize that which he had been exposed to during his preparation – he fell back on strategies that he had long felt comfortable with despite the fact that he agreed they were not good pedagogy. Such strategies were largely those he had experienced as a student.

Each of the individuals was noticeably affected in their classroom endeavours by their conception of what it meant to be a teacher. The realities and fantasies associated with teacher role identities were very significant for the subsequent development of practice in the classroom. This view is supported, for example, by Britzman, Crow, Eddy, Ryan and Woods.[86] Both Mona and Dwayne were greatly influenced by the sometimes rigid educational experiences they had as students in educational environments outside the United States: Mona in a positive way, in that she took the exhibited strengths from the teachers she had been exposed to and incorporated their practices in her teaching; Dwayne in a negative way, in that he was unable to break free of the poor teaching methods under which he had been taught and, in practical terms knew no other way of acting, despite having observed several experienced competent teachers in American classrooms. He feared failure enough not to be willing to risk anything that was beyond his realm of experience.

The major components of teacher role identity that were evidenced in the cases include: (1) childhood experiences; (2) teacher role models; and (3) teaching experiences; and less importantly, (4) significant or important people and significant prior experiences other than very early formative experiences. A discussion of the perceived strength of individuals' teacher role identities concludes this section.

Childhood experiences

Family and early childhood experiences significantly affected performance in the classroom. In particular, learned social behaviours were important elements of a successful student or beginning teaching experience. Rules of family conduct learned as a young child were ingrained to such an extent that, in the case of

Cynthia, she was unable to supplant them with the classroom management strategies learned in the university classes. Patterns of family interaction and values are important components of early experiences.

Parents' orientations and beliefs about education were significant in the case of Elizabeth and Mona. From the time Elizabeth was a young girl, she had been exposed to the inner workings of classrooms through many family discussions at the dinner table. She adopted an educational philosophy and framework for classroom actions that were almost exactly like those of her mother, an accomplished and experienced teacher. Long after leaving home, her parents' views, particularly those of her mother, remained an important filter through which she viewed the problems of the classroom.

Mona's parents had definite views about the value of education. They insisted that their children obtain the highest educational qualifications, yet, objected to her entry to the teaching profession. Their views also prompted Mona, so she said, to accept for her own teaching the rigid teaching practices of her native land with the exclusive focus on academics, something that had typified her early experiences in schools.

Dwayne had some important early experiences to work through as he began his intern teaching. Early recollections of school and family in Africa also involved the 'trauma' of being educated at home by his mother because there were no English speaking schools. This initial and stressful introduction to learning induced Dwayne to have 'adverse attitudes towards education' for a long time. Separation from family occurred later because he was sent to a boarding school. Because his younger siblings did not experience the traumas of separation Dwayne became very resentful of them. Consequently, Dwayne's thoughts of learning and family included many negative images. Besides, in the years when he was with his parents, his father was often separated from the family, and Dwayne only has faint memories of a happy childhood. According to him, his 'parents provided weak role models'. As a result, Dwayne was often left to this own devices. However, one of his strong points as a teacher was reflected in his self-reliance and perseverance in solving his own problems, highly evidenced in his journal writing.

Kristen's experience was unique. She grew up in a neighbourhood where there were many older people and she was often in the position of being taught informally by them. She felt very comfortable being in situations where she 'learned a lot inadvertently'. Learning was a very 'natural' and exciting experience. This same view was evident in her actions as a pre-service teacher. Being the youngest in her family, she often created her own learning environment, an opportunity which she believes should be made available to all learners. Her classroom practices reflected the same attitude, and she placed on her students similar responsibilities for learning.

Childhood experiences contributed greatly to the ways in which the individuals thought about teaching and acted in the classroom. Personality, socialization skills, self-confidence, habitual ways of dealing with situations, work habits and orientation to work and responsibility were important arenas of experience that surface in their practices, particularly their coping strategies, and many of these have their origins in patterns of family interactions and demands. These conclusions are congruent with those of Munro who noted the importance of personal work habits in the identity of pre-service teachers.[87] The reliance on family experiences is also recognized as being an important component of the 'micro-self' as suggested by Woods.[88]

Early teacher role models

All the individuals were greatly influenced by their experiences with teachers. Elizabeth tended to be positively influenced and had clear conceptions of her role as teacher. A number of factors amplified her perception of self as teacher. Not only did she have teacher role models in the home but her teachers consistently recognized her teacher-like skills, and to some extent, she was inculcated for the role of teacher because she was the kind of student that teachers like, commend, and induce to become teachers. Consequently, she had a strong sense of the role of teachers in public schools. On the other hand, Cynthia had clear conceptions of the teacher she did not want to be, rather than an image of herself as teacher.

Mona grew up in Europe. Her recollections of schools were very important in her classroom practices. Schools were remembered as being very serious places where there was organization, strict discipline, concentration on academics and not the 'frivolities' of extracurricular activities as common in American schools, firm expectations of students and respect for teachers. Mona's student teaching practices exhibited an almost perfect reflection of her images of school and of teachers. This component of her teacher role identity, as a result, was very different from the American-born and raised pre-service teachers.

For Dwayne, the experience of attending boarding school in South Africa was very stressful: rote learning, unimaginative classes, 'cruel teachers', strict requirements, lack of freedom, and failure. Dwayne's experience of school provided 'few positive images of teachers' or of appropriate teacher practices. Beginning intern teaching was difficult because he did not possess a reper- toire of learned and appropriate teacher practices. He had no clear image of what it meant to be a teacher and this was some- thing that plagued his year of teaching. His immediate response was to treat the unruly students in ways that he was treated, and indeed he did, but to his good fortune he was not taken to task by either students, parents or principal – although, according to his journal entries, and based on the resulting tension, he had some close calls.

Kristen was inclined to view teachers negatively even though they tended to 'love [her] because she was a good student' and because she was 'quiet, passive, and obedient'. She affirmed that her teachers were 'generally great people but were lousy instructors' because they were not effective for her. The more traditional teachers provided opportunities for development of skills but it was the non-traditional and innovative approaches, adopted by a few teachers, that were mostly remembered, especially the experiential activities provided by early grade school teachers. Another aspect of her school learning was significant. She seemed to induce many teachers to regard her as 'different'. These teachers related to her in ways that made the curriculum different for her. Consequently, she had a strong sense of the importance of curriculum relevancy and the concern for indi- vidual needs of students and, as she began teaching, her methods were far from traditional. Later, as a first year teacher the administrator who evaluated her described her teaching not only as 'outstanding', but 'caring', and 'incredibly creative'. On the other hand, schools were not always kind to her. As a student she was discontent with the administrative and bureaucratic functions of schools and the emphases on class and status. She had often been discriminated against because of her working-class origins. As a pre-service teacher she had problems with the structural and

administrative aspects of schools and later, as a teacher, had difficulty bringing herself to teach the predominantly upper middle-
class accelerated, or 'gifted', students.

Positive experiences in schools clearly placed Elizabeth and
Mona in advantageous positions while for Kristen school provided
mixed role models and experiences. For both Cynthia and
Dwayne, the experiences of junior high school were better forgotten and only contributed to their difficulties in the classroom.
I concluded as Crow did: 'These recollections of former teachers
and experiences had been internalized into the informants' own
teacher role identities.'[89] The conclusions also concur with those
of Britzman.[90] The degree to which negative role images contribute to malfunctioning in the classroom is unclear. The model,
'Interaction of biography and school environment: Influence of
biography on practice', provides a simplistic explanation of how
negative school environments exacerbate and affirm the components of negative teacher role identities, and how positive school
environments encourage the implementation of aspects of positive
teacher role identities and practices of pre-service teachers.

Teaching experience

Prior teaching opportunities were highly significant for some
individuals. In Elizabeth's case, prior teaching experiences provided an important base for classroom actions. Cynthia's and
Mona's experiences teaching small groups of people were also
formative, as was Kristen's tutoring. Dwayne had no prior teaching
experience whatsoever.

Elizabeth taught in Germany for her church. She learned an
important principle for dealing with potential proselytes: 'When
they become disinterested in the message, you stop teaching.'
Elizabeth's students refused to pay attention in ways that she
thought appropriate and so she stopped teaching. When she
resumed teaching after restructuring her classroom she did not
instruct in the ways in which she believed she should teach. She
had also taught in her local church. The focus of her teaching in
church meetings was on small group activities, discussions and lots
of questions. By the time she began student teaching she was very
familiar and skilled in these approaches. Consequently, in her
school classes she regularly used the same methods.

Cynthia's previous and occasional teaching experience was in
small informal groups. She felt comfortable dealing with indivi-

duals on a one-to-one basis or in small groups and it was in this manner that she operated in the classroom. As a result, while she tutored or assisted one or two students, the remainder of her classes ran amok. She was unable to deal with the whole class group.

Similar experiences with small group tutoring had a different effect on Mona. She developed skills of interaction and took the opportunities to impress upon her students the importance of one-on-one communication and of gaining experience in oral testing – something that she continued with in the classroom.

Recent peer tutoring opportunities also provided Kristen with perspectives for dealing with students on a one-to-one basis. It gave her strategies for instruction. For example, the importance of being able to rephrase ideas and instructions when dealing with individuals carried over to classroom activities. Very clear communication became an essential mark of her teaching style. The tutoring responsibilities provided insights into the skills that she needed to develop in the classroom and that were important for her students to acquire. Kristen's tutoring of peers provided opportunities for her to try out teaching strategies and ideas for curriculum and lessons. Many of the instructional strategies she implemented in her student teaching were tried out first in the peer setting. Interestingly, the role of tutor was a long-term one, one that she began in sixth grade when she spent much of each day in another classroom tutoring students and helping the teacher.

Early teaching experiences provide an additional framework to which the experience of subsequent classroom practice was added. For some of the individuals, the prior teaching occasionally made the university preparation experiences more relevant or, at other times, redundant – depending on their view of their earlier experiences. The data support the hypothesis that earlier experiences are more important than later experiences in the formation of a teacher role identity. It was later experiences that were often most evident in the classroom practices. But, as difficulties arose in the teaching setting, it was often the latter experiences that were first peeled away as pre-service or beginning teachers attempted to cope with difficult situations. Consequently, they tended to rely on deep-seated experiences and life-long ways of coping and dealing with problems. Behaviours learned in previous teaching activities that were not necessarily congruent with public school classrooms were difficult to overcome or negate in the classroom.

Significant people and experiences

Most of the pre-service and beginning teachers' classroom practices were only weakly affected by their university education experience. What was taken from the university, however, were those viewpoints and orientations to practice in the classroom that were congruent with previously held images of teachers' work and that provided reinforcement and validation of their positions.

Kristen, the youngest of the pre-service teachers, was positively influenced by the teaching styles of several of the university teachers – more so than by the theories and viewpoints they presented. She felt that their concern for individuals, their intellectual rigour, their flexibility and their specific teaching methods provided invaluable models for future classroom practice.

While she had wanted to become a teacher at an early age, it was not until a high school teacher approached Kristen and suggested that she apply for a pre-service teacher scholarship that, as a college student, she began to think seriously about the profession. She has continually denied her future role as teacher, primarily because of the many negative associations she, and others, placed on the teaching profession. She did not like the disparaging remarks made by her peers about the profession of teaching. Her perception was that most teachers were not able to motivate students to learn and were often incompetent. But, interestingly, she recently unearthed a journal that she wrote as a 16-year-old and a short story written when she was in junior high. Both records affirmed the fact that she recognized in herself, as a young person, the desire to be a French teacher.

The long but laboured experience of success at the university level was an important factor in Dwayne's renewed perceptions of self, his attitudes, and his ability to learn. While the realization did not provide clear images of a teacher role identity, it did induce him to be receptive to ideas about becoming a teacher and to acknowledge that learning can be enjoyable. Specifically, he wanted other children who had failed to be able to succeed. It was this goal that was present in his rather weak view of teacher's work. Yet, while he was receptive intellectually to the theories and skills presented at the university, he was able to implement only a very few aspects of his formal teacher preparation and relied on methods he had been subjected to as a student.

The other women, Elizabeth, Cynthia and Mona, were only mildly affected by the theoretical and skill aspects of their university experience, at least as evidenced in observations and according to their own admissions. But, like Kristen, they were influenced by individual teachers who either exhibited vastly different teaching methods and styles to their own images of teachers or, alternatively, were congruent with those images of teachers or teaching.

Other influences that affected their teacher role models emanated from: experiences of travel; recognition that different people learn in different ways; realization that some systems of education emphasize and utilize varied kinds of teaching; experience of culture and recognition of the needs of others; work and life experiences; relationships with children; and reading. Some of the more encompassing of these experiences are similar to the components of the 'macro-self', as suggested by Woods,[91] while the 'micro-self' components are more closely akin to the early experiences of family and school.

In no case was the university preparation experience strongly evident in the individuals' teacher role identities or in their classroom behaviours. While the university teacher education experience appeared to help make cognitive changes in the pre-service teachers' thinking,[92] there appears to be no significant evidence of the university's influence on practice – at least during the early months of teaching. In a report on a longitudinal study of her original pre-service teacher subjects, Crow suggests there is a lag time – or 'latent effect' – before the cognitive changes originating from the university education experiences are put into effect.[93] From the case studies what is strongly evident, particularly in one of the cases, is the influence of individual university teachers. To a small degree, the teaching styles, as opposed to the subject matter, of university teachers provide the most recent layer of verification of pre-service teacher's role identity, in as much as they confirm or disconfirm the pre-service teacher's beliefs about appropriate actions for teaching. These findings are congruent with those of Martinez.[94] The difference between intellectual learning and experiential learning may account for the fact that the consequences of university classes are not obvious in classroom practice. Student teaching is experiential learning and is interpreted to be 'more valuable' to pre-service teachers because it has a 'ring of truth and relevance'. Student teaching has traditionally been regarded by teacher educators, cooperating teachers and student teachers as a 'trial by fire' experience, one in which both past and present experiences are of more value than theories in determining outcomes.[95] That belief appears to be validated in the thinking and actions of the five teachers.

Strength of teacher role identities

More so than any of the other pre-service teachers, Elizabeth had a strong sense of her teacher role identity before she entered the programme. During the early weeks she made it plain that she had a clear perception of the work of teachers. The origin of the strength of her teacher role identity was linked with her strong family and church orientations to teaching. Mona also had firm views about teaching practices and regularly talked about appropriate teacher actions. Her teacher role identity was also strong and was mainly linked with experiences of family and school.

Conversely, Cynthia had a weak teacher role identity. While she had solid views of teachers' actions that she did *not* want to replicate in the classroom, there was no evidence, apart from in matters of curriculum design, that she had determined appropriate ways for herself to act in front of students. She not only had a low opinion of herself but she had not imagined herself clearly in teaching roles or in schools. Her failure was closely tied to this omission. Dwayne also entered the programme with no clear image of himself as teacher. His weak teacher role identity was a reflection primarily of his early school experiences.

Kristen's teacher role identity seemed to be placed between those with strong identities and those with weak teacher role identities. She appeared to be the most capable of the pre-service teachers as she was able to intellectualize about her teaching to a very high degree, make links between theories and practice, and be highly reflective of her actions in the classroom. She was the most creative and innovative of the pre-service teachers. The university had been more influential for her than the other people, perhaps because she was the youngest, and while Kristen's teacher role identity was initially a product of her negative school experiences, it evolved further as she began work as a contract teacher. However, she maintained her negative attitudes towards schools and threatened several times in the first months to resign, despite the school administrators praising her teaching efforts.

Mona appeared to be in a similar position to Kristen. While she appeared to strongly impose her personality and methods upon her classes, she claimed that she had no firm view of herself as teacher, a position that I questioned because of her forceful actions in the classroom. Nevertheless, she did not have a long-standing desire to be a teacher and it was only a relatively recent decision that she enter the teaching profession – and that decision was based on her long-term goal to become a public health educator. Indeed, her struggle with the administrative and planning functions of teachers represented her opposition to the profession.

The data provide support for the notion that those pre-service and beginning teachers with strong positive teacher role identities are better able to deal with the rigours of teaching than those with negative and weak teacher role identities. A strong teacher role identity, in practical terms, means that the individual has a much larger repertoire of appropriate and well thought out teacher actions on which to fall back; an accumulation of countless hours observing positive role models and reflecting upon strategies that best suit their personality and perceived needs. The data also hint that those with either very strong teacher role identities, or those with very weak identities, often teach in the manner in which they were taught and grew to accept as 'normal' teaching. In other words, the long apprenticeship of students observing in classrooms enables individuals to develop conceptions of what teaching is.[96] Those views are composites of all the many experiences in classrooms and express beliefs about the teaching and 'life in the average classroom'.[97]

Biographical transformation model

One way to view the effect of student teachers' and beginning teachers' biographies and their effect on practice is through the interactive 'Biographical Transformation Model' (see Fig. 1). This section is arranged as follows: the theory of the model; examples of the model in practice; and use of the model to explain the antecedents of teacher role identity.

The theory of the model

The model very loosely draws on schema theory in which texts are made meaningful.[98] Yet, the terminology used in explaining the

Figure 1 Biographical Transformation Model linking experiences with
beginning teacher behaviours

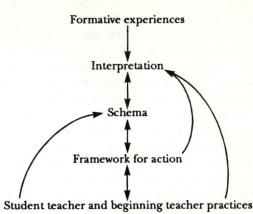

model, while similar to that used in schema theory, ought not be
confused with it. In the model, the early and pre-teacher education
'formative experiences' of childhood, teachers and schools are
first interpreted by the individual. The experiences have both
immediate inherent and reflective assigned meanings.

The inherent meaning is the meaning of an event at the time
the event is enacted. For example, a teacher's reprimand is taken
at face value by the student who had misbehaved. Later, another
meaning is derived. For example, the teacher reacted harshly,
beyond what was reasonable for the misbehaviour, because she
'did not like' the student's attitude towards her class. The assigned
meanings are, and become, the bases of the 'interpretations' of
the experiences; understanding at a later date what the early
experience meant to the individual at the time of the event. The
various experiences of family and school are analysed through the
lenses of other prior experiences and reference points,
particularly the values that each person comes to accept. Later,
individuals give the event – the formative experience – and the
inherent meaning of the event a reflective or assigned meaning; a

137

result of stepping back and analysing the experience. This is the interpretation. The particular interpretation assigned an experience is transformed into a 'schema'.

The schema, a way of understanding or resolving present and future contexts, is a cognitive filter and a basis for future teacher-centred classroom practices. The interpretation, and subsequent schema developed by the individual regarding classroom and other relevant experiences, is obviously highly idiosyncratic; individuals experiencing a singular event have multiple perspectives of that event because there are different interpretive slants that can be assigned. But, through the interpretation, role models and practices are either upheld or rejected by some function of the individual's prior perspective, relations with role model teachers, or the assigned meanings of various situations. The schema is also organizational and enables information to be categorized so that it can be meaningfully used. For example, the recognition of positive teacher role models advances the meaning of future observed teacher actions. The schema, in turn, determines the manner in which future encounters with teachers or learning environments are interpreted and acted upon. Consequently, the schema becomes an evaluatory tool for examining other teacher practices and is transformed into a 'framework for action'.

At this point, the individual begins to establish a more formalized, yet still embryonic, philosophy of teaching or idealized ways of acting in classrooms. The schema is probably the basis for fantasies, as discussed by Ryan[99], where student and beginning teachers have idealistic visions of their future teacher actions, something that may indeed not be diffused or dismantled until well into the first months of teaching.

From the schema and framework for action emerges the 'teacher role identity'. In weak teacher role identities, the effects of prior positive experiences tend to be overrun by negative prior experiences. In other words, given that they have equal strength, negative prior experiences predominate over positive experiences in pre-service teachers' actions in the classroom and, as a result, individuals holding weak teacher role identities do not have clear conceptions of their future actions in the classroom. Teaching then, becomes an arena in which the self is tested and cajoled by students who sense a flaw or weakness in the façade and in the structure of the teacher. If the teacher role identity is strong, whatever kinds of prior experiences are predominant (i.e. negative or positive), the effects and images of those experiences will tend to dominate weaker prior experiences in the classroom actions of the beginning teacher.

Embedded in the framework for action are the formulation of personal goals and agenda for behaving in the classroom. The pre-service teacher may, or may not, think carefully through appropriate or inappropriate ways of acting and dealing with problems. As philosophies of teaching grow in the thinking of individuals the framework of action represents the ideal – yet somewhat slanted towards the practical – actions of teachers in the classroom. Such actions are well-represented by ways teachers say they are going to act or, perhaps, more accurately, by the ways they romanticize and tell their peers about their classroom actions in the faculty room.

The realities of the classroom and context modify the framework for action but, invariably, the biography of the individual is played out in their 'teacher practices'. The idealized actions are quickly modified by the urgency of the situation and the polyphasic nature of teaching. Indeed, while teacher practices are a product of a complex set of conditions and modifications of prior experiences, they are buffeted and moulded by the context of the school and classroom. Despite the power of time, of school and classroom contexts, and of teacher preparation, the classroom practices exhibit convincing evidence of the strength of biography in the actions of beginning teachers.

It is these teacher practices, particularly coping strategies in relation to early experiences, that have provided the crucial evidence of the power of biography in the actions of beginning teachers. The intermediary links of the model are speculative, for it is difficult to reconstruct with any real degree of certainty the linking pathways. However, the separate experiences of Elizabeth, Mona, Cynthia, Dwayne and Kristen support the concept of the 'Biographical Transformation Model'.

The model in practice

Brief examples from the experiences of Elizabeth and Cynthia illuminate the usefulness of the model for understanding the links between biography and student teacher and beginning teacher actions.

139

Elizabeth Prior teaching experience had a significant effect on Elizabeth's teaching. Elizabeth worked for her church in Germany and the experience of dealing with people whom she was proselytizing had a particular and inherent meaning. The 'interpretation' Elizabeth determined as having application in the field of teaching was: 'When people are not interested, you back off, because, when opinions, beliefs or actions are forced upon individuals, they are likely to reject both the teacher and the message.'

Elizabeth transformed the interpretation into a 'schema': 'Stop teaching when individuals (i.e. students) are no longer interested in the subject matter.' In the setting of the classroom it was not applicable to stop teaching although she did briefly, so Elizabeth modified the schema into a 'framework for action', in which the schema was translated into several appropriate remedial actions to fit the classroom situation: 'Tighten up on discipline; deny the range of learning opportunities; lecture more and discuss less; have more structured lessons; change students' seating positions, and others.' She chose the 'best' perceived solution to her problem. As each potential solution was tried, and failed, she adopted another strategy. The solution, evidenced by her 'beginning teacher practices', was the reorganization of the seating arrangement of the classroom and the changed tactics for dealing with discipline and subject matter. While initial responses to the situation were made from the basis of her immediate and prior teaching experience, the subsequent peeling away and discarding of strategies that did not prove successful resulted in Elizabeth adopting deep-seated teacher role identity strategies that were based on her participation in the traditional kinds of classrooms of her childhood.

Cynthia Family values were impressed upon Cynthia. She was taught not to be assertive. She experienced being 'put down' whenever she even looked like acting in an assertive manner. The 'inherent meaning' of these kinds of experiences was that assertive behaviours were not appropriate ways to act because, as her parents told her, it was not 'socially correct'. The 'ascribed meaning' was that she would feel unaccepted if she was assertive. Through Cynthia's 'schema', the actions of others, for example, her teachers, were viewed and filtered. She was able to recognize behaviours in others that she either supported or rejected. Negative or positive teacher role models were recognized as were appropriate role models of family. The 'framework for action' was evidenced when Cynthia used the constructs of her philosophy of education and teaching to decide on a strategy of unobtrusively providing learning opportunities to students. She would not be assertive or authoritarian but, instead, focused her preparation and efforts on designing an effective and innovative curriculum. From the schema and framework for action, Cynthia developed a 'teacher role identity'; it was doubtful that Cynthia had formed a substantial teacher role identity. That identity, one which she only faintly recognized, was framed in negative teacher actions by the time she began student teaching. Certainly she had images of what she did not want to be in the classroom, but had only very weak impressions of what role she would actually need to take. The evidence suggests that the positive teacher role models influenced her thinking about curriculum while the negative experiences of teacher actions did nothing to provide a framework for positive actions in the classroom – for dealing with difficult and unruly students.

For the present, the 'Biographical Transformation Model' seems a reasonable way to explain how the formative experiences of Elizabeth and Cynthia were translated into teaching practices. Further testing of the model will result in its refinement and, perhaps, its sophistication.

Using the biographical transformation model to explain teacher role identity

In a recent paper, written after the five case studies were completed, Crow and Kauchak raised some questions about the concept of teacher role identity:

> The construct of Teacher Role Identity, while being intuitively attractive, is also nebulously unclear. What are the antecedents, i.e., when does it appear and to what extent do personality, personal history (e.g., home, parents, hobbies, friends) and formal schooling experiences interact to create a TRI [Teacher Role Identity]? In a similar way, what are the major sub-concepts that undergird the concept?[100]

While the constructs may be unclear, the concept provides a useful framework with which to examine the biographies of pre-service and beginning teachers. In response to the questions of Crow and

Figure 2 Developing teacher role identity, a model linking stages of development of teacher role identity with phases of the Biographical Transformation Model

Stages of development of teacher role identity	Phases of the Biographical Transformation Model
Family experiences as a child	
Experiences with teachers	
School experiences	Formative experiences
Meaning of family experiences	
Meaning of experiences with teachers	
Meaning of school experiences	Interpretation
Family role models	
Negative teacher role models and	
Positive teacher role models	
Development of educational philosophy	Schema
Ideals of adult–child relationships	
Ideal instructional strategies	
Ideal instructional environment	Framework for action
Significant recent experiences and people	
Teacher role identity ———————	Teacher role identity
	Student teacher and beginning teacher practices

Kauchak, Fig. 2 suggests a model for understanding the progressive development of some of the antecedents of teacher role identity. The speculative model, 'Developing Teacher Role Identity', suggest's the various stages of the construction of teacher role identity based upon the phases of the Biographical Transformation Model. As experiences are transformed into teacher actions, so too are the antecedents to the teacher role identity transformed into more complex constructs.

First, experiences of family, school and teacher are interpreted and are assigned meanings. The collective meanings of family, teacher or school experiences are modified, augmented and generalized to become family role models, positive or negative teacher role models or a personal philosophy of education. In turn, the constructs of the role models and philosophies are transformed into ideas for working in the classroom. From the idealized strategies, relationships and environments, the individual enacts classroom practices. Those behaviours may be modified by the context of the situation.

Influence of biography on practice

A list of coping and instructional strategies that were used by select individuals in relation to their biography, specifically the origins of their teacher role identity, is presented in Table 2 (pp. 120–1).

The speculative model, 'Interaction of biography and school environment: The influence of biography on teaching practice', is presented in Fig. 3. The model considers the nature of both the teacher role identity and the nature of the school environment. Teacher's role identity, a product of early experiences, can also be viewed as affecting a student beginning teacher's classroom practices in either negative or positive ways. By negative ways, I mean the tendency to engage in inappropriate classroom behaviours or actions. Positive teacher role identities result in positive classroom practices.

Although the pre-service teachers who had weak teacher role identities also tended to couch their early experiences in negative terms, it may not be reasonable to suggest that those with negative experiences will automatically develop weak teacher role identities. Depending on the kinds of early experiences, the development of ideals and influences of significant people or experiences, a teacher role identity may be strongly negative or strongly positive. What is significant, chronologically, is that over the course of the early experiences of family, school and teachers, and later, prior teaching, significant people or experiences, the teacher role identity evolves and is wrapped in negative or positive orientations.

Pre-service teachers come to teacher education programmes with a teacher role identity. Some individuals have sophisticated notions of what it means to be a teacher, others do not, but student teaching becomes the arena in which the teacher role identity, in whatever state it is laid out, is put to the test. For a pre-service teacher with a negative teacher role identity when the school environment is also negative, resulting practices tend to be negative and inappropriate. Those individuals are usually ill-equipped

Figure 3 Interaction of biography and school environment: The influence of biography on teaching practice

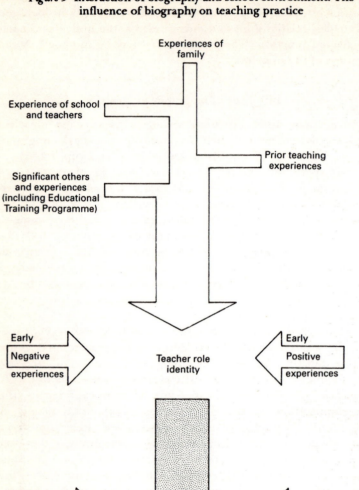

to handle the rigours of classrooms in positive ways. A negative school environment is one in which the classroom operating atmosphere, the support of the cooperating teacher, the size of the classes, the mix of personalities, students' view of the subject matter, curriculum requirements, instructional resources and other factors, do not provide solid support or congruence with the teacher role identity and 'framework of action' that the pre-service teacher holds. Conversely, a positive school environment reinforces the positive teacher role identity and the actions of the pre-service teacher are seen as being appropriate because they are congruent with the operating atmosphere of the classroom. The school environment reinforces or nullifies the strength of the teacher role identity so that classroom practices are enhanced or depreciated. In this way, the contextual elements of the teaching environment are importantly formative but lack the great power that has been attributed to them.[101]

While I have obviously over-simplified the description of the process and orientation by which neophytes operate in the classroom, it is important to acknowledge that the classroom teaching environment is extremely complex, making the interactions and responses of individuals difficult to categorize. It is not the intention of the model to deny the complexity but, similarly, one of the ways in which student and beginning teachers begin to get a handle on the classroom is to reduce the complexity of the situation. In effect, they try to enhance the positive factors of the classroom environment in order to remain a dynamic and operative force in the room.

By enhancing the positive environmental factors, neophytes increase their chances of acting out appropriate behaviours. An illustration from Elizabeth's experience supports this notion. Her student teaching at the senior high school was under the supervision of a forceful, young and energetic woman teacher. Elizabeth began her student teaching under the shield of a serious yet pleasant classroom environment. The students were used to sitting in an arrangement that promoted interaction between themselves and the teacher. Classes tended to be highly interactive and her student teaching went extremely well. Later, as a beginning teacher in another class, she tried to replicate a similar working atmosphere that she had previously enjoyed. In the new situation, there were high levels of disorder because she had not attended to matters of discipline and classroom management, and she was not able to maintain the positive images of her teacher role identity such as, for example, the openness, interactive discussions and round table seating arrangements. In order to maintain control, she gradually removed practices from her repertoire that she perceived were inducing some of the problems. First, she adopted stricter disciplinary tactics; then she rearranged the desks; later she altered her teaching approaches by increasing teacher-directed activities; and last, she reduced the autonomy and decision-making opportunities of the students. While her teaching practices were still positive, Elizabeth reduced the complexity of the classroom environment in order to cope and to maintain the implementation of components of her teacher role identity.

The issue of control seems to be a major factor in the successful implementation of the elements of teacher role identity. Further, control is indispensable. If a student or beginning teacher does not have control they are, invariably in an untenable position. Experienced teachers can maintain control in much looser environments than the situation Elizabeth experienced because they are often less threatened by disorder. Most student and beginning teachers must experience high levels of control in order to feel safe and to maintain a positive teacher role identity. With their limited repertoire of teaching practices, the only option student teachers and beginning teachers have is to streamline the classroom environment to reduce the possibilities of loss of control. They may revert to deep-seated role models of traditional teachers as they attempt to cope with the disarray of student behaviours and situations. Those with teacher role identities that are comfortable in unstructured or non-traditional classrooms, for example, are better able to deal with disruptive situations than those pre-service teachers with negative role identities, as the case of Cynthia illustrates.

The importance of understanding biography

The theories attempt to explain the value of understanding the role of biographies in classroom practices. Acknowledging that biographies are a significant factor in the classroom practices of pre-service and beginning teachers will be an important activity for teacher education programmes. The implications are significant from a variety of perspectives. One dominant issue these studies raise relates to the effectiveness of current components and models of teacher education for meeting the needs of students who have vastly different perspectives on the role of teachers and the teaching process from either those of cooperating teachers or programmatic role models. While a certain degree of discontinuity between pre-service teachers and school personnel may stimulate questioning and reflection, there is a point when the discontinuity of experience may be destructive for further development.

These studies, and the small but growing body of knowledge about teachers' biographies, suggests that it is not primarily the pre-service teacher education programmes that establish teacher role identity but, rather, previous life experiences as they relate to education and teaching. To understand how to harness the life experiences of pre-service teachers and channel them into contributing to more developed and effective teacher role identities will be a valid activity for teacher educators.

University pre-service teacher preparation programmes are usually too short, too structured and too insensitive to individual needs and backgrounds to do anything but provide a thin overlay experience, one that usually does not meld with previous life experiences and beliefs about teaching. Rather, university programmes often create further discontinuities about teaching for the pre-service teacher, particularly if the negative aspects of previous experiences are not dealt with. By not accommodating and dealing with the biography of teachers in preparation, future beginning teachers are bound to become teachers who teach in the manner in which they were taught and who will be limited in the ways in which they can professionally develop. Consistently resorting to coping strategies in the classroom is, to a degree, an acknowledgement of the powerful effect that biography has on teaching practice and points to the need not only to modify the negative effects of biography but to alter the contexts within which student teachers and beginning teachers operate.

NOTES

1 Woods, P. (1986) *Inside Schools: Ethnography in Educational Research*, London: Routledge and Kegan Paul. See also: Zeichner, K. and Grant, C. (1981) 'Biography and social structure in the socialization of student teacher: A re-examination of the pupil control ideologies of student teachers', *Journal of Education for Teaching*, Vol. 3, pp. 299–314.
2 Recent examples of studies related to biography include: Britzman, D.P. (1985) 'Reality and ritual: An ethnographic study of student

teachers', *University Microfilms International*, No. 8517084, Ann Arbor; Crow, N.A. (1987) 'Socialization within a teacher education program', Unpublished doctoral dissertation, The University of Utah, Salt Lake City; Knowles, J.G. (December 1987) 'What student teachers' biographies tell us: Implications for pre-service teacher education'. Paper presented at the First Joint Conference of the Australian and New Zealand Associations for Research in Education, University of Canterbury, Christchurch, New Zealand; Martinez, K. (1987) 'Encounters of the first kind: A progress report on research into changing perspectives of beginning teachers'. Paper presented at the First Joint Conference of the Australian and New Zealand Associations for Research in Education, University of Canterbury, Christchurch, New Zealand; Munro, R. (1987) 'Personal biography in the shaping of teachers'. Paper presented at the First Joint Conference of the Australian and New Zealand Associations for Research in Education, University of Canterbury, Christchurch, New Zealand; Traver, R. (1987) 'Autobiography, feminism and the study of teaching', *Teachers College Record*, Vol. 88, No. 3, pp. 443–452; Woods, P. (1984) 'Teacher, self and curriculum' in Goodson, I.F. and Ball, S.J. (eds) *Defining the Curriculum: Histories and Ethnographies*, London: Falmer, pp. 1–26.

3 Ball, S.J. and Goodson, I.F. (1985) 'Understanding teachers: Concepts and contexts' in Ball, S.J. and Goodson, I.F. (eds) *Teachers' Lives and Careers*, London: Falmer, pp. 1–26.

4 Crow, 'Socialization'.

5 To date there have been several reports including: Knowles, 'What student teachers' biographies tell us'; Knowles, J.G. (1988) 'The failure of a student teacher: Becoming educated about teachers, teaching, and self'. Paper presented at the First Joint Conference of the Australian and New Zealand Associations for Research in Education, University of Canterbury, Christchurch, New Zealand; Knowles, J.G. and Hoefler, V.B. (1989) 'The student teacher who wouldn't go away: Learning from failure', *Journal of Experimental Education* (Summer).

6 Crow, 'Socialization'. See also Measor, L. (1985) 'Critical incidents in the classroom: Identities, choices, and careers' in Ball, S.J. and Goodson, I.F. (eds) *Teachers' Lives and Careers*, London: Falmer, pp. 61–79; Sikes, P. (1985) 'The life cycle of the teacher' in Ball, S.J. and Goodson, I.F. (eds) *Teachers' Lives and Careers*, London: Falmer, pp. 27–60.

7 Zeichner and Grant 'Biography and social structure'; Crow, 'Socialization'.

8 See, for example, Copland, W. (1980) 'Student teachers and co-operating teachers: An ecological relationship', *Theory into Practice*, Vol. 18, pp. 198–199; Edgar, D. and Warren, R. (1969) 'Power and authority in teacher socialization', *Sociology of Education*, Vol. 42, pp. 386–399; Friebus, R. (1977) 'Agents of socialization involved in student teaching', *Journal of Educational Research*, Vol. 70, pp. 263–268; Karmos and Jacko (1977) 'The role of significant other during the

student teaching experience', *Journal of Teacher Education*, Vol. 28, pp. 51–55; Zevin, J. (April 1974) 'In thy cooperating teachers' image: Convergence of social studies student teachers' behaviour patterns with cooperating teachers' behaviour patterns'. Paper presented at the annual meeting of the American Educational Research Association, Chicago, Illinois.

 9 See, for example, Hoy, W. and Rees, R. (1977) 'The bureaucratic socialization of student teachers', *Journal of Teacher Educational*, Vol. 1, No. 28, pp. 23–26.

10 See, for example, Yee, A. (1969) 'Do cooperating teachers influence the attitudes of student teachers?', *Journal of Educational Psychology*, Vol. 60, pp. 327–332; Zevin, 'In the cooperating teachers' image'.

11 See, for example, Copland, 'Students teachers'; Doyle, W. and Ponder, G. (1978) 'The practicality ethic in teacher decision making', *Interchange*, Vol. 8, pp. 1–4.

12 Feiman-Nemser, S. and Buchmann, M. (April 1983) 'Pitfalls of experience in teacher preparation', Occasional paper no. 65, National Institute of Education, Washington, DC. See also: Knowles, 'The failure of a student teacher'; and Knowles and Hoefler, 'The student teacher'.

13 Zeichner and Grant, 'Biography and social structure', p. 301.

14 Lortie, D.C. (1975) *Schoolteacher*, Chicago: University of Chicago Press, p. 79.

15 Zeichner and Grant, 'Biography and social structure', pp. 307–308.

16 ibid., p. 311.

17 Woods, *Inside Schools*, pp. 11, 139.

18 Pollard, A.J. (1982) 'A model of classroom coping strategies', *British Journal of Sociology of Education*, Vol. 3, pp. 19–37.

19 Benyon, J. (1985) 'Institutional change and career histories in a comprehensive school' in Ball, S.J. and Goodson, I.F. (eds) *Teachers' Lives and Careers*, London: Falmer, pp. 1–26.

20 See, for example, Goodson, I.F. (1981) 'Life histories and the study of schooling', *Interchange*, Vol. 11, No. 4, pp. 62–76; Goodson, I.F. (1983) 'The use of life histories in the study of teaching' in Hammersley, M. (ed.) *The Ethnography of Schooling*, Driffield, England: Nafferton.

21 Middleton, S. (ed.) (1988) *Women and Education in Aotearoa*, Wellington, New Zealand: Allen and Unwin/Port Nicholson.

22 See, for example, Barone, T.E. (1987) 'Educational platforms, teacher selection, and school reform: Issues emanating from a biographical case study', *Journal of Teacher Education*, Vol. 38, No. 2, pp. 12–17; Eddy, E.M. (1969) *The Passage to Professional Status*, New York: Teachers College Press.

23 See, for example, Britzman, 'Reality and ritual'; Crow, 'Socialization'; Knowles, 'The failure of a student teacher', Martinez, 'Encounters of the first kind'; Munro, 'Personal biography'; Woods 'Teacher, self'.

24 Barone, 'Educational platforms'.

25 Eddy, *The Passage*.

26 Woods, 'Teacher, self', p. 239.

27 ibid., p. 260.

28 ibid.
29 Britzman, 'Reality and ritual', p. 9.
30 ibid., p. 519.
31 ibid., p. 526.
32 Britzman, D.P. (1986) 'Cultural myths in the making of a teacher: Biography and social structure in teacher education', *Harvard Educational Review*, Vol. 56, p. 443.
33 ibid., p. 453.
34 ibid.
35 Martinez, 'Encounters of the first kind'.
36 Munro, 'Personal biography', p. 1.
37 ibid.
38 Crow, 'Socialization'.
39 Crow, N.A. (1987) 'Pre-service teachers' biography: A case study'. Paper presented at the Annual Meeting of the American Educational Research Association, Washington, DC, p. 9.
40 Crow, 'Socialization'.
41 ibid.
42 Woods, *Inside Schools*, p. 283.
43 Zeichner, K.M. (1983) 'Individual and institutional factors related to the socialization of teaching' in Griffith, G.A. and Hukill, H. (eds) *First Years of Teaching: What are the Pertinent Issues?*. (Proceedings of the National Working Conference, pp. 1–60), Austin: Research and Development Center for Teacher Education, The University of Texas at Austin, p. 45.
44 Lacey, C. (1977) *The Socialization of Teachers*, London: Methuen.
45 Veenman, S. (1984) 'Perceived problems of beginning teachers', *Review of Education Research*, Vol. 54, pp. 143–178.
46 Ryan, K. (1986) *The Induction of New Teachers*, Bloomington, Indiana: Phi Delta Educational Foundation.
47 Lacey, *The Socialization*, p. 78.
48 ibid., p. 83.
49 ibid., p. 87.
50 ibid., p. 93.
51 See Hargreaves, A. (1977) 'Progressivism and pupil autonomy', *Sociological Review*, Vol. 25, No. 3; Hargreaves, A. (1978) 'The significance of classroom coping strategies' in Barton, L. and Meighan, R. (eds) *Sociological Interpretations of Schooling and Classrooms: A Reappraisal*, Driffield: Nafferton; Hargreaves, A. (1979) 'Synthesis and the study of strategies: A project for the sociological imagination' in Woods, P. (ed.) *Pupil Strategies*, London: Croom Helm; Pollard, A.J. (1979) 'Negotiating deviance and "getting done" in primary school classrooms' in Barton, L. and Meighan, R. (eds) *Schools, Pupils and Deviance*, Driffield: Nafferton; Pollard, A.J. (1980) 'Teacher interests and changing situations of survival threat in primary school classrooms' in Woods, P. (ed.) *Teacher Strategies*, London: Croom Helm; Pollard, 'A model'. (1982).
52 See, for example, Woods, *Inside Schools*; Pollard, 'A model'.
53 Woods, P. (1977) 'Teaching for survival' in Woods, P.E. and

Hammersley, M. (eds) *School Experience*, London: Croom Helm, pp. 271–293.
54 Hargreaves, 'The significance'
55 Pollard, 'A model'; Pollard, 'Teacher interests; Pollard, 'Negotiating deviance'.
56 Pollard, 'A model', p. 25.
57 ibid., p. 32.
58 ibid., p. 34.
59 ibid., p. 35.
60 Woods, *Inside Schools*, p. 139.
61 McDonald, F.J. (1980) *The Problems of Beginning Teachers: A Crisis in Training*, Princeton, NJ: Educational Testing Service; Bullough, Jr., R.V. (1989) *First Year Teacher: A Case Study*, New York: Teachers College Press.
62 Calderhead, J. (1984) 'Introduction: Teacher as decision-maker' in Calderhead, J. (ed.) *Classroom Decision Making*, London: Holt, Rinehart and Winston, pp. 1–19.
63 ibid., p. 14.
64 McDonald, *The Problems*, p. 76.
65 Bullough, *First Year Teacher*.
66 Veenman, 'Perceived problems'.
67 ibid.; see Ryan, *The Induction*, for a discussion of stages.
68 Bullough, *First Year Teacher*.
69 See, for example, Hargreaves, 'The significance'; Lacey, *The Socialization*; Pollard, 'A model'; Woods, 'Teaching for survival'; Bullough, *First Year Teacher*; McDonald *The Problems*.
70 Knowles, 'What student teachers' biographies tell us'.
71 Knowles, 'The failure of a student teacher'; Knowles and Hoefler 'The student teacher'.
72 Crow, 'Socialization'.
73 See, for example, Rist, R. (1977) 'On the relations between educational research paradigms', *Anthropology and Education Quarterly*, Vol. 8, pp. 42–49.
74 Ryan, K. (1979) 'Toward understanding the problem: At the threshold of the profession' in Howey, K. and Bents, R. (eds) *Toward Meeting the Needs of Beginning Teachers*, Minneapolis: United States Department of Education/Teacher Corps.
75 See Agar, M. (1980) *The Professional Stranger: An Informal Introduction to Ethnography*, New York: Academic; Spradley, J.P. (1980) *Participant Observation*, New York: Holt, Rinehart and Winston; Spradley, J.P. (1979) *The Ethnographic Interview*, New York: Holt, Rinehart and Winston; Yin, R.K. (1984) *Case Study Research*, Beverly Hills: Sage; Glaser, B. and Strauss, A. (1967) *The Discovery of Grounded Theory: Strategies for Qualitative Research*, Chicago: Aldine.
76 See Knowles, J.G. and Kauchak, D.P. (April 1988) 'Learning to teach: A case study of teacher socialization in the context of a pilot graduate pre-service teacher education program'. Paper presented at the Annual Meeting of the American Educational Research Association, New Orleans, LA.

77 Spradley, *The Ethnographic Interview.*
78 Woods *Inside Schools.*
79 Yinger, R.J. and Clark, C.M. (1985) 'Using personal documents to study teacher thinking', Occasional paper no. 84, Michigan State University: Institute for Research on Teaching, East Lansing, Michigan.
80 Spradley, *Participant Observation*; Glaser and Strauss, *The Discovery.*
81 Ryan, *The Induction.*
82 Knowles and Kauchak 'Learning to teach'; Crow, N.A. and Kauchak, D.P. (1988) 'Teacher socialization: A quasi-experimental case study'. Paper presented at the Annual Meeting of the American Educational Research Association, New Orleans, LA.
83 Lortie, *Schoolteacher.* See also Crow, 'Preservice teachers' biography'; Zeichner and Grant, 'Biography and social structure'.
84 Crow, 'Socialization'.
85 Crow, 'Preservice teachers' biography' p. 7.
86 Britzman, 'Reality and ritual'; Crow, 'Socialization'; Eddy, *The Passage*; Ryan, *The Induction*; Woods, 'Teacher, self'.
87 Munro, *Personal biography in the shaping of teachers.*
88 Woods, 'Teacher, self'.
89 Crow, 'Preservice teachers' biography', p. 7.
90 Britzman, 'Reality and ritual'.
91 Woods, 'Teacher, self'.
92 Crow and Kauchak, 'Teacher socialization'; Knowles and Kauchak, 'Learning to teach'.
93 Crow, N.A. (1988) 'A longitudinal study of teacher socialization: A case study'. Paper presented at the Annual Meeting of the American Educational Research Association, New Orleans, LA.
94 Martinez, 'Encounters of the first kind'.
95 Feiman-Nemser and Buchman, 'Pitfalls of experience'.
96 See Martinez, 'Encounters of the first kind'.
97 Crow, 'Socialization', p. 7.
98 Anderson, R.C. (1977) 'The notion of schemata and the educational enterprise: General discussion of conference' in Spiro, R.J. and Montague, W.E. (eds), Hillsdale, NJ: Lawrence Erlbaum.
99 Ryan, *The Induction.*
100 Crow and Kauchak, 'Teacher socialization', p. 12.
101 See Copland, 'Student teachers'; Doyle and Ponder, 'The practicality ethic'; Yee, 'Do cooperating teachers'; Zevin, 'In the cooperating teachers' image'.

5

SCHOOL IMPROVEMENT AND EDUCATOR PERSONALITY

Stages, types, traits or processes?

Louis M. Smith, Paul Kleine, John J. Prunty
and David C. Dwyer

INTRODUCTION

Beyond the particular substantive concepts one uses to order the personality of the teachers and administrators engaged in school improvement a further issue lies in the form which those concepts take. Mischel[1] in the second edition of his *Introduction to Personality* specifies what he calls 'approaches', a higher level ordering of personality theories, which group the various substantive theories in terms of their more abstract structure and purpose. The approaches cluster into trait, psychodynamic, behavioural and phenomenological theories as the various theorists 'construe or cut nature apart at different sets of joints'. Addressing this further issue is the intent of our title, 'stages, types, traits or processes?' Such discussion was at the heart of the symposium, 'Teachers' Professional Life Cycle and School Improvement: What are the Links?' for which this essay was first written. In a sense the title, by its very form, takes a position on the issues we want to raise, that is, by the specification of 'life cycle'. In a fundamental sense we hope to make that part of the title problematic. The resolution, if it be that, is an enlarged conception of the issues surrounding the individuals who engage in school improvement. To do all this we need to describe the Kensington School in the Milford School District, a place where we have spent considerable time over the last twenty years.

L.M. SMITH, P. KLEINE, J.J. PRUNTY AND D.C. DWYER

METHODS AND PROCEDURES

In any essay that reports empirical data it seems appropriate to indicate the nature and kind of procedures which produced those observations. In an over-simplified sketch, the research problem started with Smith and Keith's study of the Kensington School in the mid-1960s, which was published as *Anatomy of Educational Innovation*.[2] In the late 1970s and early 1980s, we, Smith and his colleagues, Kleine, Dwyer and Prunty, returned to the Kensington School in the Milford School District with National Institute of Education (NIE) support for a second project, *Kensington Revisited: A Fifteen Year Follow-up of an Innovative School and its Faculty*. These results were published in a long six-volume final report to NIE[3] They appear now in a trilogy, for the Falmer Press in England, on the 'restudy and reconstrual of educational innovation'. One of these books, *The Fate of an Innovative School*, is a history and ethnographic study of the first fifteen years in the life of an innovative school and of the school today. The second one, *Innovation and Change in Schooling*, is an historical and contextual study of the Milford School District and community and the impact of context on educational innovation. The third, *Educational Innovators: Then and Now*, is a life-history study of the original faculty, where they came from and what brought them to Kensington, and where they have gone and what they have done since their time at Kensington and Milford. It is the latter book from which the present ideas are largely drawn.

We located both of the original key administrators of the Milford District, Superintendent Steven Spanman and Curriculum Director Jerl Cohen, and the original principal of the Kensington School, Eugene Shelby, and all but one of the original faculty of the Kensington School. We interviewed them at length, up to seven hours on tape, in an essentially open-ended style. From these rambling records we constructed a point of view about them, their careers, their lives, and their perspective on educational innovation.[4]

EDUCATOR LIVES, PERSONALITY AND INNOVATION

When one deals at some length with the lives of two dozen innovative educators, the problem of the kind of language to use in which to cast one's remarks comes vividly to the fore. Does one describe

154

the individuals in terms of stages in a life cycle, as the Levinsons and the Sheehys do? Or does one cast the accounts in terms of traits as Gordon Allport did? Are there personality types, as Kretchmer and S.S. Smith once proposed? Or is it better to deal with processes of needs and presses and careers and life choices and chances, as Murray did some years ago, and as some of the more contemporary social and cognitive theorists have urged more recently? It is into that cauldron of 'personality' that we want to dip, albeit so briefly. Further, we want that effort to help us think about the phenomenon of school improvement.

A brief glimpse at Kensington's original principal

On the surface, Principal Shelby's career is less dramatic than Superintendent Spanman's or Curriculum Director Cohen's. Yet, in some very significant aspects, that would be a misconstrual. Eugene was a true believer and a man of social action. Here in a brief statement from the interview he recalls his earlier professional motivations:

ES: Okay, I think that was described in your book as searching for the holy grail. (Laughter)
OBS: Alright, yes.
ES: Do you recall that term?
OBS: Yeah, I do. (Laughter)
ES: And I have not reviewed that for a long, long time either, but I remember that because I think it is true. I have spent several more periods of my life searching for the holy grail, until I finally gave up.

Readers of *Anatomy of Educational Innovation* will recall that Shelby had left the Kensington School, mid-semester, in the spring of 1966, at the invitation of a close friend of Steven Spanman's. It was an unusual time of the year to leave. It was a return to his home state where he had grown up, done his undergraduate and graduate work. It was also to an unusual position, as director of PS 2100, a school of the future.

Perhaps even more importantly than it being a futurist school it also involved Eugene in another round of the most difficult kind of innovation, institution building. The new situation contained an interesting complex of qualities: (1) the school was a part of a larger Hispanic/American centre, (2) it had multiple sources of

155

funding including Title III monies of the recently passed
Elementary and Secondary Education Act (ESEA), (3) it was just
beginning, Eugene was the first person hired by the overall
director, (4) the local city public school was the fiscal agent, (5) a
number of local and state political figures were involved, and (6)
eventually, it would have its own legally constituted board of
directors. Educators involved in starting research and development centres and regional educational laboratories will recognize
the issues and the difficulties.

> Eugene described for us the development of the ideas
> behind the new venture. As the idea progressed, they, I guess,
> came up with the idea of creating more than just a school and
> coming with the whole center they called it the Hispanic–
> American Educational Center, which would take over all of
> the facilities that could be used by them, and would have a
> number of major components. It was really a grandiose
> scheme and I think it grew from an initial conception of
> about four components to maybe even eight or ten. One
> component was to be a Regional Laboratory, one component
> was to be a Cultural Center, Hispanic–American Cultural
> Center, patterned after the East–West Center in Hawaii. I
> know the mayor and some of our Board members went to
> Hawaii to visit that. One component was PS 2100, The School
> of the Future, and another component was to be an Admini-
> strative Services component. The State at the same time had
> passed legislation to create a number of regional educational
> service centers.

So, Shelby's quest for the holy grail continued. Large-scale,
complex, and ideal reforms remained central items on his agenda.
Along the way, in the pursuit, he raised questions which we believe
remain fundamental in the organizational analysis of innovation:

> ES: But I really thought that the idea, okay, I still think that
> my ideas about schools have a lot of merit. I thought,
> okay, I have been through it, and instead of, you know,
> my trying to be principal of just one school to do some-
> thing, it would really be a lot more productive and have
> a lot more benefit if I could indeed work with several
> schools and have them do some things. And I was pretty

optimistic about it. Here again, searching for the holy grail. It was really a disappointing thing for me. First there is the question of can a public school district really allow a school to be different, and that was one of the issues in Milford? It was an issue in the South. And, you know, the superintendents would say, 'Hey, this is a good idea. Yeah we would like to get some of our principals in your summer workshop, and we would like to do some things, help them to be more innovative, and get some good programs going.' And yet there was not the real support. And if we let them do something different, what is that going to do to the other schools? That was an issue. We were not very selective in the people that got into the program. I'm not sure that we communicated very well to them what it was for, but, and I wasn't very good, as I was trying to be a one man show, which was a real mistake. I did a lot of sermonizing, looking back on it, I think, but we had some things going for us too. I did have some good people there. You know, I planned them out pretty well. But, I remember on one, I think this kind of describes what I was up against. One of the activities that I involved these principals in was, one of the things that we need to do is, to be pretty clear about what it is we are trying to do. You know, just have some objectives. If you want a school to do something, what do you want it to do? I said schools have been so means oriented that we have not really zeroed in on what it is we are trying to accomplish. Until we do that we are not going to do it very well. So I had them engage in an exercise to articulate their objectives. I remember one of the participants finally came up with the objective so that at the end of the year all the kids on each grade level would be at the same achievement level.

OBS: That did not fit too well with your goals?

ES: We want to *narrow* the range of individual differences? It just really depressed me.

Later in the interview, Eugene finished his story of his post-Kensington experiences with an account of his return to a principalship:

Anyway, I told you I kept asking the question, what is it that I really want to do? And the answer for a long time was nothing. And finally it was, I want to get back into the school and be a principal.

Teacher/administration personality: an abstract view

The brief interview notes, from our longer and more detailed accounts, give a glimpse of one key innovator from the Kensington School. It seems self-evident that the 'person' is an important item in any description and analysis of educational innovation. Some analytic accounts[5] have minimized this aspect of innovation. We believe the excerpts raise a major sub-issue in the nature of the conceptualization of the person in the study of innovation. It has to do with the kind of personality theory to which students of innovation appeal. At times we feel we are beating the proverbial dead horse to note that the substance of the theory we have been developing is a far cry from the dominant behaviourist view in much of the innovation literature, in much of educational psychology, and in much of the educational research community. Behavioural objectives, time on task, mastery learning, school effectiveness, are sounds that emanate from drums and drummers distant from the language and perspectives of the innovators we have studied and the language and theory in which we have chosen to couch our own interpretations and speculations. We believe that this non-behaviourist kind of reconstrual of educational innovation is one of the major outcomes of our inquiry. The unfinished nature of this agenda lies in the huge array of possibilities latent in personality theory. Even a brief scanning of books such as Mischel's[6] or Hall and Lindzey's *Theories of Personality*[7] indicates the shifting sands upon which one tries to construct a point of view. The psychological community has not done the kind and quality of thinking or produced the kinds of resolutions that those of us in education require. That agenda remains open.

Looking over Shelby's comments raises several key issues with which personality theory must deal. First, Shelby had a penchant for taking on large, complex and idealistic problems in educational improvement. These tasks involved long periods of time. Cumulatively, they added up to decades. Earlier, we had phrased this in the language of Eric Hoffer[8] as 'true belief'. Second, the degree of personal energy and effort that he contributed as an individual was enormous. It is almost as though that single-handedly, 'a one man show', and through personal powers of persuasion, 'I did a lot of sermonizing', he could make the desired events occur. Further there are commitments to their own ideas and beliefs about the 'good school' that don't permit or grant legitimacy to other ideas, 'all kids... at the same achievement level'. Finally, there are long mood swings, 'And the answer for a long time was nothing.' We believe that the implications of these comments for construing personality of educational innovators and reformers are profound.

TWO ALTERNATIVES

At this point we would like to skip into two quite disparate sources which are a long way from psychological personality theory but which were very useful in helping us think about the Eugene Shelby's of the school improvement world. Arthur Bestor is a well-known historian of the nineteenth Century, and perhaps known more infamously to educationists as one of the sharp critics of latter day progressive education.[9] So it is a bit ironical to bring his earlier work and ideas to bear on school improvement. Ernest House is a well-known educational evaluator much interested in multiple aspects of school improvement. They begin our task of synthesis.

House's perspective

One of the most provocative views on educational innovation that has appeared in the educational literature is Ernest House's essay, 'Technology versus craft: a ten year perspective on innovation'.[10] In the introduction to the article he distinguishes between educational innovation, educational reform and educational change:

> The topic of this article, however is not broad educational change as such but rather the narrower subject of educational innovation – the deliberate systematic attempt to change the school through introducing new ideas and techniques. Innovation is viewed as relatively isolated technical or programmatic alterations or as low-level change, whereas

reform involves a normative national and broad structural change. Of course, change and innovation cannot be distinguished neatly from one another.[11]

Shortly we will turn to those distinctions, as we have on other occasions.[12] Initially here we are concerned with his several perspectives on educational innovation.

The perspectives are, in effect, belief systems which have 'dominated thought on innovation over the last ten years', that is, how innovation does or, in some cases, should proceed. He argues that much of the innovation of the 1960s, fuelled by federal efforts, was based on an RD and D, research, development and diffusion model. This was the technological perspective with its elements of rationality, division of labour, hierarchical mode of control, and its assumption of commonly shared values. In its extreme form it argued for producing 'teacher proof' materials, and in the eyes of some teachers and teacher advocates reduced teachers to unthinking cogs in a mechanical system of education and schooling.

As difficulties arose in the development and use of innovations, serious flaws appeared in viewing innovation from the technological perspective. An alternative and competitive model arose that House has labelled the political perspective. The essential ingredient centred on the conflicts in values and goals within any innovation. Both within and among professional educators, disciplinary specialists of several sorts, and parental and citizen groups conflicting ideas of the desirable were clear and important. Concepts such as interest groups, conflict, negotiation, compromise and mutual adaptation entered the discussion. This was a very different point of view than the technological.

Thirdly, House categorizes a more anthropological case study approach to understanding innovation as the cultural perspective. Communities of individuals in schools and school districts, and communities of parents and patrons each with their own cultural forms, modes and meanings are going about their lives in their own ways using common sense, appealing to traditions, and renewing the meaning of life for themselves. The context of the innovation became salient in this perspective. Overall, House sees the shift moving from the innovation *per se*, to the innovation in context, to the context *per se*. This community prerogative seems broader than the 'communitarian' position raised by Bestor.

In our view we are adding here a fourth perspective, that of the person in innovation. Our book on this part of our research, by its very title, *Educational Innovators: Then and Now*, is an argument that the individuals who enter into the activity of innovation are different from the run of the mill educators in the public schools and the colleges of education in the universities. Having a mid- to long-term look at their careers and at their belief systems has been instructive. In so far as the technologists, the conflict theorists and the culturalists have ignored the 'person' in their perspectives they have presented a limited view of the phenomenon of educational innovation.

Bestor and the utopians

Arthur Bestor's view in his *Backwoods Utopias*[13] was another stimulus that pushed our thinking along substantially. He argues that the late eighteenth and early nineteenth century was a time of great hope and experimentation in American society, and that reforms and reformers were of four types. He contrasts: (1) individualism, (2) revolution, (3) gradualism, and (4) communitarianism. In regard to individualism he quotes Emerson, 'If the single man plant himself indomitably on his instincts, and there abide, the whole world will come round to him.' People of indomitable will have been planting their flags for centuries and influencing the course of events. Charisma, and perhaps stubbornness as well, have been with us a long time. Revolution in France, in America, and later throughout the world in the nineteenth and twentieth centuries has been a major second avenue of social change. Recently, the neo-Marxists have sometimes acted as though they discovered and/or owned the phenomenon. Gradualism reflects attempts at 'an amelioration of particular conditions', not a total reconstruction of society. Some political theorists, for example, Lindblom,[14] have argued that this is the 'democratic' way and have coopted into it their point of view. But it is to the communitarian movements that Bestor's book is addressed, and, surprisingly to us, he captures much of what the Kensington/Milford educators were about.

> Communitarianism does not correspond exactly to any of these. It is collectivistic not individualistic, it is resolutely

opposed to revolution, and it is impatient with gradualism. Such a position may seem no more than an elaborate and self-defeating paradox. To the communitarian it was not. The small, voluntary, experimental community was capable, he believed, of reconciling his apparently divergent aims: an immediate, root-and-branch reform, and a peaceable, non-revolutionary accomplishment thereof. A microcosm of society, he felt, could undergo drastic change in complete harmony and order, and the great world outside could be relied on to imitate a successful experiment without coercion or conflict.[15]

Although the Kensington/Milford educators did not call it that, now, in long retrospect, we are prepared to argue that their model of change was implicitly, in intent and scope, communitarian and utopian in the sense of the quote from Bestor. This makes further sense out of two ideas from our earlier description and analysis.[16] These were 'the protected subculture', an attempt to isolate the Kensington School from the pressures of the School District in general, and the Kensington School as 'a deployment center', a place for generating ideas and practices to be disseminated to the rest of the Milford District. These, too, we now see are ideas with a long history in American society and education.

A beginning synthesis

Now we view Eugene Shelby as a communitarian utopian. We have developed two pictorial ways, Figs 4 and 5, of handling the three overlapping concepts of innovation, reform and utopianism. These concepts seem to be points along two continua. The first dimension moves from a concern with specifics or elements of change to a concern with systemic wholes or total units of change. The second dimension reflects a concern with means and instrumentalities versus a concern for ends, goal or visions. In Fig. 4 we have presented the analysis as a cone or megaphone metaphor. In this form we are hypothesizing that the two dimensions, means–ends and specifics–systemic are not orthogonal. As one moves from utopia, to reform, to innovation the dimensions tend to come together. In the Fig. 5 we are hypothesizing that the dimensions are orthogonal. Further we are hypothesizing that the dimensions have midpoints of mixed

Figure 4 Megaphone metaphor of innovation, reform and utopia

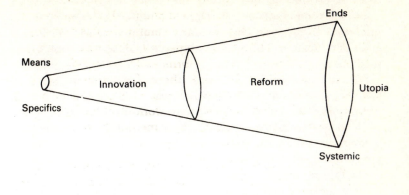

Utopia

Figure 5 Critical concerns in innovation, reform and utopia

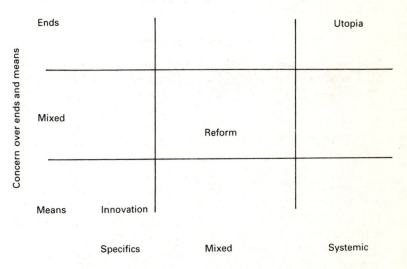

concerns. In sum, the key concepts, and the individuals who fit the types, lie on the diagonal.

Shelby's comments seem to place him rather easily among those interested in systemic change and with concerns for the broad goals of education. This seems to be what 'pursuing the holy grail' is all about.

To return to our concerns with personality theory we find that a typology has been helpful in producing an image of educational innovators. This seems to have occurred in two ways. First, it has been suggested that we must discriminate among innovators, reformers and utopians. Second, it suggests that there are multiple kinds of individuals interested in school improvement. When we analyse these 'types' into underlying 'dimensions' we find further help in terms of ideas such as means–ends and specific–systemic continua. Implicitly, if not explicitly, Shelby seemed to think and act in these terms. In the search for a label to handle that we find we resonate to 'perspective', as used by the symbolic interactionists such as Howard Becker.[17] A perspective is a point of view, a combined set of ideas and actions which solve problematic situations. The concept is nicely congruent with participant observational data in that field notes usually contain references to what individuals do and what they think about what they do. Our data from Shelby seem to allow such an interpretation.

CONCLUSION

As we cautioned in our opening remarks, we have talked little of life cycles or stages. Our follow-up study suggests that educational innovators neither die nor fade away. Personality dispositions relevant to school improvement remain. That seems a major and important finding. While the standard perspectives drawn from psychology provided some insights into the dreams, hopes and actions of our innovative educators, we found these concepts to be less than satisfying. We turned instead, with a pragmatic and somewhat uneasy eclecticism to alternative ways of construing personality issues. With indebtedness to House and Bestor, we found the typing of school improvers as innovators, reformers and utopians helped make sense of our data. In turn, these types seemed to fall into two dimensions: a specific to systemic orientation and a concern for means or ends. We depicted these dimensions as a cone-shaped model of non-orthogonal dimensions or a three by three matrix. Both conceptions appear fruitful for additional work practically, theoretically and empirically.

Substantively Bestor's fourfold classification of individualists, gradualists, revolutionaries and communitarians suggests another typology for rethinking what we called earlier,[18] the issue in the degree of change: gradualism versus the alternative of grandeur. That is a fundamental reconstruction of those ideas, and a linking of them to issues in personality types.

We believe that these ideas have major implications for the debate on the practical problem of whether one should focus on the recruitment of types of teachers for innovative school improvement projects or whether one should focus on the training and socialization of teachers for innovative projects. Further, if one expands that discussion into concerns for leadership in school improvement, the dilemma becomes a tri-lemma. Our concern for the types of persons we found at the Kensington School and in the Milford School District may not be much beyond a 'word-to-the-wise' for school administrators, but we feel that it is an important word.

Finally, this kind of thinking adds a dimension of 'personality' to House's conceptualization of innovation, if not improvement, as technical processes, as political processes, and as cultural processes. That is, there are personality processes at work as well. Now when we think of school improvement we have a conception which we can use to approach any proposal for change. That seems useful for consultants asked to help, for administrators who are pushing an agenda, and for teachers who may be less than willing actors if not pawns in the process of school improvement and educational change. In short, the linkages or 'mediations', to use Sartre's label, are kinds of people who have quite different perspectives on the nature of schools and the improvement of schools.

NOTES

1 Mischel, W. (1976) *Introduction to Personality*, New York: Holt, Rinehart and Winston.
2 Smith, L.M. and Keith, P. (1971) *Anatomy of Educational Innovation*, New York: Wiley.
3 Smith, L.M., Prunty, J., Dwyer, D. and Kleine, P. (1983) *Kensington Revisited: A Fifteen Year Follow-up of an Innovative School and Its Faculty*, Washington, DC: NIE.
4 Smith, L.M., Kleine, P., Dwyer, D. and Prunty, J. (1985) 'Educational

innovation: a decade and a half later' in Ball, S. and Goodson, I. (eds) *Teachers' Lives and Careers*, London: Falmer.

5 House, E. (1979) 'Technology versus craft: a ten year perspective on innovation', *Journal of Curriculum Studies*, Vol. 11, pp. 1–15.

6 Mischel, *Introduction to Personality*.

7 Hall, C. and Lindzey, G. (1978) *Theories of Personality*, New York: Wiley.

8 Hoffer, E. (1951) *The True Believer*, New York: Mentor.

9 Bestor, A. (1955) *The Restoration of Learning*, New York: Knopf.

10 House, 'Technology versus craft'.

11 ibid., p. 1.

12 Smith, L.M., Kleine, P., Prunty, J., and Dwyer, D. (1986) *Educational Innovators: Then and Now*, London: Falmer.

13 Bestor, A. (1970) *Backwoods Utopias*, (2nd edn), Philadelphia: University of Pennsylvania Press (originally published 1950).

14 Lindblom, C.E. (1968) *The Policy Making Process*, Englewood Cliffs, NJ: Prentice Hall (2nd edn, 1980); Lindblom, C.E. (1969) 'The science of muddling through' in Carver, F. and Sergiovanni, T. (eds) *Organizations and Human Behavior: Focus on Schools*, New York: McGraw-Hill.

15 Bestor, A. *Backwoods Utopias* (2nd edn), p. 4.

16 Smith and Keith, *Anatomy of Educational Innovation*.

17 Becker, H.S., Geer, B., Hughes, E.C. and Strauss, A.L. (1961) *Boys in White*, Chicago: The University of Chicago Press.

18 Smith and Keith, *Anatomy of Educational Innovation*.

6

USING ORAL HISTORIES TO RECONSTRUCT THE EXPERIENCES OF WOMEN TEACHERS IN VERMONT, 1900–50

Margaret K. Nelson

INTRODUCTION

The research reported here is part of a larger study of school-teachers in Vermont, designed to show both the broad parameters and the personal meaning of this occupation for women in the first half of the century. Few historical characters have been portrayed in as dismal a light as the rural New England school-teacher. Hired because she was cheaper than her male counter-part, set down with little more education than her students in a poorly furnished (and poorly heated) schoolhouse, required to leave her job as soon as she married (or confined to life as a spinster), and subject to restrictive behavioural standards, she is, perhaps, one of our favourite victims. Yet, the voices of school-teachers themselves offer a different perspective which reveals that if there were constraints, there were also ample opportunities for the teachers to negotiate the boundaries of these constraints and to employ them for their own purposes. The particular focus of this paper, then, is a demonstration of how the findings from oral history interviews challenge the impression gained from written documents alone.

Vermont provides an ideal location for using the method of oral history to explore the experiences of rural teachers. At the beginning of the century school teaching was an occupation which could be entered with as little as an eighth grade education; by 1950 there were discrete professional standards including four years of college and specific courses designed for teacher preparation. At the turn of the century most teaching in Vermont took place in one-room schoolhouses; fifty years later the site for most teaching was the graded schools located in towns and cities. This latter change brought with it increasing specialization: the rural schoolteacher taught all grades and all subjects; she also served as cook, janitor and fund-raiser. The more modern teacher had the responsibility for only one grade with the help of a range of subsidiary personnel. The single superintendent to whom the rural schoolteacher reported gave way to a whole layer of administrators and more complex rules and procedures. Because the processes of consolidation, specialization and bureaucratization occurred much later in Vermont than they did in more urban areas, information about both the earlier form of schoolteaching and the process of transformation is accessible through interviews with participants.[1]

In what follows, I briefly describe the methodology on which this study is based, including both the kind of written materials which were available and the manner in which I conducted interviews. I then discuss two ways in which information collected through interviews revealed significant insights about women's lives as schoolteachers which could not have been obtained from written sources alone. First, the interviews revealed two types of gaps in the written documents: some information was entirely omitted; other information was available only in a one-sided manner. Second, the interviews suggested an interpretation of the information which differed substantially from that which emerged from relying solely on written materials.

METHODOLOGY

From the beginning of my research I assumed that oral history interviews would be an essential component of my data collection. I knew that the written materials were scanty and if I were to fully understand how teachers experienced their work, I needed personal testimony.[2] My reading of history bolstered this conviction. Numerous studies have shown that there is a gap between what we can discover when we rely on published accounts of some historical event and what we can discover when we ask questions of the on-site participants of those same events. This gap looms larger when we are looking at women's history because of the private nature of so much of women's lives.

Written documents

The written documents on which I relied for this project included both primary source materials and secondary analyses of Vermont's educational system. Within the former category the most useful documents were reports of the State Department of Education.[3] These provided an overview of the changing characteristics of the teaching force and regulations relating to qualifications. Other resources included minutes of school board meetings, the publications of various professional associations and evaluation teams, records from teacher training institutions, and contemporary histories of education in Vermont.[4]

Many recent analyses of women in teaching focus on the process of feminization rather than women's personal experiences.[5] Numerous studies of specific groups of schoolteachers have appeared over the past ten years; rural New England schoolteachers remain under-represented in the research as well as in collections of personal testimony documents.[6]

Oral history interviews

Interviews were conducted with approximately fifty women whose teaching careers included some time in schools in Addison County, Vermont prior to (though occasionally continuing beyond) 1950. I obtained names of subjects at a Retired Teacher's Association meeting where I described my research interest and asked for volunteers. Other names were suggested by the subjects themselves, taken off school records, or offered by individuals in the community who were familiar with my project. The sample is not random. The limits imposed on the kind of individuals to be interviewed derive from both my research interests and my effort to keep the study feasible by limiting it to a single county.

Initially I used an interview schedule designed to obtain a total life history into which more detailed information about occupational involvement could be placed. As a starting point I relied quite heavily on the life-history interview guide developed by Sherna Gluck[7] and on the questions developed by the Project at the University of Michigan[8] for interviewing women in trade unions. As I became more certain about my own interests I expanded those areas of questioning which seemed to be offering the most insight. The interviews were designed to be free flowing and open ended, to allow the interviewees to tell their stories in their own words, with the interviewer directing questions only as necessary to make sure that specific areas were covered. After the initial interview, which usually took an hour to an hour and a half, I listened to the tape and designed further questions to be covered or issues to be pursued in a subsequent interview. Most of the subjects were interviewed at least twice. The interviews were conducted by students enrolled in a course in oral history at Middlebury College and research assistants made available by the Center for Field Research as well as by myself. The interviewers ranged in age from 17 to 67, in level of education from high school completion to graduate degrees, and in occupation from the undecided status of student to committed teachers.

The variety of different interviewers had a mixed effect on the research. On the positive side, as individuals with varying interests and perceptions, they brought out a wider range of responses and pursued a wider range of questions than I alone might have done. For example, when I started the research I was primarily interested in seeing how involvement in the occupation fitted into the larger structure of the lives of the subjects. But the teachers among my researchers were personally interested in gaining information about how the informants had structured a school day, classroom techniques and the content of lessons. Their persistence in asking questions along these lines brought out material which I came to learn was crucial to understanding the issues under consideration. On the other hand, some of the interviewers were totally uninterested in topics that were important to my research goals and failed to pursue intriguing lines of thought. And some failed to separate their own concerns from the attitudes of the subjects. In one particularly disastrous encounter, an interviewer became quite huffy and upset when the woman she was speaking with insisted that 'teachers today have it much too easy'.

THE CONTRIBUTIONS OF INTERVIEW MATERIALS

Filling gaps in the written documents

Omissions

Interviews with retired schoolteachers revealed a variety of issues which were entirely omitted in the published accounts of the occupation. Significant features of the life experiences of schoolteachers are lost if we rely on such sources. They will rarely cover topics pertaining to sex, hidden violations of rules, or personal experiences which are simply not relevant to official concerns.

One of my significant findings from the interviews was evidence of sexual harassment.[9] Although our contemporary consciousness has made this an issue of public awareness, if we rely on what was written in the first three-quarters of this century, it would appear that no such problems existed. The written documents might make an intriguing reference to some 'trouble' in a school or the hasty departure of a teacher, but the precise nature of such incidents are shrouded in mystery. Moreover, almost none of the (even quite recent) secondary analyses of the teaching profession mentions sexual harassment, even though violence and the use of corporal punishment is addressed.

In all honesty, I must admit that at first I did not explicitly look for evidence of sexual harassment: it takes us a long time to turn our contemporary consciousness to an understanding of the past. It took the frank discussion of one woman to alert me to the possibility of exploring the issue. However, even when sexual harassment is the precise focus of concern such material is difficult to uncover. There are multiple reasons why the interviewees would deny, forget to reveal, or actually conceal such assaults. First of all, these women were all quite elderly by the time they were interviewed and may simply have felt it was inappropriate to tell younger women about such events. Second, they would not have had the label of sexual harassment with which to classify or make sense of their experiences. They might thus have had all the shame and sense of isolation that go along with such assaults, especially before they were publicly acknowledged. Third, some of the women romanticized their teaching experiences. To reveal harassment of this sort would have undermined the picture they were attempting to create. And finally, the women were being taped by strangers they had little reason to trust. That this last was sometimes the case is strongly suggested by the behaviour of one woman who spoke about her superintendent with acute fear, asking that the tape recorder be turned off when his name came up. She implied that she had had some kind of embarrassing trouble with him but she would not give more information about it.

Nevertheless, one brave woman told me a disturbing story about being alone in a new school and having a school board member arrive to watch her prepare the building for the students:

> The first day that I was there he was really smart. I had been
> getting books off that high cupboard there and I was up on a
> stepladder and the first thing he did – and I didn't even know
> he was there – and the first thing he did was run his hands up
> my legs. Boy. Pshoo. I turned around and swatted him with a
> yardstick that was up there on that shelf. Then I found out
> who he was and I said I didn't care. I didn't even know who
> he was or anything. I had never met him or anything. He had
> a lot of nerve.

Though later interviews did not reveal additional instances as
explicit as this one, I was alerted to the fact that when women
mentioned their small size and light weight in comparison with the
older boys in the schoolroom they were telling me that they had
felt physically vulnerable and scared. Similarly I heard their discussions of how they were selected by visiting superintendents – 'and
if they liked our looks they hired us' – not just as quaint reminders
of youthful attractiveness, but as indicators of sexual overtones
running through evaluations. In fact, the whole arena of education
in rural schools (from my now possibly overly sensitive eyes)
emerged as heavily laden with instances of overt sexuality. The
boys, I was reminded, taunted the girls and the teachers with
snakes. Sometimes, these taunts assumed a more serious nature:

> They'd had so much trouble [the year before]. I tried to find
> out what the trouble was and nobody would tell me what the
> trouble was. They'd had eight teachers the year before and
> court cases. Of course it was sexual trouble and nobody
> would speak about it. It was mostly boys in that school and
> they had attacked the girls. . .. They'd just sneak off and the
> teacher couldn't control it.

With this new awareness, the tale in a professional journal about
travelling salesmen seemed to have a hidden message:

> A white schoolhouse stood beside the road in the shadow of
> the Green Hills. . .. Twenty children were working at their
> tasks, and the blue-eyed curly headed teacher at her desk was
> piloting an awkward boy through a tough problem in Stocks
> and Bonds. An automobile came to a shrieking stop in the
> road. A grim-jawed man lugging a heavy bag strode up to the
> door. . .. He pushed open the door, and invaded that peace-
> ful room. He banged down upon the teacher's desk a set of

172

books and a sheaf of impressive-looking papers. He pointed to a title, 'What To Do and How To Do It.' He shattered the stillness of the room with hypnotic speech. . ... He pushed a fountain pen into her fingers. . . . She stammered a frightened, 'no.' But would this man take No for an answer? Not on your life. . ... The frightened curly head took the pen, and signed.[10]

A second kind of material omitted from written accounts had to do with those things which were hidden from the officials. Part of the picture of schoolteachers as victims has to do with the provision that they were not allowed to teach once married.[11] It is generally assumed that this provision went unchallenged. As Tyack and Hansot argue,

> Women were thus presented with a dilemma that men did not face: the forced choice, in most cases, between a public career and the intimacy of marriage. And single women who continued in education met negative stereotypes about spinsters.[12]

Nevertheless, as my interviews revealed, many of the young women engaged to teach in rural schools, ignored this edict and settled down with a husband. If they were concerned about whether or not this would result in being fired, they simply 'forgot' to inform the superintendent and the school board members:

> I got married. I was supposed to stop but I didn't tell anybody I got married so I didn't stop. A lot of teachers in my day did that which was not very nice but we were sort of forced to do it because we felt we wanted the job.

Of course, they often lived in small towns where it is notoriously difficult to keep a private life truly private. And superintendents were delighted to share the fiction of a single teacher when there were few people qualified for – and willing to take on – the job of teaching in a rural school.

Officially, pregnancy among schoolteachers was frowned on even more severely than marriage: 'It is part of the American credo that school teachers reproduce by budding.'[13] But my subjects told me that they did not feel compelled at all to create this impression. In fact they spoke freely about pregnancies which were both acknowledged and supported:

> I taught until February and nobody knew I was pregnant, and then came February vacation and I sent [my superintendent] a note and said he better look for somebody quick. He and the school nurse came to see me during February vacation and asked me how I was and what the doctor said and so forth. And I said, '[The doctor] said I'm fine,' and [my superintendent] said, 'As long as you're all right you go right along.' And so I did.

Such pregnancies might have had a more mixed reaction in the community itself. Some teachers remember parents who objected to the appearance of a prominent pregnancy in the classroom. Mrs Staples recalls trying to convince a little boy to take off his sweater on a hot day and the boy's guardian coming into the school saying, 'I was not to tell her kid what to do and all that and anyway it was time for me to stop teaching when I was as big as I was'. And another teacher remembers that the only time she was not asked back, 'Was the year I had my twins – there was one woman who thought I stayed a little too long'. But other teachers remember communities which were at least silent, if not fully supportive:

> When I was pregnant I was down in East Middlebury and I finished right up until June. . . . There was no comment at all that I ever heard of. . . . There was another teacher there and we both of us wore smocks, she did as well as I did, and it seemed to work out all right. I never heard any repercussions.

Moreover, the evidence suggests that because the teachers located their own replacements, they could generally be assured that they would get their jobs back. Women reported that they drew on the resources of friends and family members (a mother, a sister) to take over for them. These individuals would willingly give way when the schoolteacher was ready to resume her position. If no one in the teacher's network was available, she might find an inadequate replacement to ensure her reappointment the following year. Fifty years after she left her school on a 'maternity leave' Mrs White can still get a chuckle out of remembering the incompetence of the man she selected to substitute for her:

> When I was gone that six weeks, that's the funniest thing that happened. . . . Those kids really gave [the substitute] a hard time. . . . The kids didn't like him and he didn't dare go

outside on the playground and that was the funny part of it. . .. And one noon hour they really gave him a hard time, they didn't let him out the door. And the kids stood outside and broke every window with stones and he didn't dare go outside and stop them. And right towards the end of the year he had to help take them on the school picnic. And boy, when he came back, he was a rag.

Once the babies were born the schoolteachers had to find ways to handle their double burdens. No published materials offer information about how teachers managed their private lives. Such issues were not relevant. But the interviews were rich in surprising information. First of all, they provide evidence of the kind of open role sharing that 'second wave' feminists thought they had discovered. Several women said that their husbands cared for the children because their occupations allowed more flexibility than schoolteaching. And some indicated that because their own long days made it difficult for them to handle the demands of household maintenance, their husbands did most of the cooking and cleaning. Mrs Harrington, in a matter of fact way, noted that her husband cooked dinner, 'because he was home earlier than I was'. Another teacher also remembered that the division of labour in her household was not constrained by traditional notions of responsibilities for tasks: 'My husband almost always got home from work first and started the supper; but if I got home before him then I did things like starting the fire'. In the interviews I also found evidence that some of these women had discovered 'on-site' child care. Several mentioned that they brought their children to school and included them in their classes:

I took my son to school with me when he was five. That probably was a mistake but it turned out all right. The neighborhood children were kind. The parents might not have condoned it but they were tolerant of it and it worked out.

Moreover, the teachers imply that superintendents were no more constrained than they were, by notions of appropriate roles for married women with children. Superintendents were perfectly willing to rehire teachers, even if they had stayed a bit too long with a pregnancy, and they did not allow the presence of a child to interrupt their search for a teacher. The same woman who said she had not been asked back to the school, said that later that year.

I was home with my baby – he was born in June – and during Christmas vacation of that same year the superintendent came to me and said, 'You want to leave that little baby at home? Up in Starksboro they need you in a big school up there.' I thought it over and I had spells of crying and then I took it because I was lonesome for school. So I was only out of school for six months.

Sometimes the teachers returned to work because they needed the money. But others revealed, as did the woman quoted above, a sense of loss when they could not participate in their chosen career. This commitment to teaching could provide the basis for a renegotiation of a marriage contract:

I didn't resent [being asked by my husband to give up my job] though I was very lonesome for teaching. I didn't teach for several years and I was very lonesome. I was almost willing to go into a school and say I'll pay you to let me teach. . ... And after a while I said [to my husband], 'I don't like this, why don't I go back to teaching.' And he said, 'Okay, if you really want to.'

One-sided accounts

In addition to omitting information, I found that the published reports often offered a one-sided interpretation or vision of such seemingly inevitable changes as professionalization and the transition to the graded school. In the annual State Department of Education reports increased professional training appeared as the necessary accoutrement of good education; the poorly trained teachers were lambasted:

Only those conversant with the conditions know the worthless work performed in some rural schools under the guise of teaching, and were the patrons of such schools cognizant of the flagrant injustice committed against their children by the employment of young and untrained novices, they would vigorously demand a higher quality of instruction or the transportation of their children to better schools.[14]

Not surprisingly, the professional associations also supported changes designed to increase the status of the occupation through increased occupational entry requirements. But the voices of the schoolteachers themselves suggest that there was at least some significant opposition to the new model of the teacher. They resented having to extend their working days to include travel to night courses as they raced endlessly to catch up with changing standards. Those who had been teaching for long periods of time felt that the growing emphasis on educational qualifications belittled their extensive experience. And they were doubtful that professional training was the only significant qualification for the making of a good teacher: 'I don't say they aren't as good teachers – they're probably better because they're very educated – in books. But there's something in the human touch there that's missing.'

The transition to the graded school was also lauded in the written documents. While some writers expressed a sentimental attachment to the good old days, the clear focus was on moving education to new buildings with increased standardization where students could get something better than 'twenty-eight weeks. . . in [the] depressing school atmosphere which is produced by an unkempt school room, unwholesome surroundings, and a mercenary amateur as a teacher'.[15] Interviews revealed that some teachers also welcomed this change.[16] They found that the graded schools had the touted advantages: increasing professional recognition, opportunities for collegiality, higher wages and better facilities. As one teacher said, 'It was a thrill to get into a graded school rather than a rural school. That was an upgrade.'

But many teachers found reason to be hesitant about the transition. For them it entailed a loss of autonomy. One teacher put it this way:

> For so many years I had been the one who settled everything. . .. That was one of the hardest things for teachers who had always been in a country school to come into a graded school – because you had to follow rules and regulations.

They also noted a loss of sense of mission. In the rural schools they knew that they were teaching for love rather than money, 'because we didn't get money enough to make you want to teach for the money you got like they do now'. They knew that their role was a significant one, particularly when they provided the entire educational experience for their students: 'And one little boy I know – I was the only teacher he ever had.' And they knew that they were important to the community:

And the older teachers taught for themselves and for the children and the community and the parents. I know one teacher taught down in Cornwall for years, her father had a farm – raised potatoes, raised crops – and she gave them all away to the parents that she taught their children because they were poor.

Some teachers also felt that they lost status when they went to the graded school because they no longer stood out as the sole embodiment of knowledge for a delimited community.

These attitudes, because they went against the grain of public opinion, were never published or recorded. Without interviews such voices which reveal one meaning of teaching in a rural school, and one reaction to 'progress', would be lost entirely.

Reinterpretation

Perhaps the most important category of differences between what we learn when we rely on published sources and what we learn when we rely on the voices of participants has to do with how we interpret the evidence. Nancy Cott has described changes in the understanding of the meaning of the nineteenth-century ideology of domesticity:

> The first to appear in historical writing tended to see women as victims or prisoners of an ideology. . . that was imposed on them. . . .. The second, a refinement and revision, observed that women made use of the ideology. . . for their own purposes. . . .. The third, more literally a revision, viewed woman's sphere as the basis for a subculture among women that formed a source of strength and identity.[17]

My own interpretation of schoolteachers and the rules regulating their behaviour went through a similar reappraisal.

For months I had posted to my bulletin board a copy of typical regulations applied to rural schoolteachers:

> Teachers will not dress in bright colors. Dresses must not be more than two inches above the ankles. At least two petticoats must be worn. Their petticoats will be dried in pillowcases.
>
> [Teachers] will not get into a carriage or automobile with any man, except her brother or father. Teachers will not loiter at ice cream stores.

Teachers are expected to be at home between the hours of 8 p.m. and 6 a.m., unless in attendance at a school function.

The teacher will not smoke cigarettes or play at cards. She will not dye her hair under any circumstances.

The interview data confirmed that such restrictions were commonplace. One teacher, for instance, remembered that she was asked about both drinking and smoking during a job interview and that she was refused a position because she admitted that she 'liked a cigarette every now and then'. Another teacher told about receiving criticism for square-dancing with the children: that behaviour was not sufficiently lady-like. Other features of the teachers' lives were also constrained. Miss Allen, for example noted that 'every teacher has to live in the district where she taught even though her own family might be within easy commuting distance'. Such a proviso insured that the teacher's behaviour could always be observed. The teachers also suggested that there were costs to such restraints. One teacher said she 'outwardly' conformed to the requirement that she act 'like a lady'; she added 'inwardly I rebelled'. Another teacher summed up the effects of these policies in a poignant way: 'Teachers were a thing apart,' she sighed, 'you couldn't do anything that other people did'.

The conclusion that women schoolteachers 'were victims or prisoners of an ideology. . . that was imposed on them' is easily drawn. Tyack and Strober, for example, assume such a stance when they argue that these restrictions would not have been possible if men had dominated the occupation:

The effects of the feminization of teaching. . . are also obvious in the subordination of teachers to narrow standards of propriety imposed by local communities, especially in small-towns. Had mature men constituted a majority of the teaching profession, it is hard to imagine that school patrons would have insisted on such tight supervision of the morals and mores of teachers as they did in the case of young women.[18]

At the same time, the information does not fit together to support this kind of simple interpretation. First, as already mentioned, there were frequent rule violations which cannot be explained away. Teachers remained in their classrooms after marriage in spite of regulations which insisted otherwise and commonly made

179

it known that reproduction occurred by means other than 'budding'. Second, the published sources (as well as the interviews revealing superintendents' desperate searches for teachers) indicated that teachers, whether or not they had violated the rules, could easily find positions in rural schools. During much of the time period under investigation, in fact, there was an acute shortage of teachers. In 1918, for example, the state superintendent of education said,

> The scarcity of teachers presents a very grave problem. A careful census of the teachers needed in Vermont. . . showed that there were lacking. . . more than one hundred fifty rural teachers. . .. During the existence of the war many former teachers were willing as patriotic duty to leave their homes and serve in our schools. This condition will not exist in times of peace. We must therefore prepare ourselves to deal with a most powerful shortage of teachers during the coming year.[19]

The situation was not alleviated during the 1920s in spite of the implementation of training programmes designed to make the occupation easier to enter. During the Depression when, in most places women were losing teaching jobs (especially married women), the state superintendent noted that the situation in Vermont was quite different:

> At the present time most states have a large oversupply of teachers. It is surprising to learn that Vermont's only real oversupply is for high school positions. The fact is that there is actually a dearth of well-qualified teachers for the elementary school positions. As the depression lifts, many who have now gone back to teaching in order to supplement the family income, will again take up their duties as home makers.[20]

Right before World War Two, the superintendent was still insisting that there was a shortage of teachers; the war itself exacerbated the problem.

If, as scarce labour, teachers were a potentially powerful force who could possibly shake off the restrictive covenants – not just in practice on occasion, but as the prevailing ideology as well – why did they suggest that on the whole they complied with these notions of 'proper' behaviour? If we listen carefully to what the teachers say about these constraints, a more complete understanding emerges. The teachers may have minded the restrictions, but they also speak of them with a certain pride and they link them with both protection and status.

First, given the kinds of possibilities for sexual harassment discussed previously, the schoolteachers suggested that the restrictions ensured that their behaviour would be beyond reproach:

> There were a lot of criticisms of teachers in your own private life. You had to be careful of the people you associated with. I think that was one of the things, just pick the people who had good reputations. You didn't want to be seen out with a group of people who weren't well thought of in the community. Especially the boys. You didn't want to be seen with boys that didn't have good reputations.

They were thus secure against the suggestion that they could be held responsible through their own 'provocative' behaviour for unwanted approaches. They also suggest that the restrictions might have actually protected them from abusive behaviour by male students in a manner unavailable to teachers today:

> When I was a secretary [in a graded school] there were two young teachers – both as cute as they could be – come into me and said, 'You got to help us, we're in trouble.' 'What's your problem?' And they named off two big boys, high school, junior high school boys, that had used some obscene language to them. And they said, 'What would you do if they talked to you that way?' And I said, 'They wouldn't talk to me that way.' 'Why?' 'Because I wouldn't talk to them that way.' And that's it.

Second, and perhaps even more importantly for this re-analysis, to the extent that the restrictions defined teachers as 'a thing apart', they gave them a unique status that they could draw on to accomplish their twofold tasks of education and community development.

In 1925 the median age of teachers in rural schools was 23.2; she could enter the occupation after only one year of training.[21] Yet, in spite of her youth and limited preparation, she had to command respect in the classroom and in the community as a whole. The teachers unvaryingly remembered having this respect. Mrs Crowell, for example, when asked about the position of the teacher in the community, responded: 'The teacher was quite somebody. . . [she had] a great deal of respect. . . I was always invited to everyone's house for a meal or a party.' And Mrs Ulland said, 'Teachers and ministers used to be right together in terms of respect, prestige.'

They also spoke of being called upon by members of the community to help with a wide variety of problems, suggesting that they were seen as being both knowledgeable and wise. Mrs O'Hara remembers being asked by a farmer to help him figure out the volume of a silo, and Miss Winter recalls even broader expectations:

> They expected the teacher to do everything and know everything. If there's a child was sick, they'd send word down, want to know what to do. They'd send down the bottle of castor oil if they couldn't make the kid take it and wanted the teacher to make her take it.

It is possible that the restrictions, by identifying teachers as individuals with distinctive attributes, helped them to solidify a position which would have been difficult to achieve in the absence of maturity and training. Their separateness ensured that they could represent morality and knowledge.[22] In fact, the teachers themselves suggest as much when their memories link respect and constraints:

> [There was] this great respect for the teacher in the rural school. So they set me up at the end of the dining room table and set a place for me to eat, and I ate alone. I almost died, I was so homesick.
>
> I know teachers were [respected]. It's an intangible. Teachers today – and I'm not saying this is wrong – are free to lead their own lives. And I've known teachers – I'm sure you have too – whose personal lives don't bear close scrutiny. And parents are aware of this and children are too. So perhaps it was in some way good that certain standards were expected of teachers.

Teachers were not just responsible for the content of the educational process; they were responsible for creating the opportunities for that process to occur as well as for creating the conditions of their own employment. The district in which the school was located was a geographic area defined by distance from a central point and designed to insure that the children within a single neighbourhood could walk to school. The district had no independent existence as an entity: it had no political, religious, mercantile or social meaning. What held the district together, or defined it as a unit with common interests, was the presence of the school. But the school which served a district stood in an uneasy or paradoxical relationship to its environment: if the presence of a school was what defined the area as a community, without the unified action of the district people to sustain it, there would be no school. The teacher, if she wanted to keep her job, had to engender community support, not only for her performance, but for the school itself. If she wanted heat and indoor plumbing, she had to create sufficient community enthusiasm that it would be willing to supply these conveniences. And, because her salary was geared to the quality of the school (through state rebates to the district), she had an additional material incentive for getting the community involved in such projects as painting the schoolhouse and planting shrubbery around it. The teacher, then, who was hired by the district would have to create that district and rouse it to joint activity. Mrs O'Connor gives us a good description of how this worked:

> And I went around on snowshoes to some of the houses about this time of year. And I'm interested in them because there was a great drive on in the state to make our school-houses come up to standard. . ... The teacher received more pay and that wasn't only it, we really looked better from the state and the amount of money that the state gave to each school was more. So it was something to the parents, and people of the district, to have the school in better shape. Many times we raised money by various ways, having dances and having dinners and so on and then many times the fathers and interested people in the community would come on and do the carpenter work. So that, between the two helps we really had some good standard schools. It was in that school that I started P.T.A. And that's how we standardized that school while I was there.

Other teachers similarly recalled creating holiday entertainments for their communities to impress upon them that they were good teachers, as well as to raise the community spirit necessary for maintaining the school:

> Every holiday – that is, Christmas, Thanksgiving and
> Memorial Day – we always had programs at the school and all
> the people of the district came. It was kind of an entertain-
> ment. Every teacher was expected to by the district
> people. . .. If you didn't do those things you weren't a very
> good teacher – and it was really quite a problem that these
> teachers nowadays don't have at all. . . I would never have
> tried getting out of it. If I had, they wouldn't have thought I
> was a good teacher, I guess.
>
> Cornwall was a very good community and I used to have a
> lot of entertainments at the school and I raised money for
> new seats. . . and, well, we started just doing it, you know, for
> the community to get together. Card parties we had. And I
> always had entertainments at Halloween and Christmas.

The 'difference' of teachers may have been relevant to this
process: it enabled them to stand apart and to be seen as free from
an involvement with particular factions. One teacher, albeit unwittingly, suggested as much when she linked community service with
the restrictions. After describing her involvement in 'entertainments' she was asked whether she had other responsibilities
towards the community: 'I wasn't aware that I had any,' she said,
'except that I walked a straight and narrow path character-wise.
You just knew that that was expected of you.'

Of course, the impression we gain from the written documents
is not entirely wrong. Rural New England schoolteachers in the
first half of the twentieth century were paid less than their male
colleagues (in any situation) and less than their female colleagues
in graded schools, taught in inadequate surroundings, had abbre-
viated careers, and were subjected to 'restrictive supervision'.[23] Yet,
as we have seen, this is not the whole picture. They also took
enormous pride in their careers, fought to retain their jobs and
created opportunities to improve the conditions in which they
worked. And they employed the rules which constrained them to
their own advantage. Rather than a simple mark of their
oppression, these restrictions became a resource, the basis for the
accumulation of influence within the community, the school and
their personal lives. The fact that they could even abandon them,
on occasion, suggests that we should see teachers as a relatively
powerful and inventive group. Nancy Cott's conclusion that the
tenacity of the ideology of domesticity 'owed as much to women's

184

motives as to the imposition of men's or "society's" wishes,' applies as well to the persistence of standards of good behaviour among early twentieth century schoolteachers.[24]

At the same time, a counter truth exists. Schoolteachers could violate rules, but they could not change them. To the extent that they embraced restrictions as a source of personal empowerment, they eliminated the possibility of achieving a collective basis for effective resistance. Outward conformity to the norms of lady-like behaviour – though paired with inward rebellion – limited the terms in which the battle for occupational improvement could be waged.

CONCLUSION

I have focused on ways in which published materials limit our access to material which reveals what it meant for women to be rural schoolteachers in the first half of this century. Public history often ignores minority views. But women's lives are further hidden because important information is overlooked, consciously avoided or distorted. On the other hand, oral history can also lead us astray. The method is notoriously bad for giving us an overview or an accurate sequence of events. Moreover, there may be problems in the interview process itself, particularly when respondents are asked to remember things that happened a long time ago. Even when recall is accurate, there may be enormous incentives for distorting the representation of the past. But when the two methodologies are combined, we can obtain important insights which help us answer questions that should stand at the centre of inquiries about the meaning of schoolteaching in the lives of its participants.

NOTES

1 Stone, M.S. (1935) *History of Education: State of Vermont*, Montpelier, Vermont: Capital City Press; Tyack, D. (1974) *The One Best System: A History of American Urban Education*, Cambridge: Harvard University Press.
2 Clifford, G.J. (1978) 'History as experience: The uses of personal-history documents in the history of education', *History of Education*, Vol. 7, No. 3; Clifford, G.J. (1978) 'Home and school in 19th century America: Some personal-history reports from the United States', *History of Education Quarterly*, Vol. 18, No. 1.

3 Vermont Board of Education (1900–16) *Vermont School Reports*, Rutland, Vermont: Tuttle Company.

4 Bailey, F.L. (1939) *A Planned Supply of Teachers for Vermont*, New York: Bureau of Publications, Teachers College, Columbia University; Carnegie Foundation for the Advancement of Teaching (1914) *A Study of Education in Vermont*, New York; Stone, *History of Education*.

5 Bernard, R.M. and Vinovskis, M.A. (1977) 'The female schoolteacher in Ante-Bellum Massachusetts', *Journal of Social History*, Vol. 10, No. 3; Clifford, G.J. (1983) '"Daughters into teachers": Educational and demographic influences on the transformation of teaching into "Women's work" in America', *History of Education Review*, Vol. 12, No. 1; Strober, M.H. and Tyack, D.B. (1980) 'Why do women teach and men manage? A report on research on schools', *Signs*, Vol. 5, No. 3; Tyack, D.B. and Strober, M.H. (1981) 'Jobs and gender: A history of the structuring of educational employment by sex' in Schumuck, P.A., Charters, Jr., W.W. and Carlson, R.O. (eds) *Educational Policy and Management: Sex Differentials*, New York: Academic Press.

6 Jones, J. (1980) *Soldiers of Light and Love: Northern Teachers and Georgia Blacks, 1865–1873*, Chapel Hill, North Carolina: University of North Carolina Press; Hoffman, N. (1981) *Women's True Profession: Voices from the History of Teaching*, Old Westbury, NY: Feminist Press; Kaufman, P.W. (1984) *Women Teachers on the Frontier*, New Haven, Connecticut: Yale University Press; Rinehart, A.D. (1983) *Mortals in the Immortal Profession: An Oral History of Teaching*, New York: Irvington.

7 Gluck, S. (1977) 'Topical guide for oral history interviews with women', *Frontiers*, Vol. II, No. 2.

8 Project at the University of Michigan (1977) 'Interview guide for the twentieth century trade union women: Vehicle for social change', *Frontiers*, Vol. II, No. 2.

9 Nelson, M.K. (1988) 'The threat of sexual harassment: Rural Vermont school teachers, 1915–1950', *Educational Foundations*, Vol. 2, No. 2.

10 Vermont Teachers Association (1930) *Vermont School Journal*, p. 4.

11 Tyack, D.B. and Hansot, E. (1982) *Managers of Virtue: Public School Leadership in America, 1920-1980*, New York: Basic, p. 192.

12 ibid., p. 8.

13 Tyack and Hansot, *Managers of Virtue*, p. 175.

14 Vermont Board of Education, *Vermont School Reports*, 1938, pp. 7–8.

15 ibid., p. 8.

16 Nelson, M.K. (1983) 'From the one-room schoolhouse to the graded school: Teaching in Vermont, 1910–1950', *Frontiers*, Vol. VII, No. 1.

17 Cott, N. (1977) *The Bonds of Womanhood*, New Haven, Connecticut: Yale University Press, p. 197.

18 Tyack and Strober, 'Jobs and gender', p. 145.

19 Vermont Board of Education, *Vermont School Reports*, 1918, p. 13.

20 Vermont Board of Education, *Vermont School Reports*, 1934, pp. 11–12.

21 Bailey, *A Planned Supply*.

22 Tyack and Hansot, *Managers of Virtue*.

23 Tyack and Strober, 'Jobs and gender', p. 145.

24 Cott, *The Bonds of Womanhood*, p. 197.

7

WHY DO PROGRESSIVE WOMEN ACTIVISTS LEAVE TEACHING?

Theory, methodology and politics in life-history research

Kathleen Casey

INTRODUCTION

The abandoned careers of trained teachers have been a persistent subject of concern in educational literature, as demonstrated by the twenty years of relevant research cited by Chapman[1] and Rosenholtz and McAninch.[2] Yet, although we know that personnel continue to disappear from school district payrolls, existing conjectures as to why they have left and where they have gone remain inadequate. This chapter argues that the conceptual categories structuring this area of research have been narrowly conceived and prematurely foreclosed; it aims to re-open the discussion of teacher attrition by presenting a set of teachers' own explanations for leaving school employment.

A certain set of taken-for-granted assumptions control the way in which the problem of teacher attrition has normally been defined, one which presumes managerial solutions. Inquiries have generally been oriented by administrative demands for a stable workforce. Rosenholtz and McAninch talk of teacher 'defection'; Bowers[3] of 'teacher turnover'; Ornstein's[4] and Arnold's[5] articles on the job market for teachers are framed in terms of demographic 'supply and demand'. In the same vein, recent statements from the Holmes Group warn of an 'imminent shortage of qualified teachers'.[6]

A limited number of research strategies have been employed in investigating this topic. Former members of the teaching profession have often been traced statistically, rather than in person, and information has typically been collected from such sources as district files,[7] state departments of public instruction,[8] or through researcher-conceived surveys. The correlations which Schlechty and Vance[9] choose to investigate, and the explanations which they propose, are based on their own interpretations of social trends, rather than on consultations with those studied.

The particular configuration of selectivities and omissions which has been built into this research frame slants the shape of its findings. By systematically failing to record the voices of ordinary teachers, the literature on educators' careers actually silences them. Methodologically, this means that even while investigating an issue where decision-making is paramount, researchers speculate on teachers' motivations, or at best, survey them with a set of forced-choice options. Theoretically, what emerges is an instrumental view of teachers, one in which they are reduced to objects which can be manipulated for particular ends. Politically, the results are educational policies constructed around insti-tutionally convenient systems of rewards and punishments, rather than in congruence with teachers' desires to create significance in their lives.

UNDERSTANDING TEACHERS' LIVES

The collection and analysis of life history narratives, as I shall demonstrate below, offers a radically different approach to under-standing teachers' lives. The power of this alternative mode of inquiry to challenge the dominant research configuration is just beginning to unfold as increasing numbers of scholars explore its capacities. As I discuss at length elsewhere,[10] my own practice has been guided by the theory, methodology and politics outlined by the Popular Memory Group,[11] by feminist revisionist scholarship and, in the field of education, by the work of Hoffman,[12] Nelson,[13] Kaufman[14] and Spencer.[15]

My research is, therefore, informed by several interrelated notions. I place teachers' own understandings of their experiences at the centre of my agenda, since I believe participants can supply different, and perhaps better, knowledge of prevailing conditions than can the detached observer. This means that life histories are not elicited simply for the 'information' which can be extracted; the 'interpretations' which are an integral part of the narratives are considered to be equally, and possibly more, valuable com-ponents.

The difference between the existing teacher retention research and the emerging area of life-history studies is not simply a question of whether researchers collect data about subjects or from them; nor of the degree to which investigators directly elicit information from participants, although these are important. What is at stake is the power relationship between researcher and subject. Essential to my approach is a respect for the authenticity and integrity of the narrator's discourse. The speaker is seen as a subject creating her own history, rather than as an object of research.

The open-ended format which I have employed in my own research allows the interests of the narrator, rather than those to the interviewer, to dominate. The political relations of research are designed so that the voice of the teacher can be given equal status with that of the academic researcher. Thus the act of interpretation is largely relinquished to the subjects themselves, while the researcher concentrates on discovering the patterns of priorities in the narrative texts.

The contrasts between teachers' own formulations and those which are generated in the academy can then be revealed. Disparities between teacher-generated texts and public policy documents can also be studied. This notion of a 'dialogue' between 'social texts' is explained in more detail in 'Teacher as author'.[16]

The analysis which follows creates a dialogue between the teacher attrition literature and a set of life histories narrated by thirty-three women who have been teachers and progressive activists.[17] Even though such teachers might be characterized as atypical, since conservatism is considered to be the norm for the occupation,[18] it would seem particularly valuable to focus on such a group in connection with life choices. If we suppose, by virtue of their activism, that these are deeply thoughtful, highly articulate and socially dynamic individuals, then their narratives should provide both illuminating analyses of their lived experiences, and exemplary strategies for positive social change. I believe that they do.

The format which follows deals first with the questions which have been raised in the academic literature on teachers, primarily those relating to the influence of gender on the profession, and teachers' relationships with their students. I then address the issues which appear in the women's own life histories, and which have been neglected in previous appraisals. The narrators' perceptions of systemic rather than personal problems in education, and their indictments of administrative authority, are discussed at length. Finally the constructive life choices which these women have made subsequent to leaving school teaching are presented.

WOMEN'S CHANGING LIVES

Contemporary reports are concerned with the effects of the profound economic, political and social changes in American women's lives on the stability of the teaching force. In the past, a persistent explanation for occupational induction has been its compatibility with 'female' roles; more recently, however, the same qualities have been construed as reasons for professional attrition. Do women still see teaching as work which they can combine with their responsibilities as wives and mothers,[19] or, do the best and brightest women seek more challenging and better paid jobs else-where?[20] The answers presented in the life-history narratives of this group are more complex than that simple dichotomy suggests.

In this study, it is clear that teaching as temporary, pre-marital employment is a pattern of the distant past. Only the two oldest of the twenty-three married women stopped working after marriage and both of these later returned to teaching. Of the twenty women with children, only five interrupted their work lives beyond the taking of maternity leave, and all of these later returned to the paid labour force.

That the relationship between marital status and occupation has clearly changed is also evident in the life histories of the nine divorced and three widowed women in this study, who did not either enter or leave teaching as a direct result of these life changes. The work lives of these women appear to be relatively autonomous of those of their husbands, both in terms of economic need and moral reputation. Remnants of a cult of respectability appeared in only one woman's story; she was threatened with the loss of her job teaching on a military base because she separated from her husband. According to the male administrators, 'you came on this base as a married person, and that's the way you are supposed to stay.' But in the end she was not dismissed because she stood firm on her legal rights: 'I said they could force me on that plane physically. But I said when I got off this island, I would hire a lawyer and I would sue for my job back.'

Marriage still has a potential effect on women's work in the form of career conflict between spouses. Three women in this study left school teaching because their husbands took jobs which required moving to a different location; but the details of these changes are worth noting. When one woman was relocated in a city with a surplus of teachers, she took the opportunity to write novels for teenagers, and to become more involved in political work. A Black American woman teacher decided to live with her West Indian husband in the Caribbean; rather than teach in a system which she felt to be authoritarian, she planned to do political work. For both of these women, leaving employment in a school system did not mean that they were no longer teachers; they considered their political activities to be educational work.

A combination of factors were involved in the third woman's leaving school teaching: at the same time her husband's new job required moving to a different city, she was pregnant for their second child, and became seriously ill with diabetes. Some time after the move, her husband also became ill, and, inspite of her own physical problems, she took a part-time job teaching music in a church organization. Here again, teaching was redefined under force of circumstance, rather than completely abandoned.

The emphasis on marital status in discussions of the lives of women teachers is, and always has been, too narrow a focus. This is all too obvious in the narratives of the seven Catholic women religious ('nuns') included in this study, for whom neither marriage nor child-rearing were issues. The reasons why only one of these women is still teaching in a conventional classroom must be found elsewhere.

THE VALUE OF WOMEN'S WORK

While compatibility with marriage and children has been described as an attraction to teaching, it has also been the basis for allegations of women's 'lack of commitment'.[21] The women in this study are highly sensitive to the devaluation of 'female' professions. Gender stereotyping of the occupation was considered to be a strong disincentive, particularly among the younger public school teachers, who explained their initial reluctance to join the profession in terms of its poor public reputation.

And I always felt sorry for teachers. I thought they, you know, they were teachers 'cause they couldn't do anything else. . ..

191

They. . . really weren't successful in any other career, and as a last resort, turned to teaching. Especially males. And women. . . I guess I thought they were teaching because they weren't allowed to do anything else. I'm *sure* I got that idea from my parents, who were very. . . upwardly mobile and. . . aggressive in that sense.

Finally, however, neither the attraction of more glamorous and better paid careers, nor education's tarnished reputation prevented the women in this study from becoming or from remaining teachers. While they continue to be conscious of public criticism, experience has taught them the value of their own work and that of their colleagues. A Black inner-city school teacher credits her own efforts: 'I work like a dog. I work like two people. During lunch hour. I have no free time.' A woman who formerly taught in inner-city public and alternative schools praises those who continue to do so: 'I think teachers are amazing, wonderful people to be doing this work right now. And given what the teaching conditions are like.'

BLAMING THE SYSTEM

According to these narratives, the trouble with American education is not its teachers, but the oppressive system within which they must work. In conjunction with the larger social structure, the educational organization generates problems which are then blamed on its victims. The same hard-working Black teacher quoted above analyses the reasons why she regrets becoming a teacher in this way:

I wouldn't encourage my child. I wouldn't do it again myself. There are so many negative things. The harder you work, the less you are appreciated by some people. There is nothing to be proud of. I don't tell people I'm a teacher. Maybe society has a lot to do with it. And too much politics. I don't dislike kids. Even the worst ones. I dislike the system.

'The system' even 'destroys certain people', she records, giving an example of a close friend who was forced to resign her job. She herself plans to take early retirement, like many of her colleagues have done: 'People are getting out if they are old enough to retire. Some people even quit before their twenty-five years are up. They can't cope. I always cope. I don't complain. For that day I enjoy.'

It is worth noting that two other women in the study did not see their retirement as a 'natural' source of occupational attrition; both retired teachers described the end of their careers as a deprivation of meaningful work hastened by inflexible regulations, not as a taken-for-granted consequence of age.

Besides censuring the system in general, these teachers give a clear analysis of which particular aspects of schools they find blameworthy, and which admirable. Their analysis is most concerned with the quality of human interactions, and their relationships with other members of the school population are clearly differentiated: students are almost universally seen as positive partners; administrators are widely condemned as the executors of the arbitrary and excessive controls of the system, and colleagues are generally just taken for granted.

RELATIONSHIPS WITH STUDENTS

Problems with students are not mentioned as reasons for leaving teaching in these narratives. On the contrary, one of the few pleasant memories of school teaching for one woman is the political influence which she had on her students:

> And I still have kids, you know, kids who are in their thirties now. . . one girl who I didn't even remember from that time, *found* me ten years later. . . .. She said that my class and the politics that I'd presented had made this big impression on her. And that was very satisfying, 'cause I just hit a point finally, after about the third year, where I was getting. . . a political message across and I was doing it in a pedagogically interesting way, and I felt comfortable with who I was in the classroom.

'I loved the people I taught' is a typical comment made by the Catholic women religious in this study. Speaking of the inner-city children with whom she works, a Black elementary school teacher says: 'They love your very soul'.

The desire to help particular groups of children motivated several women to expand their sphere of activity beyond schools. One woman laments the limitations of the teacher's role within the school system:

And given what the teaching conditions are like, and how little you can do for these kids. . . I mean, they're in such *terrible* emotional, financial, psychological. . . physical condition! And there's so little you can do as a teacher in that situation. There is *so* little. I mean, they really need you. And you know that. But it is. . . it's just so hard to. . . keep doing that.

Among the out-of-school, child-oriented projects with which these women have worked are community meal programmes, chaplains to children in detention, chaplains to gay and lesbian adolescents, and in-prison classes for women, the majority of whom are mothers of small children. Children are also mentioned as a motivating force in more general social change projects.

Persistent exceptions to the accounts of positive relationships with children are the reports of racist behaviour by white students against four Black, one Native American and one Jewish women in the study. Although none of these women left teaching for this reason, the Jewish woman came close when racist abuse was added to the other stresses she was experiencing as a beginning, substitute teacher:

I got offered another job at a junior high that was *so* racist. . . . This was pre-integration, you know, before busing, and it was totally white. . .. The kids were. . . I found them almost impossible to be around. They were very anti-semitic. I found swastikas all over my stuff all the time and I was miserable there. I was teaching *ancient* history to these kids. And I almost quit teaching in the process.

A Black high school teacher analyses the political reasons why she was not subjected to overt racism in her early teaching career:

And that's not to say that the first years that I taught there that racism didn't exist, and that people were not racist. But, they kept their mouths shut. And they were on their guard about not letting it come forth because that was in the early seventies and it just didn't look like the anti-racist whites and people of colour were going to be tolerant of overt racism.

But then in the late seventies and early eighties people began to feel free to come forth with it and during my last couple of years at —, once I got a note pushed under my door, you know, saying, 'Nigger something,' and once a boy in my class was passing around this note in one of my ethnic culture classes, talking about those 'slanted eyes' and using cuss words, and talking about H-bombs, and I was *furious*, you know. And I had to deal with that.

But, because she was an established and confident teacher in a generally positive context, these and other political incidents did not play a disruptive role in her life: 'There were a couple of times that I was called a wild-eyed communist, you know, which may have been the truth! But those incidents do not stand out as my over-riding experience there.'

RELATIONSHIPS WITH ADMINISTRATORS

Administrators are the source of the most persistent and profound school problems recorded by the women in this study. Teachers acknowledge positive exceptions (e.g. 'I have had a lucky position that I could work with principals who relatively speaking had love and respect for me'), but complaints about specific implementors as well as against the system itself resound throughout the narratives. Even those women who have themselves served in administrative capacities reject particular aspects of the existing system. One describes efforts to abolish authoritarian hierarchy in her school; another relates her difficulty getting an appointment in a large North-eastern state with only four other female high school principals. Underlying all these criticisms is a rejection of the masculine privilege upon which the organizational structures of schools are seen to be based. According to these interpretations, male administrators are situated to exercise authority over their subordinates, and, even under the best conditions, female teachers and school children are in a vulnerable position. Indeed, many women were anxious to recount their experiences in the worst of conditions.

Women teachers in this study leave particular schools, and teaching in general because of the systematic suppression of children. One member of Catholic religious order recounts:

And the reasons I left that school was that I didn't agree with a lot of the philosophy in the school. I really believe that a school is a place where people come together, and form some kind of a community, and it's *not* a prison, and if it's likened to anything it's likened to a family rather than a prison. And, my experience in that school was that it was *much* closer to a prison. And I was not into prison ministry at the time! So I decided, I will get out of here.

Another nun explains:

I left teaching because I got tired of trying to change the system. You know, I couldn't do it. And I couldn't fight any longer. I couldn't stand to watch the injustices against the kids, and I felt there was a lot of oppression. Towards children. And *because* of that, I wanted to stay *in* it, so that there'd at least be a *few* voices, because the, some of the teachers I worked with were *super*, super people. You know, and were *for* the children. It doesn't make sense to me if you're in the teaching and really not for the kids.

So rigid is the system of control that even the teacher's solidarity with the children harms them:

It seemed like the hierarchy, you know, the *administrative* people in the education system, were just so *blind*, to who the children were. You know, and they were just like the Pope, throwing down these rules and, and all these things they wanted you as a teacher to *do*. . ..

And, then, the difficulty for me in the all Catholic school thing was too, that I had to do things. . . *this way*. . . and if I didn't, then my class suffered. It wasn't just me.

In another version of the conflict with administrators, a woman who formerly taught art on a military base recalls how her high school students were able and willing to help her:

He came in and kicked the bag of clay, made a hole in it and it drained down on the floor. And he said, 'You need to clean this up, it's making a mess.' And these high school boys saw it. . . and it was like a moment of recognition. They looked at me, and they said, 'Don't worry, Miss —, we'll clean it up.' And then the kids got more supportive than ever 'cause they saw I was in a *bad* situation. And being harassed constantly.

Teachers are also subject to systematic administrative depreciation of their selves by analogy with the children they teach. One woman recalls being mistreated 'like a child':

I have never in my life liked this school system, where I have been treated so much like a child. And it certainly was from the very start an *enormous* rage in my heart, strictly personal rage at how I was treated. From the first time that I went to get certified and was shouted at by matrons and you know had to carry your urine sample in and I mean the whole thing the impersonal debasing way in which you were treated. It enraged me.

The same kind of anger is recounted by a nun who experienced the same kind of administrative disregard for herself. Her work 'wasn't really valued'; she was 'just another cog in the wheel' in the eyes of six different male principals, who 'never knew what had come before and cared less'. When she was transferred after seventeen years teaching in the same school, she 'left without even a plastic plaque with my name on it', symbolic, in her eyes, of the non-being accorded to her person. An administrator's reaction to the death of a colleague confirmed that this was not just an individual problem:

I remember when this Brother who was a very nice man died and the principal stood up and said, 'Well, we had a problem. I was away in Europe this summer and when I got back, I found out that he had died. Brother died, and we didn't have anybody to take his place, but fortunately, we were able to fill the gap.' I was just appalled, you know. Like I finally said. . .that's all the administration want, you know, someone to fill the hole.

Administrative manipulation of teachers' time in school is usually seen as a chronic irritation, but it has the potential to cause a major crisis in a teacher's life. One woman's narrative established a convincing relationship between the actions of an administrator and the serious accident which finally caused her to leave teaching. Her description of her job echoes the complaints of many teachers of special subjects:

I had eight classes a day. One right behind the other. All different kids. Assembly line. Sometimes I didn't have time to go to the potty. I was seeing over four hundred kids in elementary, and over one hundred in the high school, every week. I had the hundred high school kids every day. In the morning, and then the elementary started right after that and I saw them on a weekly basis 'cause there were so many.

At the same time, she was trying to organize a two-week art appreciation trip for a group of high school students, prepare a three-day in-service programme for art teachers, and write a paper for a national conference. Because her request for the teacher's aide had been repeatedly refused, she does not hesitate to blame the administration for the overload which preceded her accident. Her description of the principal's reaction to the accident itself completes the indictment:

Well, I was running around during, you know, when they were having an auditorium thing with all the kids, thinking oh, 'I've got thirty minutes, go xerox off these papers for the trip, go do this, go do that,' and was really racing around, and I fell down the steps. I tripped on the carpet and fell. . .down the steps.

Well, I was laying there. I couldn't get up. I looked down at my feet, I mean, I knew I'd done something terrible right away. I'd never had an accident in my life. It was so bizarre. It was like a movie.

I was so used to rushing *so fast* with this job. I mean the days were just *extremely* fast-paced, neurotic. . .and I looked down and here came this second grade class that I was supposed to teach. Coming down the hall, little kids trooping along. And they found me. I couldn't get up. Everyone else was in the auditorium, you know. And this guy comes along. I mean, I'm still laying on the floor. I can't move. The leg is just like huge, immediately. I mean I lay there and watched it grow gigantic.

So he looks at me and says, 'Well, are you gonna be able to give this in-service?' I mean they haven't called an ambulance, they haven't done anything. He is only thinking about can I hold up for all the work I had.

Well, I said, 'I'll send somebody for my papers, to work on while I'm at the hospital.' So I did, I sent a student down to get my bags, that had all my notes and stuff in it, and the ambulance came, and they carted me off to the hospital.

This same administrator, in apparent retaliation for her past assertive behaviour, later attempted to sabotage her workmen's compensation:

Within a month after the accident, his secretary came to me and said, 'You really need to make sure that the proper forms have been filled out, because,' she said, 'now you can't tell this, where you heard this, because I'll lose my job,' she said, 'but this man was saying, "Well, I haven't sent in the forms, and in a little bit, you know, as time passes, she won't even have a leg to stand on"', making a pun about it, '"ha, ha".' She said, 'He really means to do you in on this.'

So egregious was this particular man's abuse of power that he was finally fired by the school board, but not before many other teachers quit their jobs. This woman refused to be intimidated; however, she was finally forced to leave teaching altogether because of her physical problems.

The leg, you know, falls asleep, swells up, no matter what. So the doctor here says, 'Did you know you have a permanent disability? You're a fool not to have already applied for disability through even social security.' To me, I was raised kind of like. . .I *still* feel awkward about it.

In these stories, the administrative repression of teachers operates as a chronic, covert, psychological force, causing many teachers to withdraw themselves from school employment without any appearance of crisis. Confrontations between individual teachers and administrators never end in outright dismissal; although several women were intimidated by threats of firing, the one woman who actually lost her job was forced to resign. Only two women's job crises are directly attributable to their political activities, and these incidents were reconstructed by administrators as personal and professional failures.

One woman felt that she was sabotaged by a colleague when she showed a film on El Salvador to her ESL students:

We had a Cuban teaching in the department. Who came in the fifties, and was really anti-, anti-communist. So he told the kids that my trip (to Cuba) had been paid for by the Communist Party, and that I was a communist and I was trying to change all of them, and that they should watch out for me, et cetera, et cetera. It was pretty hard for them to all believe, and *certainly* because I was very friendly with all of them. And they really didn't like him. But he had a real hold on them, 'cause he was older and he was like a grandfather figure.

Anyways the day of the El Salvador film, he refused to let the kids come. I told all the kids that had him seventh period that they had to go to him also *sixth* period, because I didn't want them disturbing in the middle of the class. They were very reluctant, but he, Mr. — hadn't signed their pass so they had to go. Ok.

Well, what he did was once he gathered them all in his classroom, he said 'Ok, *now* you can go to Miss —'s room.' And so they all came back up en masse, and starting pounding on the doors, 'We wanna get in, we wanna get in.'

Finally, it was the havoc of 150 kids milling around in the halls, not the political content of the film, which caused the department head to 'scream and yell', and the headmaster to call the teacher down to his office, and threaten dismissal: 'And he said "From now on, you are gonna report to me whenever you have a movie," and "Who gave you permission to see it anyways?" And then he sent out a memo the next day.'

The woman who lost her job did so because of her solidarity with her feminist and radical students. She started a women's group at the high school where she taught, which according to her account,

ended up getting me in a fair amount of hot water because they decided to have a women's day, and they invited people from gay liberation. And a couple of the men *totally* freaked out some of the kids, to a point where a complaint was filed against me, and I was censured. . .in my record, because the report was that they had performed obscene sexual acts in the school. Which was *totally* untrue. This was all the fabrication on the part of some football player, but. . .anyway I got into terrible trouble and the principal basically told me they wanted to get rid of me.

At the same time, she was involved with a student group 'that called a student strike, around the Kent State stuff, so, you know, fifteen students were standing up on a balcony in the middle of the school yard, and I was the one teacher up there with them.' Even more than the particular political issues involved, the conflict centred around her refusal to assume an authoritarian persona in relationship to her students. Developing an alternative style had been so difficult for her as a beginning teacher that she had literally developed an ulcer. So, the summons to the principal's office represented both a denial of her accomplishments and a release from unbearable tensions.

> Because it's very civilized there, and they don't fire people, the principal just called me in and said that I had this letter of censure in my file and. . .he'd be willing to overlook it if I'd be willing to leave. . .! And he didn't think I was real happy there anyway. So, I agreed with him that I was not real happy there. And, I quit. And that was in '71.

While administrators may be able to minimize the effects of individual teachers' infractions, strikes represent wide-scale ruptures of their system. Teachers record an interesting combination of emotions connected to such events.

During one strike, a Black activist teacher received bomb threats, and needed to be escorted into school by a policeman. This woman plans to take early retirement, but it is not because of this experience. 'I kind of enjoyed it too', she says, smiling ironically; she was exhilarated by the breakdown of a system which she sees as ordinarily messed up. In many ways, her life was more difficult when things returned to 'normal' after the strike, the administration retaliated against her. She 'had a pretty hard time', because the principal put 'a dirty letter' in her file, and started to give her 'under-hand trouble'. But, in her own words, 'nothing would stop me inspite of the trouble.'

During the same strike, a union activist put her future professional life in jeopardy by joining the picket lines inspite of threats of retaliation from parents. Yet, she remembers that year as one of the happiest in her teaching career, free as she felt of the usual constraints of the school system:

> I had an opportunity to contact the kids and their parents, and what I told them was I'd be picketing, and then I would meet them at nine o'clock at the corner of — and we would spend the day together. And the parents were welcomed to join me. And we went to — park, and we went various places, public museums, and we had a wonderful time. I really regretted [the end of the strike] because it was a wonderful way to get to know a family and a kid in an informal setting outside of school.

MAKING CHANGES

Although I have spent the better part of this chapter outlining serious complaints of teachers, the life-history narratives themselves are not dominated by negative descriptions. These women do find many positive aspects to teaching, and almost without exception, they present their lives subsequent to school employment with enthusiasm. The same configuration of progressive values which characterized these women's lives as schoolteachers appear in their subsequent choices of activities, whether they go on for further education, move up into administration or university teaching, move over to alternative schools, or move out into other fields.

One direction in which the lives of these women move is towards more education for themselves. The level of academic qualifications among the women in this group is exceptionally high. Four women received their Bachelors' degrees in middle age. Twenty of the thirty-three women surveyed have studied for higher degrees: PhDs are held by five women, and five others are in the final stages of that degree; nine women have received Masters' degrees. Areas of graduate study include art, music, political science and theology, as well as aspects of education, such as curriculum and administration. For these women, further education is seen not only as a necessary path of career advancement or change; they also speak of its benefits in developing their sense of self, their intellectual understanding, and their political perspective.

Vertical movement up into administration is a strategy used by five teachers in this study to increase their personal and political power within the educational system. One woman describes her decision to become an administrator as a pragmatic move in a time of fiscal crisis:

> Well, originally. . .I was laid off, and then I was rehired, and then I was laid off again the following year, because they laid off more people, and then I was rehired. And transferred. And that was a real difficult couple of months for me to adjust to a new school. It was a very bad school. Um. . .and I started thinking 'Jesus, if I'm gonna get laid off every year, this is no way to live.' So I started thinking of other alternatives, and that's when I got into this.

Her experiences as a teacher also led her to believe in coopting the most powerful forces in the structure to one's own cause. When she worked without the support of the administration, she recounts, she was censured for unauthorized political activities in her classroom; but when she enlisted its cooperation, she was able to introduce a progressive curriculum into all the city's high schools.

However, this option is not acceptable to all. Another woman who spent most of her teaching career in an alternative school continues to envision public school administrators as 'the enemy', even though she is equally anxious to solve her problem of unemployment:

> So I *really* don't know what I'm gonna do. I. . .you know, I could think about working in some way for some school department somewhere, you know, I certainly. . . have lots of skills in administration stuff, but that sort of makes me feel sick. There are a number of jobs at various times I could have had in the — school department. But I never wanted to do that, 'cause I feel like. . .they're sort of the enemy in some ways!

A vertical progression also occurs in these women's career trajectories as they move into higher levels of teaching. Seven teachers have held a series of positions, spanning elementary, secondary, higher education and administrative posts, a phenomenon which is invisible to the usual measures of teacher attrition. Interestingly, these progressions are not touted as promotions by their narrators, but are related in a very matter-of-fact tone. Neither is university teaching presented as the pinnacle of a successful career; of the seven women who have taught in universities, three have deliberately chosen to leave that job. One woman refused to teach a medical subject in which she was not qualified; two others were attracted by more politically satisfying work. One woman recalls:

> The most radical thing I ever did was when I gave up my college teaching job, and said 'No, I'm gonna do (an alternative working class high) school full time.' What I was deciding to do was to make a commitment which was clearly going nowhere in terms of career, but was very important to me politically. And I very clearly chose it and I've never regretted it. I'm still, you know, in a mess because of it, financially and

in terms of career, but it was real clear. I never regretted that decision.

This woman is one of many who described themselves as having 'alternative' philosophies and modes of teaching. Among the strategies used to gain more autonomy, members of this group have chosen to work in alternative programmes within public schools in alternative schools and at alternative sites, such as through YMCA programmes, in campus ministry or with women in prison. But, while they have gained, at least temporarily, more politically compatible conditions, these women have also experienced a great deal of financial instability both personally and as members of organizations. This same woman recounts the trials of maintaining an alternative school for ten years:

> We raised a fair amount of money eventually. Just foundations and. . . feds, we got federal money, we got state money. We got drug money, we had juvenile delinquency prevention money. We had everything but taxpayer money, essentially. We couldn't get school money. And *all* these other monies required that we *do* special projects. They would never just give us money to be the school, right? So we were *constantly* having to dredge up something new to do, and. . . a lot of that turned out to be curriculum development.
> So that's when we developed the idea of a women's curriculum. And got a foundation to give us like $30,000 to do the book, which, of course, came out of our hides. Then we put all the money into the school. They'd give us thirty thou to. . . pay the support, you know, taking time off, and we'd do it, you know, all night and stuff.

But, these were not the only problems the school faced. Although there were 'fabulous', 'exciting' years, after some time students did not understand the uniqueness of this project:

> The older the school got, the more established it got, the more people sort of took it for granted as an institution. And would come in and see it as an already established institution and not one that they had to build. And would begin to act out against the institution, and frankly we didn't know how to handle that. Because for the first six years nobody had acted out against the institution!

204

This woman's decision not to work in the public system had been strongly reinforced by her years at the alternative school; when it closed, she left teaching altogether.

Almost all the women in this study who have moved out of education into different fields are Catholic women religious. While this chapter cannot cover all the profound changes in these women's lives in recent years, it can take note of at least one explanation for these career changes. Speaking of the time when virtually every nun worked in a school or a hospital, one woman criticizes male church administrators:

> We had so few choices. What avenues were open to you professionally were dependent upon what bishops would allow. And the only thing the bishops kept pressuring sisters for were hospitals and schools. They were institutionalizing a concept. They were thinking in big chunks of labour.

When the stress on occupational conformity was lifted, she explains, career decisions were made by each woman in 'co-responsibility' with her community, and Catholic women religious began to think 'in terms of the broader society and each one having an individual gift to do something'.

These former teachers have chosen to work as a psychologist, a youth worker, a campus chaplain, a chaplain to gay and lesbian Catholics, a music director and a peace minister; one works at a mission for street people; another with women in prison. The only woman still employed in a classroom has begun to make a transition to a career in fine arts. But, the new kinds of work chosen by the Catholic women religious still fall within the category of 'women's' occupations – the helping professions. It is not surprising, therefore, that they see continuity in their callings, rather than distinct career changes.

CONCLUSION

Judging from the narratives quoted here, the inclusion of women teachers' own assessments of their experiences significantly enlarges our understanding of the complex phenomenon of teacher attrition. Of course one could argue that male teachers, as well as other female teachers, might produce very different explanations. Indeed, these narratives raise such important issues that I would recommend an increasingly wide range of teachers be included in any future studies.

But the potential consequences of using life-history narratives go beyond an expansion of explanations. As Nelson[22] has observed in connection with her own work, listening to women teachers' own interpretations of their experiences can result in the radical reconstruction of the researcher's own understanding of the problem. Because they present alternative definitions of the very fundamentals of the schooling system, these narratives ultimately stand to challenge dominant interpretations of teacher attrition.

Teaching takes on a distinctive meaning in these narratives; it becomes much more than the paid employment for classroom work in a specific school. Many women define being a teacher as a fundamental existential identity. When she was unable to get a teaching job, one woman explains, 'I cried and cried because I was really upset. You know, I wanted some meaning to *my* life, and some meaning for having gotten that education.' Another woman mourns the loss of her profession in this way: 'I'm a teacher at heart. I will *always* be a teacher. And I miss teaching. I miss teaching.' One woman opens her narrative with the announcement: 'I have been a teacher in one way or another for forty years', although only twenty were spent in classrooms. For these women, teaching is an activity which can take a variety of forms in a variety of settings.

These women work for children, not for those who pay their wages. The narratives are full of examples of an 'ethos of nurturance and growth',[23] yet this aspect of teaching has virtually disappeared from the ongoing academic debate. While Schlechty and Vance, as quoted above, acknowledge its existence, they do not interpret it as a positive force for teacher retention in itself, but only as a 'tendency' which is discouraged by the management structure.

Perhaps the most serious omission in the literature on teacher retention is its neglect of the antagonism between teachers and administrators, a major explanation in these narratives. This exclusion is partly due to the widespread and unquestioning adoption of an administrative perspective by writers on this subject; it is also caused by the not-unconnected selective filtering of women's experiences through male, and in some cases, masculinist perspectives.

While some recent work has attempted to correct earlier stereotypes of women teachers, this has sometimes resulted in a simple reversal of those constructions. Instead of claiming that 'women on the average are more amenable to administrative control than men',[24] it is now assumed that women teachers will wish to pursue a career based upon upward mobility within the hierarchical structures of schools.[25] Such an option was generally not a major attraction for the women in this study.

The recent profound changes in American women's lives extend beyond increased employment opportunities of some. The feminist perspective which all these narratives share needs to be recognized in academic studies of women teachers' motivations. Seen from this angle, teacher attrition (in the limited meaning of leaving employment in a school) may not be such a negative phenomenon, given the conditions under which these women have laboured and the positive alternatives which they have chosen.

NOTES

1 Chapman, D. (1983) 'A model of the influences on teacher retention', *Journal of Teacher Education*, Vol.34, No.5, pp. 43–49.

2 Rosenholtz, S. and McAninch, A. (1987) 'Workplace conditions and the rise and fall of teacher commitment'. Paper presented at the Annual Meeting of the American Educational Research Association, Washington, DC.

3 Bowers, K. (1981) 'Keeping young teachers' options open', *Independent School*, Vol.40, No.4, pp. 19–22.

4 Ornstein, A.C. (1979) 'Teacher surplus? Trends in education's supply and demand', *Educational Horizons*, Vol.57, No.3, pp. 112–118.

5 Arnold, A.J. (1983) 'Teachers on the move: In and out of the job market', *Learning*, Vol.1, No.8, 24–27.

6 Sedlak, M. (1987) 'Tomorrow's teachers: The essential arguments of the Holmes Group Report', *Teachers College Record*, Vol.88, No.3, p. 317.

7 Allfred, W. and Smith, R. (1984) 'Profile of Utah teachers leaving the teaching profession', *Rural Educator*, Vol.5, No.3, pp. 2–5.

8 Schlechty, P. and Vance, V. (1981) 'Do academically able teachers leave education? The North Carolina case.' *Phi Delta Kappan*, Vol.63, No.2, pp. 106–112.

9 ibid.; Schlechty, P. and Vance, V. (1983) 'Recruitment, selection, and retention: The shape of the teaching force', *Elementary School Journal*, Vol.83, No.4, pp. 469–487.

10 Casey, K. (1988) 'Teacher as author: Life history narratives of contemporary women teachers working for social change', PhD dissertation, University of Wisconsin; Casey, K. and Apple, M.W. (1989) 'Gender and the conditions of teachers' work: The development of

understanding in America' in Acker, S. (ed.) *Teachers, Gender and Careers*, New York: Falmer.

11 Popular Memory Group (1982) 'Popular memory: theory, politics, method' in Johnson, R., McLennan, G. Schwartz, B. and Sutton, D. (eds) *Making Histories*, London: Hutchinson.

12 Hoffman, N. (1981) *Women's 'true' profession: Voices from the History of Teaching*, Old Westbury, New York: Feminist Press.

13 Nelson, M. (1983) 'From the one-room schoolhouse to the graded school: Teaching in Vermont, 1910–1950', *Frontiers*, Vol.7, No.1, pp. 14–20.

14 Kaufman, P.W. (1984) *Women Teachers on the Frontier*, New Haven: Yale University Press.

15 Spencer, D.A. (1986) *Contemporary Women Teachers: Balancing School and Home*, New York: Longman.

16 Casey 'Teacher as author'.

17 The thirty-three tape-recorded narratives upon which this analysis is based were collected in five American cities in 1984–85 as the first phase of a long-term research project on the life histories of contemporary teachers. All of the women in this group have at some time in their lives been employed as teachers, twenty in elementary, twenty in secondary schools. Only ten remain in conventional classroom jobs. Six women left school employment within the first five years of teaching; three are still in the early years of their careers; but the overwhelming majority (24/33) taught for ten or more years. For more details about the larger project from which this material was taken, see Casey, 'Teacher as author'.

18 Lortie, D. (1975) *Schoolteacher: a Sociological Study*, Chicago: University of Chicago Press.

19 Dreeben, R. (1970) *The Nature of Teaching: School and the Work of Teachers*, Glenview, Illinois: Scott, Foresman and Company.

20 Schlechty and Vance, 'Do academically able teachers'; Sedlak, 'Tomorrow's teachers'.

21 Lortie, *Schoolteacher*.

22 Nelson, 'From the one-room schoolhouse'.

23 Schlechty and Vance, 'Do academically able teachers'.

24 Etzioni, A. (ed.) (1969) *The Semi-professions and their Organization: Teachers, Nurses, Social Workers*, New York: Free Press, p. xv.

25 See, for example, Biklen, S.K. and Brannigan, M. (1980) *Women and Educational Leadership*, Lexington, Massachusetts: D.C. Heath; Ortiz, F.I. (1982) *Career Patterns in Education: Women, Men and Minorities in Public School Administration*, New York: Praeger; Schmuck, P., Charters, W.W. and Carlson, R. (eds) (1981) *Educational Policy and Management: Sex Differentials*, New York: Academic.

8

VISITING LIVES

Ethics and methodology in life history

Lynda Measor and Patricia Sikes

The past decade has seen a 'Small world' renaissance of research based on life-history method.[1] 'Across academic disciplines and national boundaries scholars have increasingly found value in inspecting "a life".'[2] We wonder why?

We aim to explore this question in this chapter, and to examine some of the methodological and ethical issues which arise when the life-history model is employed. Our overall aim has been to identify the theoretical issues, but also to offer a reflexive account of our own practices to illuminate the theoretical matters.

Together with our colleague, Peter Woods, we were involved in a project which aimed to use life-history methods as a way of investigating the careers and the lives of teachers.[3] All the data in this chapter arise from that work. Five years after completing the project we were given this opportunity to take a critical and retrospective look at what we did, and to examine the ethical issues that were involved.

As a starting point we need a clear picture of what life history is, and we may be able to find help in this through a comparison with biography. Life history is perhaps best defined as 'sociologically read biography'.[4] Biography itself is currently in vogue, it even has economic credibility; as the huge payments made to Holroyd on the publication of his recent biography of George Bernard Shaw make clear. We began by questioning why life history has experienced this second lease of life and popularity. Perhaps some of the answer lies in the fact that biography gives access to the doings of others, albeit in a written form. Biography, whether sociologically 'read' or not, is something of a parasite, depending on someone being prepared to give an account of themselves. It involves the author and then the reader in a form of 'licensed voyeurism';

tapping our wish to know what goes on behind closed curtains. The reticence of our friends on such matters leaves a space which biography can fill. Life history, like other biography, offers one respectable way of indulging our wish to have evidence from the lives of others that we are not alone in our difficulties, pains, pleasures and needs.

In biography we see a life recreated. Biographers work in the 'tone of intimacy', their business is that of 'imaginative identity' with their subject.[5] Life history does share in this same enterprise, but there are differences. If we refer back to Bertaux's point about life history being 'sociologically read biography' then certain of the issues come into sharper focus; and we can get a purchase on some of the ethical issues involved here. We want to suggest that it is the intimacy which raises some of the sharpest ethical questions in this kind of research. Because the material is intimate, it means that the potential for harm is greater. The life history 'taker' is bound to 'observe and record things potentially damaging to individuals',[6] and the question is what do they do with them?

On this question a comparison with biography is useful. As the literary biographer observes and documents the process of 'remaking the self' they are free to use compassion and insight in their treatment. Life history works under a different set of coordinates, in aiming for 'sociologically read biography'. In this chapter, we hope to trace the ways that the life history taker is constrained and directed by this factor.

Before we can begin to look in any detail at these issues, there is one matter which requires attention. It is the question of the value base which underpins the ethical stand we take, and the question of where we derive this from. We want to claim that the principles and theories that underlie the practices of qualitative research in fact constitute a number of ethical safeguards in themselves. However, they may not be enough, there are other values at stake.

Questions of ethics are invariably difficult to address, let alone to answer. We want to suggest that the question of a value base for sociological research is rather neglected, very little about ethics has been spelled out.[7] In relation to education too, teachers have not confronted the issue, values have been implicit, perhaps uncontested – until the 1980s in Britain. We need to refer to the issue of a value base. Otherwise we are left floundering. Woods has discussed the importance of having an honest project, and of confidentiality. But why are these values given privileged status, and where do we get them from?

We seem to be thrown back to the eighteenth- and nineteenth-century formulations of ethics and social contracts when we try to provide answers. It is Kant with his notions of 'respect for persons' which forms the root of much of our thinking. His argument is that respect for persons is the fundamental value, and that other ethical principles follow from it. Liberal, democratic society has identified those of confidentiality and acceptance. We are then left with three major values with which to work; they are respect for persons, self-determination and confidentiality. Given that they stand at the base of liberal society, we are on strong ground with them, they are a majority view. Later in this chapter when we have looked at some of the issues in more detail, we want to question whether these values are enough.

QUALITATIVE RESEARCH PRINCIPLES

We have claimed that the principles of qualitative research carry a number of ethical safeguards within them. Our project was based on the premise that, 'The objects studied are in fact subjects, and such subjects produce accounts of the world.'[8] This meant it was crucial to keep in mind that 'knowledge does not have "the other" as its object, instead it should have the inextricable and absolutely reciprocal interaction between the observer and the observed'.[9] This position has implications for what counts as ethical practice. For researchers it means that the people in the research should be treated as 'persons, as autonomous beings'[10] and therefore they need to find practices which 'honour the principle of respect for persons'. Researchers have an obligation to protect people from being managed and manipulated in the interests of research.

RESEARCH AS SOCIAL PROCESS

Hammersley makes the point that we must recognize that social research is a social process. 'Society is seen to be constituted through a ceaseless stream of interacting people, piecing together their separate lines of activity.'[11] It is important to recognize that when researcher and respondent meet, these same principles operate. A life history is not told in a social vacuum. Plummer draws our attention to the fact that life histories are one example of 'joint actions' and that they are social objects. 'Self story telling is a ceaseless, empirically grounded, process of shifting truth.'[12] On the one hand this implies that the life story is never 'fixed once and for all'.[13] But, there is another implication, 'The meaning of a life is emergent, it is context based.'[14] The sociologist is in the action and a part of the context. Therefore, there is an obligation upon them to unpick, or at the very least document their own place in what happened. The sociologist is not a passive trans-criber, nor a dispassionate observer. Atkinson asks that accounts of research manifest these principles, by including the 'reflexive, subject–object who is the interactionist's social actor'.[15]

It is also important to take this into account at the report-writing stage of research. Woolgar shows how sociologists have demon-strated the ways in which scientific knowledge is socially con-structed. The problem is that they have failed to apply the same analysis to their own research. There is a scaffolding of artifice and contrivance behind sociological accounts, which mostly remains hidden. Latour's recent work is useful here. He distinguishes two versions of reflexivity; one which he calls meta-reflexivity, involving a constant deconstruction of the text; the other (his own), which he calls infra-reflexivity entails a self-conscious recognition of the artificiality of the text with the aim of producing the most convincing possible account.[16]

We need, therefore, modes of writing which show the kind of scaffolding and stages that went into its building. Hammersley argues, 'The principle of reflexivity leads to the recognition that the activities of the researcher are not to be left out of the research report.'[17] However, he suggests that qualitative accounts are typi-cally written in such a way as to suggest that they simply reflect how the world is. Their authors and the kind of work that went into the account are 'suppressed' from the finished account. Atkinson points out that this style 'runs counter to the interactionist model of how people generate accounts of their world.'[18] In conclusion then, there is a mounting body of theory which shows how there is both an ethical and a methodological failure involved in not recognizing the role of the researcher in the construction of the narrative and the text.

RESEARCH BARGAIN AND RELATIONSHIPS

Martin Hammersley has written of the 'research bargain' that is struck, it is a bargain with a number of clauses. The most significant deal with the 'understanding reached by the researcher and the participant, regarding what the nature of their relationship is.'[19] He suggests that the research bargain also establishes rules about what each is allowed to do in the context of the research. Additional clauses outline what each expects from the other. Furthermore, there is a sense that both sides regard this agreement as fair.[20]

Ethnographers in particular and social scientists in general, usually recognize and acknowledge the importance of the relationship established between the researcher and the person supplying the data in interview situations.[21] We want to suggest that there are features of the life-history method that make the issues especially sharp. When we look at life history,

> Its chief feature is the 'prolonged interview' which in fact consists of a series of interviews, in which the subject and the interviewer interact to probe and reflect on the subject's statements.[22]

The life-history method involves developing relationships and trust, doing so enables us to penetrate several layers of access. 'There would have to be a relationship between us that transcended the research, that produced a bond of friendship, a feeling of togetherness and joint pursuit of a common mission rising above personal egos.'[23] The relationship progresses with the research, and the hope is that by the latter stages of the research one may not be asking questions at all. Ball prefers to regard this not as 'interviewing' but as 'interactive research'.[24]

If we turn to our own practices it seems that there are questions to be asked about the 'relationship bargain' we struck. The research relationship was initiated by the researcher; the first stages of negotiation took place when the research project was introduced to potential participants, who were then invited to take part. This first encounter usually took place over the telephone. We would introduce ourselves and explain where we had got the teacher's name from. We either already knew the teacher in question or had been given their name by a mutual acquaintance. We would then go on to explain the project. (This explanation is dealt with later in this chapter.) It is at this point that some of the ethical difficulties become clearer. It is possible that we did not make the contract explicit, that what was to be exchanged was left vague. This meant that there was a space left for both participants to read their own views in; and these views could be widely different.

We have emphasized the stress we placed on the quality of the research relationships, but we need to acknowledge that the relationship was, after all, one primarily developed for the purposes of collecting data. None of the researchers maintained any of the relationships after the period of data collection was over. We, as researchers, were primarily in those relationships for research purposes, not for more general purposes of friendship. That was made clear to the respondents.

We also have to note that the relationships were confined to interviewing sessions. Interviews are odd 'social constructions' with highly asymmetrical interaction. Ball has pointed out, 'The rules of conversational discourse are flagrantly disregarded in the name of social science.'[25] Interviews are about rapport and inter-subjectivity, but they are also about research, they involve listening, but they also involve a process we have called 'listening beyond' listening for more than is being said on the surface.

Social research can be exploitative, and we have already discussed the ways that life-history accounts can have a voyeuristic attraction. Participants and researchers have not always been fully aware of this. In the light of our own practice, it is clear that there was an element of instrumentality in our concern to establish good relationships with our teachers, but was this ethically acceptable. In any dealings with people one thread is always to get on amicably.

The relationship between life history 'taker' and life history 'giver' is an artificial one. But then the notion of a 'natural' relationship is, perhaps, problematic. We meet people in all sorts of situations in the course of our lives; our meetings are variously coincidental or contrived, official or informal, equal or unequal. It is the case that certain expectations are attached to different types of relationship. One of the important questions is what expectations of us as interviewers did our teachers have. One of the ethical difficulties is that we did not ask them.

In retrospect, if we try to theorize about this, then it is possible to speculate that the teachers may have hived off 'encounters' they had with us into 'social and business' categories. We may have been largely seen as a 'business' kind of relationship, one that falls into the contrived, formal, semi-official category. However, what confounds this analysis is the factor of intimacy that we have discussed earlier. We, as researchers, were interested in data about lives that were intimate, and yet we met the teachers in a 'business' context. We crossed some important boundaries, and mixed signals in a way that contains ambiguities.

Some researchers have discussed the issue of self-disclosure as an important strategy in interviewing. As the respondent tells about their life, so the interviewer gives details about their own views and attitudes. There are a number of advantages seen to derive from this tactic. The first is its efficiency. 'Reciprocity is an excellent data gathering technique.'[26] The interviewer gains access to more personal areas of data as they move from the status of stranger to friend.[27] For Bertaux there are significant methodological issues, in that the data gathered will then 'become a mutually shared knowledge, rooted in the intersubjectivity of the interaction'.[28] Self-disclosure then underpins the recognition that social research is a joint action in ways that we have already discussed.

Other researchers have claimed that self-disclosure carries ethical safeguards too. Oakley argues that in research there should be 'no intimacy without reciprocity'.[29] Catani goes on to make some more claims. 'The price to be paid by the observer will be to be reciprocally known just as thoroughly by the object. Knowledge thus becomes what sociological method has always wished to avoid; a risk.'[30] One way of looking at this tactic is that it involves a kind of mutual baring of the soul and psyche, which diminishes the distance between 'taker' and 'giver' of the life history.

However, there is another view of this process, Hammersley discusses what often happens.

> What is involved in the process of self disclosure is the presentation of those aspects of one's self and life that provide a bridge for building relationships with participants, and the suppression of those which constitute a possible barrier.[31]

It is important to question which of the two approaches we more nearly followed. We have already given an account of the ways in which we did disclose areas of the self.[32] With one informant, Pat

Sikes discussed the shared experience of being an only child. Pat felt that this deepened the area of trust. Pat comments, 'We understood one another.'[33] But if we look retrospectively at Pat's notes on this, some ethical issues emerge. She wrote, 'Give personal details to solicit personal details.' The conclusion is a severe one, that while we talked about the importance of relationships it nevertheless seems that we viewed them as exploitable, they could be sacrificed for the pursuit of data.

Lynda Measor has discussed elsewhere the importance of 'staying bland';[34] of not letting too much of the self show. She has given details of the difficulties she encountered, for example, when her views on 'page three pictures' in the *Sun* were known in a school where she was doing research. It seems important to question the ethics of this. Ball puts the issue with uncomfortable directness, 'The interviewer comes to know his subjects without necessarily having to engage in a reciprocal process of personal "social striptease".'[35] Extending the metaphor even further Campbell asks, 'Should the quest for the "inside life" of others strip away every fig leaf?'[36]

Perhaps all we can say is that we acted professionally, and that we established some relationships that were work-related and which provided some satisfaction to both sides. But we need to question what the respondents got from the relationships.

What the researchers wanted from the respondents was their story, was fact and reflection on their lives as teachers. It is much more difficult to know what the respondents wanted from us. Woods has suggested that sympathy, reassurance and advice may be crucial elements. The act of being 'listened to' counts for a lot. But it remains the case that at the time we did the research, we didn't ask.

We did have some clues as to what the answers might have been. Lynda thinks it is significant that all of the retired teachers she interviewed offered her tea, and it was always served in the best family china. Such actions said something about the importance of the interviews, and also spoke of the distance that was to be kept. The essential fragility of the relationships involved was clear with one teacher, Mr King. Two days after Lynda had interviewed him, his house was burgled. When Lynda telephoned him three days later he was distinctly frosty, and asked point blank whether she had been responsible for 'casing the joint'. Lynda comments, 'I felt horrified, but on reflection I realised that Mr King did not after all know who I was, he had no real proof of my identity, he had taken me "on trust". I think it shows what an odd line we tread doing this kind of work.'

In the course of writing this chapter Lynda had the opportunity to talk about this issue with one of the teachers in the original sample. She had a brief and informal discussion with Mr Ray. He commented with some heat about the fact that very little is offered to respondents. He suggested, for example, that interviewees should be paid, and that at the very least they should be sent copies of the book when it is published. He also felt that he wished he had been sent copies of draft chapters. We have no way of knowing how widespread this reaction is, the discussion was not set up with the same rigorous concern for methodology as the initial interviews were. It is also important to note the reaction of another teacher who heard Mr Ray's comments. He felt that it is not payment that is at stake, but rather the opportunity for professional self-enhancement that could be made available to teachers through this kind of work, and it is to this issue that we need to turn next.

COVERT AND COLLABORATIVE MODELS OF RESEARCH

The next clause in the bargain concerns the 'account of the goals, purposes, methods and likely consequences of the research'.[37] This is a cause of some difficulty in much research for it seems rare for researchers to be entirely open in their accounts. Hammersley takes one position on the issue: 'The researcher must compromise between ethical considerations, the requirements of the research and what participants are prepared to accept.'[38] There are strategic considerations in this matter, which Hammersley privileges.

It is important to note that other views have been expressed. Heron comments that people, 'Have a moral right to participate in decisions that claim to generate information about them.'[39] He demands that we 'share power' with the respondents, this should be done, 'not only in the application of research. . .but also in the generation of knowledge'.[40] In these ways Heron considers that we respect persons, and that we enhance their opportunities for self-determination. In other words we work with an ethical code.

It seems to us now in retrospect that there may be serious ethical and methodological issues involved in concealing part of the research intention, and we felt it might be useful to explore our practices in the area. Our position on this issue was a kind of

217

halfway house. We were very concerned that collaboration and reciprocity should be – and should be seen to be, a central aspect of the research. Our reasons for this were to do with our methodological commitments, and associated with these, our feelings about the morals and ethics of research relationships.

We explained to teachers that we were interested in collecting life histories of their careers and experiences in schools. We also explained the structure of the project, that we were interviewing teachers of different ages and at different stages of their careers. We made it clear that we were only including art and science teachers in the project. This information meant that we could then explain to teachers that they had been selected and approached because they fitted these categories, rather than for any ulterior motive. We also explained that if the teacher agreed to take part it would involve a number of meetings for us to talk about their perceptions of and experiences in teaching.

Our introduction was truthful, albeit sometimes in an economical sense. We were a bit shifty sometimes on the issue of how much time we thought we might need from teachers. Collecting and collaboratively analysing life histories is a time-consuming process. We did not initially share this knowledge with people for fear of putting them off. Nor were all of the teachers we approached chosen just because they fitted our categories. There were some occasions where we had particular knowledge about a teacher which made us keen to include them; knowledge that we did not always admit to. For example, Lynda was interested in one teacher, Mr Quilley, because she had been told by a number of sources about his reputation as a violent disciplinarian; and Pat was aware that staff at one of her schools held starkly contrasting perceptions of one retired teacher.

At the first interview we usually described the main aims of the project. Particularly in the early days we could not say very much, because we were taking a grounded theory approach and were waiting to see which themes emerged from the data. One thing we did stress, however, was that we hoped that our findings might have some practical value for the teaching profession.

Looking back, little or no 'negotiation' regarding process and procedures, or 'ownership' use and dissemination of data took place at any stage of the project. In this respect as in most others the agreement was very informal. In fact we feel that the cues we gave about these issues were all embedded in the quality of the relationship we struck with the teachers.

> I would get a sense of this through what the interviewer said, and how it was said, by how much they put into the discussion, by how they looked at me, listened to me. I would definitely not have the feeling that I was being 'researched' by a superior agency, who ultimately would put all these little cogs together into a grand machine that would be for the use of others.[41]

It is possible to question whether this is enough. It may be that some sort of written document which outlined the aims of the project, set the expectations of both parties, and agreed procedures, would have given a stamp of professionality. It might have also offered further reassurance that the researchers would stick to 'ethical codes'. The idea of such a contract was never discussed, nor did respondents ask for it. However, it would have served perhaps to emphasize our aims that the research be participative.

It seems to us that the best ethical safeguards actually derived from the process of respondent validation. 'Returning the processed accounts to the informant for appraisal and to check the accuracy of the data.'[42] When we did this we found we had misunderstood on occasion and respondents had the opportunity to put us right. We were also interested in testing out analysis of the data with respondents, and we took our early 'hunches' to the teachers for their commentary.

We found that respondents advanced the analysis in some fruitful ways. Bertaux has asked that we see 'sociology as participation' and the practice of respondent validation moves toward this approach, as well as having the added virtue of mopping up many of the ethical issues that we have dealt with here. Some of the work that Kushner and Norris have done also has relevance to our concerns. They ask that we work towards practices that give respondents, 'the dignity of contributing to theorizing about their words. . . [and] through sharing meaning production. . . [to] develop significant understandings of schooling and education.'[43]

Recent research has moved this debate on. It is interesting that in the contested area of anti-racist education the issues have been sharpened. Troyna and Carrington in a recent paper on ethics[44] have criticized the 'elitist and undemocratic nature of research'.

They see this exemplified by the denial of 'the subject's capacity to scrutinize and change the mode of the research act and their role within it'. They work with Lather's epithet that research has operated on a 'rape model'. It is research which in her view, 'takes rather than gives, describes rather than changes and transmits rather than transforms'.[45]

In the light of this it seems important to acknowledge that we did not work with a fully collaborative model, where the objectives of the research were discussed with the teachers in an entirely open manner. We want to suggest in the light of data collected recently that this may carry not only ethical problems, but major methodological ones too.

Recently, Lynda was interviewing a teacher who had worked in a region of England where the schools were very frequently researched by a local university team. The teacher exploded mildly for a few moments about how deeply he and the rest of the staff of the school had come to resent this; and how belittled they had all felt because they were never included in the research design, or fully informed about the research objectives. In the end the teachers had retaliated, a group of them from a number of schools had spent an evening in the pub, and had agreed on the story they would tell the researcher. It was a nonsense account, which disguised their real views. The teacher involved told Lynda that the researcher had swallowed the story and had incorporated it into the report.

It is a worrying fact that we do not know how widespread this kind of practice is. While we do not know, there needs to be some thought put into ways that we can find out, researchers ought not to be easily deceived. There should be methodological safeguards, plausibility and consistency need to be monitored and triangulation should provide some check. This story has important implications for researchers, we tell it not to suggest that we see teachers as tricksters, whom the researcher needs to be alert to. We want to suggest that if we work with a model which treats respondents as unable to participate in some of the ways we have discussed, then we may create major research difficulties.

The teacher who told Lynda the story is now involved in doing research himself. He works exclusively with a model that fully incorporates teachers into the research design. However, we have to acknowledge that such an approach has enormous difficulties, and could impose real limitations. One example would be the ethical and practical difficulties in working with teachers who may be racist or sexist, in ways that do not implicitly support and reinforce their racism and sexism.

However, it has a number of advantages. Firstly it stops treating teachers as if they were fools or dupes of the system. (Cole (1984) has a discussion of researchers who have done this.) It also suggests that areas of difficulty can be discussed openly and negotiated.

THE ROLE OF 'THE COAXER'

In life-history work there are important ethical questions associated with the actual and the perceived power of the person doing the interviewing. In his recent work, Plummer raised the matter of 'the role of the coaxer', who is the life history 'taker'. He comments that their line of activity is that of 'seducing stories out of people'. He comments that as sociologists 'we are all heavily implicated in this process. Most of us spend a lot of our professional lives coaxing "stories" out of people.'[46]

Others, like Woods caution against this view. He discussed the way that the interviewer can provide respondents with the opportunity to raise topics which are significant to them. This is done through the provision of an appropriate relationship, situation and atmosphere.[47] A symbolic interactionist perspective also reminds us that the person being interviewed also has power over what they choose to tell.[48]

In this context, the relationship again becomes important. It is clear, as Hammersley points out, that 'participants are not interested solely or perhaps even primarily in the ethnographer's research identity, but also in his [sic] personal attributes.'[49] This material 'prompted' Lynda to look again at some data she collected on Mr Tucks. This teacher was beginning to describe a 'critical incident' in his career.

> Mr. Tucks, . . . 'I hesitate to repeat it, I can't. . .I don't know what. . . you know. . .its difficult to repeat it. . .don't like it. . .'. At this point, Lynda applied pressure, 'Do you want to talk about it or not,' and applied sympathy. . .and got the tale.[50]

Recently Lynda was teaching a research methods course to a group of teachers, and was using this material. Their reaction to this account was one of shocked disapproval. When questioned they said that this was a highly sensitive area for any teacher, and that the researcher had applied too much pressure. They felt that it is too easy to pressure people to tell things, which later they may come to regret. Lynda feels that this commentary, coming as it does from within teacher culture carries a weight that we must acknowledge.

In retrospect it seems that we may have given a double message to the teachers we interviewed. As interviewers we made it plain to people that they should not feel obliged to tell us anything they did not want to. We were, we thought, mindful of the way in which it is possible to get caught up in events and perhaps reveal more than one would in other situations. Yet in retrospect it seems that we did simultaneously put pressure on our respondents to do just this.

A related question is how we handle the involvement of others in the tale, that is when the person giving the life history refers to others in a way that may be construed as demeaning. It might illustrate a point nicely at the time, but they may come to regret it later, especially when it appears in print. Peter Woods cites an example of this, when some teachers mentioned that they got on better at meetings without their local advisor present. This was because the advisor fixed the agenda, and in turn was briefed by his chief. Thus these meetings did not always deal with *their* problems in the way that they wished. For the sociologist this was a splendid example to support the 'bottom up' model of school and other management.[51] All were thinking quite objectively at the time of the interviews, and the personal implications only emerged later. Two guidelines would seem appropriate here. A research report should make it clear that a general, theoretical point is being made (in this case about management models and inter-role, not inter-personal relationships); and secondly the point should not be made at all, if in the opinion of any of those involved in the discussions, at a later stage of reflection (that is when material has been prepared for publication) it is likely to affect adversely their working situation or their own role performance.

There are problems of the 'intimate and painful' areas in life histories that may be full of purport and intellectual interest for the issue under discussion, but raise traumas for the individual. Self-reflection is a fashionable and useful tool, but there are things in perhaps every life that the individual prefers to forget, and emotionally it may be necessary for them to do so. The critical incidents that we asked people to dwell on may be one example.

The problem is the one identified at the beginning. A life history does deal with intimate material, and carries a high ethical load as a result.

SELECTION, PRESENTATION, INTERPRETATION

When a life history is being collected and compiled and used as a data source, both interviewer and interviewee are involved in a process of selection, presentation and interpretation. Ethical questions do arise about the ways that we elicited, interpreted and used the life stories we collected. These questions include: Were we aiding and abetting a misrepresentation? Were we basing theories in false or untrue data? Were we making invalid claims?

We want to suggest that the validation techniques that have been developed in qualitative methodology go some ways towards answering these questions. What we were doing was working from how people theorized and presented themselves in the data. We built on their categorizations and classifications, which were grounded in the data. We built from their ways of perceiving and making sense of the world. It is another way in which qualitative methodology carries ethical safeguards within it.

Lather quotes Morgan in suggesting that, 'The goal of theoretically guided empirical work is to create theory that possesses "evocative power".'[52] Many of the teachers have remarked that the lives we recorded and the final interpretations we made in the book 'ring bells' for them. They invoke an accurate sense of what it is like. We take this to mean that our interpretations represent a view of teaching which our teachers recognize, and we also see it as a safeguard.

We were explicitly interested in allowing the concerns of teachers to emerge and shape the research. This arose partly from our own commitment to symbolic interactionist methodology, partly from a practical concern to do research that practitioners would find useful, and partly from ethical concerns.

The question that arises in this kind of ethical retrospective is did we do enough? Were there issues that teachers wanted to discuss that we downplayed either when we interviewed, or later in terms of the way we selected data?

In answer to these difficult questions, it is possible to point to themes that arose only as the data were collected. The idea of 'becoming a proper teacher', for example, was one that did not have any foreshadowed place in our notebooks. We would also like to suggest that working in a research team had some advantages here. We have explained elsewhere how the bias one individual had about an issue could be balanced by the others.[53] We worked toward a notion of team triangulation, to guard against selection oversight, but it may be that this needs to be explored more rigorously if we are to build in proper safeguards to ensure that any theory generated is truly grounded theory.

This is one example of a team working to free material and analysis, but we know from other work done on groups that they also put people under pressure to conform, and that they do not only, nor always facilitate.[54] One example is dealt with in detail later in this chapter when we argue that our research was gender-blind, that it failed to take enough account of gender.

TELLING THE STORY

There is a further ethical issue over the question of what is the impact upon a life of telling the life story. Plummer points out, 'The stories we weave into our lives play a hugely important task in reorganizing our pasts, permitting the present and anticipating the future.'[55] It seems important to identify the intellectual co-ordinates of his comment. If we are discussing the role that past experience comes to play in the construction of 'a life' then it is difficult to work without making reference to work done in the field of psychoanalysis: where recent work has relevance to the field of life history.

Part of the problem in using such sources is the multiple perspectives from the psychoanalytic tradition. Plummer refers to Freud's work, as having a 'traditional archaeological approach' and largely dismisses it. Lacan offers different insight. He is interested in the pursuit of repressed material, the analysts' job is to recover it and parts of the self with it. In this way a 'truth' is discovered. However, this truth is always being purloined by the various strategies of the unconscious. This unconscious is indefinable, but its machinations are observable. This challenges the sociological notion of there being no 'truth', but only a series of subjective views in some fundamental ways. Spence's recent work develops the argument; he asserts that there is a truth lodged in the narrative that people tell. That truth can be quite different from the 'historical truth' of what happened in their lives, but nevertheless it has a force in their attitudes and actions. Sarbin pursues the idea that our minds work with truth in 'narrative' and therefore psychoanalysis must put narrative at the centre of its concern.

Such theories, whatever branch of psychoanalysis they are drawn from raise enormous and difficult questions for the sociologist taking a life history. Are there any ways in which we can take their ideas on board and use them to deepen our understanding? It is no doubt simpler to dismiss them all as just another theory, or as another 'meta-narrative', a piece of script we take from the world and apply. Nevertheless the psychoanalysis theories do represent a challenge.

In our life-history research we did aim to trace connections at an empirical level, between the teachers' past experiences and their current story. Mr Shoe discussed the effect of growing up in rural poverty on his wish to become a teacher. The question is should we and could we have taken this further?

If Spence and Sarbin are right about the way we employ narrative truth in our attempt to structure reality and our lives, then it means that we need to examine the life histories we obtained in some different ways. It means they are altogether different objects, and they need more sophisticated connections between past and present to be made. To understand them we may be required at least to take account of some kind of notion of the unconscious. It is anything but a simple matter to do so, as we discovered with our work with pupils.[56] Unless we begin to work with what is known from other disciplines about the workings of the mind and the emotions, then we may fail to grasp the emotional processes that are at work as a life story is told; and we may miss the ethical risks involved in dealing with material that has this quality of intimacy.

It is possible to criticize sociology for ignoring the affective areas of people's lives; but if we take up Sarbin's notions, then it may be that life history can stand as a methodology which opens up this hidden area. At the very least we need to begin to weave a knowledge of the way that 'talk' operates symbolically, and is in some senses a rule governed. We cannot claim to have made much advance in this area, as we were not fully aware of many of the issues at the time when we did most of the research.

The point is that when we began the project, we honestly did not know whether taking part in it would have any effect on people's lives, or rather whether they would perceive it to have any effects. One of the issues that emerged was the way that some of our respondents took advantage of the counselling potential of the interviewing sessions. There were some limited points of comparison with a Rogerian style of counselling, in that we listened, reflected back, asked questions which encouraged people to reflect on their actions and did not pass judgement. We also dealt with the intimate. We did make it clear that we were researchers, not anything more, but we had initiated the interactions and we were employing the techniques, and there is a wonderful luxury in being listened to.

It created difficulties for us, though we felt that it was not part of the bargain, and we did not want the responsibility. At one level it may be that we had not worked through the likely consequences and implications of what we were doing. Pat, for instance, had not considered that a teacher might make the decision to leave teaching as, he said, a result of talking through his perceptions and experiences. It was perhaps inevitable that people should respond in this way. Maybe sociologists should be more realistic and accept that they cannot remain as distant and detached as they sometimes hope. It does seem that there is a responsibility there, which should be acknowledged – and that it is a basic human responsibility to other people. We should not initiate situations that we are not prepared to see through to their potential conclusion.

GETTING THE FULL PICTURE – THE VIEW FROM WOMEN TEACHERS

In the area of gender, it is also possible to see ways in which methodological and ethical issues intermingled to create problems and insights. It is possible to criticize our life-history work for being 'gender-blind'. We studiously tried to select a balanced sample, where half of the teachers were women; however, we only researched teachers in current full-time employment. Our method of sampling did, therefore, leave out many women whose careers have followed a different path, for example if they have given up teaching to have children or if they work on a part-time basis. This had a number of implications. We failed to establish any picture of women's objective career patterns. It may well be the case that they follow a different trajectory from those of men. Acker's book on women teachers redresses this balance.[57]

However, there are other implications, for the construction of theory at stake here. Our work leaned on Levison, who researched men and aimed to construct a model of the life cycle and career that referred only to men. We did not attempt to open up and extend this model to include women. Feminist scholarship has clearly revealed the difficulties that can arise for and in a theory if it is based on research and thinking which only includes one gender; this is perhaps particularly true in the field of human development, and identity construction.

Isabelle Bertaux-Wiame has suggested some ways forward in the context of life-history research. She indicates that men and women tell their stories differently, that they portray the lived experience of social relations in different patterns. She emphasizes the point that women put everything in a frame of personal relationships. At first sight this seems little more than a piece of commonsense, and somewhat sexist knowledge. Feminist work on theories of human development and processes of identity construction, however, have a different tale to tell.

Gilligan is one author who has looked at theories of development from a feminist point of view. She is critical of the fact that psychoanalytic theory has implicitly accepted male life as the norm. In her view it may be that in order to grasp the processes involved in identity construction we need the view from both sexes. She starts from the fact that women have been found not to 'fit' the theories of human development as they now stand. She explores what this means for the theories, and for people.

Levinson used the psychoanalytic model. He focuses on the development of individuated self in relation to work. Men in Levinson's study were distant in their personal relationships. 'Such studies show a view of adulthood, where relationships are subordinated to the ongoing processes of individuation and achievement.'[58] Gilligan and others have traced alternative developmental constructs for women, from a study of their lives. Baker Miller, for example, suggests that women's development goes along a different route. For her it is significant that women's development is different from men's, because of its recognition of the continuous importance of attachment in the human life cycle. Gilligan makes the point, 'Girls tie their experience of self to the activities of care and connection.'[59]

The implications for theory are significant. Gilligan suggests that there is a different dynamic at work in terms of life cycle and development of identity, for men than for women. The problem is not just that one voice has been left out, the consequences are more fundamental. 'Male and female voices typically speak of the importance of different truths.'[60] For life-history research, this feminist work has implications for our view of what identity formation is, our sense of that, and of what maturity is, can shift when it is portrayed by men rather than by women. Women were left out of the original processes of theory construction, on life-cycle development, and it is not enough to simply bolt on a woman's-eye view after the theory has been constructed.

For qualitative sociology working with an interactionist model, there are significant theoretical implications. Life-cycle models like Levinson's are based implicitly on stage theory, and it may be the case that we accepted it too uncritically. Qualitative sociology continues to struggle for methodologically sound ways to make links with the macro-level and to generate grounded theory. We have discussed the challenges elsewhere.[61] We want to suggest that this is a useful example of such a case here, we aimed to work with stage theory, and ran into methodological difficulty as a result.

However, there ought to be methodological safeguards within qualitative sociology which can prevent such difficulty. The central issue is to remain faithful to the interactionist focus on the world of subjective meanings, realities and intentions of participants within situations. We must provide a rich ethnographic background of empirical detail against which the hypotheses can be tested; and when we present the analysis it needs to be laced with a great deal of the members, own accounts to enable the reader to make his own judgements.

We need to aim for a close fit between what participants say and what the researcher infers, and in Schutz's terms any second-order constructs must have a close logical relationship with first-order constructs. From a methodological point of view we are failing to do this if we only allow in one voice; and only tell half of the story.

LIBERAL VALUES – ARE THEY ENOUGH

The context in which we work in education has changed rapidly in recent years. The process had begun at the time we did this research, but five years later the changes are substantial. Educational research has decisions to make about its place in and its attitudes to these changes; it is faced with the need to make decisions and commitments which have political overtones. Questions of ethics and values have new significance in the light of the educational situation in which we now find ourselves. We want to suggest that sociologists need to begin asking serious questions about the ethics of mostly researching those in our society who have less power.

> That is to say that the eyes of sociologists, with few but honourable exceptions have been turned downwards and their palms upwards. Eyes down to study the activities of the lower classes. Sociologists stand guard in the garrison, and report to its masters the movement of the occupied populace. The more adventurous of the sociologists don the guise of the people and go out to mix with the peasants 'in the field' returning with books and articles that break the protective secrecy in which a subjugated population wraps itself, and makes it more accessible to manipulation and control.[62]

Nicolaus states his case with intensity, but people from quite different perspectives have warned of the dangers inherent in turning sociology into 'deprivation studies'.[63] If we collect information which is otherwise 'secret', it does raise questions about the uses to which that knowledge is put. It may be that sociologists need to consider the steps they could and should take to protect the autonomy of the group they are researching.

It may not be enough in Britain in the 1980s to say that sociological investigation is self evidently desirable.[64] There has been 'A decline in government interest in investing in independent questioning and self criticism'.[65] We need to take care to ensure that we do not imply that we see teachers as deprived underdogs, nevertheless teachers do work in a context which currently threatens their working autonomy and their conditions of employment and choice over the ways they teach children.

By carrying out research which aims for imaginative identification with the subject, does qualitative research open up this issue even further? We want to suggest that qualitative research has projected an image of itself as the 'cottage industry' of sociological enterprise. The status has perhaps been seen as protecting its practitioners from some of the ethical considerations that should dog the work of the number-crunching, survey-wielding, white-coat-wearing cousins on the other side of the tracks. However, to read Foucault is to be robbed of any innocence about the doing of research, Roy Porter brings to our attention the fact that schools are spaces which fall within the disciplines whose job is control; and researchers need to be aware of their place and their role there.[66]

Some areas of sociological thinking ask the researcher to go further, to take a Stoic line.[67] The Stoics believed that all activity had to be 'moral' otherwise it was worth nothing. Strong suggests that sociology should take on not only an ethical line, but also a committed line, in the C. Wright Mills tradition, and take on some of the ethical implications of the discipline. It is at this point that we need to pick up one of the questions raised at the beginning of this chapter. We began by identifying the need for a value base, and by delineating the values that are readily accepted within it. It may be that this is a new demand, to assert that education and research should define its value base. There is another issue too. We began from Kant and from the value base of liberal society. The question is whether that is any longer adequate. Do we need to go further and make different claims, especially in the context of government changes in the education system in Britain in the 1980s?

CONCLUSION

The issues raised are difficult ones, and we do not claim to have answers. There are two observations, however, that can help. Firstly that, 'No hard and fast rules can be laid down; these are matters of conscience rather than science.'[68] There are decisions which have to be made by researchers, and we have tried in this chapter to look at what foundations there are upon which to make them. The second point is drawn from symbolic interaction theory. In research relationships there is no 'natural' bargain that would be recognized as fair by all. The research bargain 'is a social construction, the result of assessments by each side of what the other has to give and what they are prepared to offer in return for these things.'[69] Hammersley applies a useful astringent here. Respondents are not fearful victims who open up their lives and souls because they are told or asked to. People have boundaries and strategies to protect themselves in research situations.

ACKNOWLEDGEMENTS

We would like to gratefully acknowledge Peter Woods' help. He initiated the research upon which this chapter is based, and made a significant contribution to earlier drafts of this chapter.

NOTES

1 Campbell, J. (1988) 'Inside lives: The quality of biography' in Sherman, R. and Webb, R. (eds) *Qualitative Research in Education: Focus and Methods*, Barcombe: Falmer; Sherman, R. and Webb, R. (eds) (1988) *Qualitative Research in Education: Focus and Methods*, Barcombe: Falmer; Smith, L. *et al.* (1986) *Educational Innovators: Then and Now*, Barcombe: Falmer.
2 Plummer, K. (1988) 'Herbert Blumer and the life history tradition: Critique, emergence, practice'. Paper presented at Interactionist Research, 1988, University of Windsor, Ontario.
3 Sikes, P., Measor, L. and Woods, P. (1985) *Teachers' Careers*, Barcombe: Falmer.
4 Bertaux, D. (ed.) (1981) *Biography and Society*, London: Sage.
5 Holroyd, M. (1988) *Bernard Shaw Volume 1: 1856–1898 – The Search For Love*, Chatto and Windus.
6 Woods, P. (1986) *Inside Schools*, London: Routledge and Kegan Paul, p. 59.
7 Burgess, R. (1985) 'The whole truth: Some ethical problems of research in a comprehensive school' in Burgess, R. (ed.) *Research Methods in the Study of Education*, Barcombe: Falmer.
8 Hammersley, M. and Atkinson, P. (1979) *Ethnography, Principles in Practice*, London: Tavistock, p. 179.
9 Ferrarotti, S. (1981) 'On the autonomy of the biographical method' in Bertaux, D. (ed.) *Biography and Society*, London: Sage.
10 Heron, J. (1981) 'Experimental research methods' in Reason, P. and Rowan, J. (eds) *Human Enquiry*, New York: Wiley, pp. 34–35.
11 Plummer, 'Blumer and the life history tradition', p. 7.
12 ibid., p. 11.
13 ibid.
14 ibid., p. 12.
15 Hammersley and Atkinson, *Ethnography*, p. 140.
16 Woolgar, S. (ed.) (1988) *Knowledge and Reflexivity: New Frontiers in the Sociology of Knowledge*, London: Sage.
17 Hammersley and Atkinson, *Ethnography*, p. 97.
18 ibid., p. 43.
19 ibid., p. 116.
20 ibid.
21 Finch, J. (1984) 'It's great to have someone to talk to: The ethics and politics of interviewing women' in Bell, C. and Roberts, H. (eds) *Social Researching: Problems and Practice*, London: Routledge and Kegan Paul.

22 Sikes *et al., Teachers', Careers*, p. 13.
23 Woods, *Inside Schools*, p. 63.
24 ibid., p. 75.
25 Ball, S. (1983) 'Case study research in education: Some notes and problems' in Hammersley, M. (ed.) *The Ethnography of Schooling: Methodological Issues*, Driffield: Nafferton, pp. 93–95.
26 Everhart, R. (1977) 'Between stranger and friend: Some consequences of long term fieldwork in schools', in *American Educational Research Journal*, Vol.14, pp. 1–15.
27 Lather, P. (1986) 'Research as praxis', in *Harvard Educational Review*, Vol. 56, No. 3, pp. 257–277.
28 Bertaux, *Biography and Society*, p. 20.
29 Oakley, A. (1981) 'Interviewing women: A contradiction in terms' in Roberts, H. (ed.) *Doing Feminist Research*, Boston, p. 49.
30 Bertaux, *Biography and Society*, p. 20.
31 Hammersley, p. 125.
32 Woods, *Inside Schools*, p. 63.
33 ibid.
34 Burgess, 'The whole truth', p. 24.
35 Ball, 'Case study research', p. 95.
36 Campbell, 'Inside lives', p. 59.
37 Hammersley, p. 117.
38 ibid., p. 99.
39 Heron, 'Experimental research methods', p. 34–35.
40 ibid., p. 35.
41 Woods, *Inside Schools*, p. 63.
42 ibid., p. 83.
43 Kushner, S. and Norris, N. (1980) 'Interpretation, negotiation and validity in naturalistic research', *Interchange*, Vol. 11, No. 4, p. 26.
44 Troyna, B. and Carrington, B. (1989) 'Whose side are we on? Ethical dilemmas in research on 'race' and education' in Burgess, R. (ed.) *Ethics of Educational Research*, Barcombe, Falmer.
45 Lather, 'Research as praxis', p. 263.
46 Plummer, 'Blumer and the life history tradition', p. 16.
47 Woods, *Inside Schools*, p. 132.
48 Ball, S. (1985) 'Interviewing pupils' in Burgess, R. (ed.) *Strategies of Qualitative Research*, Barcombe: Falmer, p. 13.
49 Hammersley, p. 118.
50 Woods, *Inside Schools*, p. 79.
51 Woods, P. Commentary on an earlier draft of this paper.
52 Morgan (1983), p. 298; Lather, 'Research as praxis', p. 266.
53 Woods, *Inside Schools*, p. 176.
54 Asch, S. (1956) 'Studies in independence and conformity: a minority of one against a unanimous majority', *Psychological Monographs*, Vol. 76, No. 9, p. 416.
55 Plummer, 'Blumer and the life history tradition', p. 11.
56 Measor, L. and Woods, P. (1983) *Changing Schools*, Milton Keynes: Open University Press.

57 Acker, S. (ed.) (1991) *Teachers: Gender and Careers Failure*, London, New York and Philadelphia.
58 Gilligan, C. (1982) *In A Different Voice*, Cambridge: Harvard University Press, p. 154.
59 ibid., p. 172.
60 ibid., p. 98.
61 Measor and Woods, *Changing Schools*, p. 67.
62 Nicolaus, M. (1972) 'The professional organization of sociology' in Blackburn, R. (ed.) *Ideology in Social Science*, London: Collins, p. 39.
63 Sir Douglas Hague, Speech to the British Association, November 1988.
64 Prior, S. 'The commodification of the body'. Paper presented at The Politics of Fieldwork Conference, Goldsmiths College, University of London, April 1988.
65 Hargreaves, A. (1986) 'Research, policy and practice in education: some observations on SSRC funded education projects', *Journal of Education Policy*, Vol. 1, No. 2, pp. 115–132.
66 Porter, R. 'Researching former mental hospital patients in California'. Paper presented at The Politics of Fieldwork Conference, Goldsmiths College, University of London, April 1988.
67 Strong, P. 'Means and ends in sociological research'. Paper given at The Politics of Field Research Conference, 1988.
68 Beattie, J. (1965) *Understanding An African Kingdom: Bunyaro*, London: Holt, Rinehart and Winston, p. 55.
69 Hammersley, p. 120.

9

STUDYING TEACHERS' LIVES
Problems and Possibilities

Ivor F. Goodson

STUDIES OF TEACHERS' LIVES

This volume has grown from a conviction that we require more analytical and systematic studies of teachers' lives. Above all the conviction grows from the belief which I will re-state that 'in understanding something so intensely personal as teaching, it is critical we know about the person the teacher is'. Put this way it seems almost self evident, commonsensical, and so I believe it is, but the fact remains that we still have an underdeveloped literature on the personal, biographical and historical aspects of teaching. Particularly underdeveloped is a literature which locates the teachers' lives within a wider contextual understanding.

In an era of new reforms and attempts to restructure schools this literature becomes even more important. Studies of teachers' lives thereby re-assert the importance of the teacher: of knowing the teacher, of listening to the teacher and of speaking with the teacher. Such studies work against the grain of political process for, as I write, this week's *New York Times* defines the US system of education in this manner:

> The current system of public education is built to control the schools from above. Politicians and bureaucrats are vested with authority to tell the schools what to do, and they are under constant pressure from constituents and interest groups to put that authority to use.

The implications for teachers and schools are clear:

> The result is that schools are buried in policies, rules and regulations that specify what they are supposed to be doing and how they are supposed to be doing it. This destroys

school autonomy and with it, the foundations for effective learning. As for management reform, it preserves the current system by giving principals and teachers 'new' powers that are actually highly circumscribed.[1]

A number of other nations, notably Britain are seeking to emulate many of these characteristics of the US system. In such times, educational studies which re-assert the importance of the teacher's voice are particularly valuable in building a knowledgeable counter-culture to stand against some of the cruder simplicities of political and 'managerial' views of schooling.

In this volume we have taken, as a starting point, work which focuses on studying teachers' lives. The intention has been to bring together a range of work within this genre so as to highlight the breadth of approaches and methodologies currently on offer. The volume therefore acts as a complement to the work of scholars already established in this field.[2] Some of the scholars in this volume are new to the field, but their work is, I think, both innovative and generative and points to exploration of new directions in studying teachers' lives.

In fact one of the most striking features of the studies in this volume is the range of approaches employed by the authors in studying teachers' lives. Such a range of studies provides its own set of opportunities: for the reader can assess the strengths and weaknesses of different approaches and focus on a number of important themes which emerge from within this collection. In this, the concluding chapter, I want to raise some methodological and ethical issues which I think the studies in this collection confront.

Some of the methodological questions are best raised by pointing to differences between the studies. To start with there is the question of the *process* that has been employed in developing the accounts provided in this collection. Specifically, the question of how explicit the authors are about the process of generating and interpreting data. Some authors provide very little account of process (for instance, Knowles), most authors provide some account, while some authors provided very detailed accounts (for instance, Butt *et al.*, Casey, Nelson). For instance, on pages 62–4 (Butt *et al.*) or pages 168–70 (Nelson) one is provided with a fairly clear description of the process and methodology of the research.

This I found most valuable in reading the subsequent account and seeking to develop insights into the nature of interpretation.

The nature of interpretation, the role of the commentary and the nature of the text are all matters of deep and abiding concern in studies of teachers' lives.

> A life lived is what actually happens. A life experienced consists of the images, feelings, sentiments, desires, thoughts, and meaning known to the person whose life is . . . . A life as told, as life history, is a narrative, influenced by the cultural conventions of telling, by the audience, and by the social context.[3]

The 'life as told' needs, I think, to be further divided into two distinctive modes: the 'life as told' by the person who lived and experienced the life (the life story) and the 'life as told' when the life story teller and another researcher collaborate to produce an intertextual/intercontextual account (the life history). We are left with four levels: life as lived, life as experienced, life as told and life history.

The teacher's life then operates at a number of intersections. First, there is the personal intersection for as Denzin has argued a life is lived on two levels which he characterizes the *surface* and the *deep*.

> At the surface level, the person *is* what he or she does in everyday doings, routines, and daily tasks. At the deep level, the person is a feeling, moral, sacred inner self. This deep inner self may only infrequently be shown to others.[4]

Second, the life operates at the intersection of context, as in issues of race and gender. For instance, as Gilligan and also Freccero have noted, while male life stories are recounted as orderly and linear, and concerned with conflict and authority, female life stories seen are often less concerned with linear striving and conflict.[5]

Third, the teacher's life operates at the intersection of life as experiences and life as text. The life account seeks to make the life textual. This rendition is profoundly problematic. Derrida, for instance, has examined this problematic through his concern with what he calls the metaphysics of presence. Building on this work, Denzin summarises the position thus:

There is no clear window into the inner life of a person, for any window is always filtered through the glaze of language, signs, and the process of signification. And language, in both it's written and spoken forms, is always inherently unstable, influx, and made up of the traces of other signs and symbolic statements. Hence, there can never be a clear, unambiguous statement of anything, including an intention or a meaning.[6]

At root, the relationship between life as lived and experienced and life as reported and rendered in text is distinctive. Within this constraint, the life account should be produced in a way which achieves as much harmony as is possible across these levels. When there is a sharp and evident disjuncture between life as lived and experienced and life history as reported and written, then we are witness to poorly conducted life studies.

In assessing the nature of interpretation Bertaux has reminded us that moving from personal life testimonies to wider life histories involves questions of methodological process and of power: 'What is really at stake is the relationship between the sociologist and the people who make his work possible by accepting to be interviewed on their life experiences.'[7]

The ethics of the relationship between the life story 'giver' and research 'taker' are considered by Sikes and Measor in Chapter 8 but the question of power is most clearly dealt with by Casey whose summary position is very similar to that of Bertaux.

What is at stake is the power relationship between researchers and subject. Essential to my approach is a respect for the authenticity and integrity of the narrator's discourse. The speaker is seen as a subject creating her own history, rather than an object of research.

Casey, then, proceeds by stating her position, her *value* position, and then devises or adopts a process of research which reflects that position, in particular as it relates to the power relation between the academically-located researcher and the teacher. The academic division of labour that Casey develops is, however, not without its problems. She argues that:

The political relations of research are designed so that the voice of the teacher can be given equal stakes with that of the academic researcher. Thus the interpretation is largely relinquished to the subjects themselves, while the researcher concentrates on discovering the patterns of priorities in the narrative texts.

It should be noted that, given the nature of the academy, this is a division of labour not without convenience for us as academic researchers. Moreover I wonder how it would deal with Measor and Sikes's nonsense account (see p. 220).

The relationship of studies of teachers' lives to the academy sits, I believe, at the centre of one of the major ethical and method-ological issues facing this work. Of course, views of the academy cover a wide spectrum from a belief in its role in the 'disinterested pursuit of knowledge' through to the assertion of the Situationist International that 'The intelligentsia is power's hall of mirrors.' In general, I would take a position which stresses the *interestedness* rather than disinterestedness of the academy. I see a good deal of empirical evidence that David Tripp's contention in this matter may be correct for he argues that: 'When a research method gains currency and academic legitimacy, it tends to be transformed to serve the interests of the academy.'[8]

Becker has commented on the 'hierarchy of credibility regard-ing those to whom we tend to listen'. This has general relevance to our research on schooling and school systems and specifically to our desire to listen to the teacher's voice.

> In any system of ranked groups, participants take it as given that members of the highest group have the right to define the way things really are. In any organization, no matter what the rest of the organization chart shows, the arrows indicate the flow of information point up, thus demonstrating (at least formally) that those at the top have access to a more complete picture of what is going on than anyone else. Members of lower groups will have incomplete information and their view of reality will be partial and distorted in consequence. Therefore, from the point of view of a well socialized participant in the system, any tale told by those at the top intrinsically deserves to be regarded as the most credible account obtainable of the organizations' workings.[9]

He provides a particular reason why accounts 'from below' may be unwelcome:

officials usually have to lie. That is a gross way of putting it, but not inaccurate. Officials must lie because things are seldom as they ought to be. For a great variety of reasons, well-known to sociologists, institutions are refractory. They do not perform as society would like them to. Hospitals do not cure people; prisons do not rehabilitate prisoners; schools do not educate students. Since they are supposed to, officials develop ways both of denying the failure of the institution to perform as it should and explaining those failures which cannot be hidden. An account of an institution's operation from the point of view of subordinates therefore casts doubt on the official line and may possibly expose it as a lie.[10]

For these reasons the academy normally accepts the 'hierarchy of credibility': 'we join officials and the man in the street in an unthinking acceptance of the hierarchy of credibility. We do not realize that there are sides to be taken and that we are taking one of them.' Hence Becker argues that for the academic researcher:

> The hierarchy of credibility is a feature of society whose existence we cannot deny, even if we disagree with its injunction to believe the man at the top. When we acquire sufficient sympathy with subordinates to see things from their perspective, we know that we are flying in the face of what 'everyone knows'. The knowledge gives us pause and causes us to share, however briefly, the doubt of our colleagues.[11]

Research work, then, is seldom disinterested and prime interests at work are the powerful, Becker's 'man at the top', and the academy itself. Acknowledgement of these interests becomes crucial when we conduct studies of teachers' lives; for the data generated and accounts rendered can easily be misused and abused by both powerful interest groups and by the academy. Middleton notes that 'in schools people are constantly regulated and classified' but this surveillance extends to teachers themselves. Plainly studies of teachers' lives can be implicated in this process unless we are deeply watchful about who 'owns' the data and who controls the accounts. If Becker is right that 'officials lie' it is also plain that they might appropriate and misuse data about teachers' lives. Likewise, those in the academy might take information on teachers' lives and use it entirely for their own purposes.

Yet Becker reminds us that the terrain of research involves not only differentiated voices but stratified voices. It is important to remember that the politicians and bureaucrats who control schools are part of a stratified system where 'those at the top have a more complete picture of what is going on than anyone else'. It would be unfortunate if in studying teachers' lives, we ignored these contextual parameters which so substantially impinge upon and constantly restrict the teacher's life. It is, therefore, I think a crucial part of our ethical position as researchers that we do not 'valorize the subjectivity of the powerless' in the name of telling 'their story'. This would be to merely record constrained consciousness – a profoundly conservative posture and one, as Denzin has noted, which no doubt explains the popularity of such work during the recent conservative political renaissance. In my view teachers' life studies should, where possible, provide not only a '*narrative of action*', but also a history or *genealogy of context*. I say this in full knowledge that this opens up substantial dangers of changing the relationship between 'life story giver' and 'research taker' and of tilting the balance of the relationship further towards the academy.

I think, however, that these dangers must be faced if a genuine collaboration between the life story giver and the research taker is to be achieved. In a real sense 'it cannot be all give and no take'. In what sense is the 'research taker' in a position to give and provide the basis for a reasonably equitable collaboration. I have argued elsewhere that what we are searching for in developing genuine collaboration in studying teachers' lives is a viable '*trading point*' between life story giver and research taker. The key to this trading point is, I believe, the differential structural location of the research taker. The academic has the time and the resources to collaborate with teachers in developing 'genealogies of context'. These genealogies can provide teachers as a group with aspects of 'the complete picture' which those that control their lives have (or at least aspire to have).

Much of the work that is emerging on teachers' lives throws up structural insights which locate the teacher's life within the deeply structured and embedded environment of schooling. This provides a prime 'trading point' for the external researcher. For one of the valuable characteristics of a collaboration between teachers as researchers and external researchers is that it is a collaboration between two parties that are differentially located in structural terms. Each see the world through a different prism of practice and thought. This valuable difference may provide the external researcher with a possibility to offer back goods in 'the trade'. The teacher/researcher offers data and insights; the external researcher, in pursuing glimpses of structure in different ways, may now also bring data and insights. The terms of trade, in short, look favourable. In such conditions collaboration may at last begin.[12]

In arguing for the provision of histories or genealogies of context, I am reminded of V.S. Naipaul's comments. Naipaul has the ultimate sensitivity to the 'stories' that people tell about their lives, for him subjective perceptions are priority data. Buruma has judged:

> What makes Naipaul one of the worlds most civilized writers is his refusal to be engaged by the People, and his insistence on listening to people, individuals, with their own language and their own stories. To this extent he is right when he claims to have no view; he is impatient with abstractions. He is interested in how individual people see themselves and the world in which they live. He has recorded their histories, their dreams, their stories, their words.[13]

So far then Naipaul echoes the concern of those educational researchers who have sought to capture teachers' stories and narratives, told in their own words and in their own terms. But I am interested by the more recent shifts in Naipaul's position; he has begun to provide far more historical background, he seems to me to be moving towards providing the stories but also genealogies of context. He is clear that he sees this as empowering those whose stories which he once told more passively: 'to awaken to history was to cease to live instinctively. It was to begin to see oneself and one's group the way the outside world saw one; and it was to know a kind of rage.'[14]

MacIntyre has followed a similar line in arguing that man is 'essentially a story-telling animal'. He argues that, 'the story of my life is always embedded in the story of those communities from which I derive my identity'.

What I am, therefore, is in key part what I inherit, a specific past that is present to some degree in my present. I find myself part of a history and that is generally to say, whether I like it or not, whether I recognise it or not, one of the bearers of a tradition. It was important when I characterised the concept of a practice to notice that practices always have histories and that at any given moment what a practice is depends on a mode of understanding it which has been transmitted often through many generations. And thus, insofar as the virtues sustain the relationships required for practices, they have to sustain relationships to the past – and to the future – as well as in the present. But the traditions through which particular practices are transmitted and reshaped never exist in isolation for larger social traditions.

He continues:

Within a tradition the pursuit of goods extends through generations, sometimes through many generations. Hence the individual's search for his or her good is generally and characteristically conducted within a context defined by those traditions of which the individual's life is a part, and this is true both of those goods which are internal to practices and of the goods of a single life. Once again the narrative phenomenon of embedding is crucial: the history of a practice in our time is generally and characteristically embedded in and made intelligible in terms of the larger and longer history of the tradition through which the practice in its present form was conveyed to us; the history of each of our own lives is generally and characteristically embedded in and made intelligible in terms of the larger and longer histories of a number of traditions.[15]

In different ways each of the papers in this volume seeks 'to awaken to history' the study of teachers' lives. This may, of course, be facilitated by more conventional life history work (as in Smith *et al.*; Casey; and Measor and Sikes), but it may be through exploring oral testimonies historically (Nelson), through exploring the inter-action between biography and teaching context (Knowles) or through collaborative autobiography (Butt *et al.*). In many ways Middleton summarizes the aspirations which are shared by the essays in this volume when she says:

Teachers, as well as their students, should analyse the relationship between their individual biographies, historical events, and the constraints imposed on their personal choices by broader power relations, such as those of class, race and gender.

In providing such intercontextual analysis the different methodologies highlighted in this volume all provide important avenues. They all combine a concern with telling teachers' stories with an equal concern to provide a broader context for the location, understanding and grounding of those stories.

In awakening to history in our studies of teachers' lives, I have felt for some time that life history work is a most valuable avenue for collaborative, intercontextual work.[16] The distinction between life stories and life histories is an important one to restate. The life story is a personal reconstruction of experience in this case by the teacher. 'Life story givers' provide data for the researcher often in loosely structured interviews. The researcher seeks to elicit the teacher's perceptions and stories but is generally passive rather than actively interrogative.

The life history also begins with the life story that the teacher tells but seeks to build on the information provided. Hence other people's accounts might be elicited, documentary evidence and a range of historical data amassed. The concern is to develop a wide intertextual and intercontextual mode of analysis. This provision of a wider range of data allows a contextual background to be constructed. Life history data can be collected at a number of levels:

1 From the teachers' own accounts, but also from more detached research studies, it is clear that the teachers' previous *life experience and background* help shape their view of teaching and essential elements in their practice.
2 The teacher's *life style* both in and outside school and his/her latent identities and cultures impact on views of teaching and on practice.
3 The teacher's *life cycle* is an important aspect of professional life and development. This is a unique feature of teaching. For the teacher essentially confronts 'ageless' cohorts; this intensifies the importance of the life cycle for perceptions and practice.
4 The teacher's *career stages* are important research foci for 'the researcher codes the subjects' words according to certain

phases or periods in his or her life, what many qualitative researchers call a previous career'. Becker has argued in his study of school teachers in Chicago that the concept of career is 'of great use in understanding the dynamics of work organizations and the movement and fate of individuals within them'.[17]

5 Beyond major career stages there are *critical incidents* in teachers' lives and specifically their work which may crucially affect their perceptions and practice.

6 Studies of teachers' lives might allow us to 'see the individual in relation to the history of his time. . .. It permits us to view the intersection of the life history of men with the history of society thereby enabling us to understand better the choices, contingencies and options open to the individual.'[18] 'Life histories' of schools, subjects and the teaching profession would provide vital contextual background. The initial focus on the teachers' lives would therefore reconceptualize our studies of schooling and curriculum in quite basic ways.

Crucial to the move to life history is a change in the nature of collaboration. The teacher becomes less a teller of stories and more of a general investigator; the external researcher is more than a listener and elicitor of stories and is actively involved in textual and contextual construction. In terms of give and take, I would argue that a more viable trading point can be established. This trading point, by focusing on lives *in context*, provides a new focus to develop our joint understandings of schooling. By providing this dialogue of a 'story of action within a theory of context' a new context is provided for collaboration. In the end, the teacher researcher can collaborate in investigating not only the stories of lives but the contexts of lives. Such collaboration should provide new understandings for all of us concerned with the world of schooling.

This development of a trading point for collaboration does not solve or mitigate the problem of co-option through collaboration. The history of academics collaborating with teachers is not encouraging in this regard. The life history places this issue of the relationship of collaboration at the centre of our concerns.

A number of the chapters offer strategies devised in answer to the problems of data co-option by powerful interest groups or academic researchers. Measor and Sikes invoke the notion of 'sociology as participation' and argue that the best ethical safeguards derive from the process of respondent validation by which they mean 'returning the processed accounts to the informant for appraisal and to check the accuracy of the data'. One should, I think, add 'allow the respondent to decide on the dissemination of the data' for this life story giver should always be viewed as the owner of the data and the ultimate arbiter of its use.

For this and other reasons I find the more collaborative modes of research the most hopeful avenues for resolving some of the ethical and methodological dilemmas, although as we shall see they open up new questions. Collaborative work on teachers' lives would in my view seek to cut across the academic division of labour as defined by Casey, for if we see teachers as active in making their own history they must also be offered the opportunity to theorize their history. In this sense I agree with Kushner and Norris that we should offer teachers: 'The dignity of contributing to theorizing about their words. . . [and] through sharing meaning production . . . [to] develop significant understandings of schools and education.'

In the chapter by Measor and Sikes we see them moving towards a more collaborative mode as they search for a solution to the methodological and ethical dilemmas involved in studying teachers' lives.

> We would also like to suggest that working in a research team has some advantages here. We have explained elsewhere how the bias one individual had about an issue could be balanced by the others. We worked toward a notion of team triangulation, to guard against selection oversight, but it may be that this needs to be explored more rigorously if we are to build in proper safeguards to ensure that any theory generated is truly grounded theory (see p. 224).

Richard Butt and his colleagues have developed a multi-layered collaborative mode for their studies of teachers' lives. They judge that through a variety of different kinds of collaboration the teacher's life can be recounted in ways that seek to minimize 'the fallibility of memory, selective recall, repression, the shaping of stories according to dispositions, internal idealization and nostalgia'. Their methodological reflection on pages 62–4 and 91–4 make, I think, stimulating reading; above all inducing us to judge how more collaborative work does make us confront ethical and methodological issues head on and in the open. There is no method which can suspend ethical and methodological issues. There are just methods which obscure and mystify such issues (behind, for instance, claims of scientific and objectivist nature) or methods which honestly confront and openly wrestle with such issues. Collaborative work on teachers' lives is of the latter sort and this provides a major argument in favour of such work. This is especially the case if our agenda is partially to open up the socio-logical endeavour and the sociological imagination to teachers as they reflect about their lives.

The close collaborative mode particularly favoured by Butt *et al.*, Casey and Measor and Sikes leads to a wide exposure of self and of the existential identity. As Nelson comments 'many women define being a teacher as a fundamental existential identity'. But moving into existential questions moves the research closer to questions of psychology and, indeed, psychoanalysis. This intersection is an important sub-text in a number of the papers. As Lou Smith *et al.* conclude, beyond technical, political and cultural processes 'there are personality processes at work as well' or, as Measor and Sikes state, 'if we are discussing the role that past experience comes to play in the construction of "a life" then it is difficult to work without making reference to work done in the field of psycho-analysis'.

This intersection with the psychological or psychoanalytic approach opens up a new and, I believe, potentially perilous terrain for collaboration. Again Measor and Sikes honestly confront their own naivety in this regard:

> The point is that when we began the project, we honestly did not know whether taking part in it would have any effect on people's lives, or rather whether they would perceive it to have any effects. One of the issues that emerged was the way that some of our respondents took advantage of the counselling potential of the interviewing sessions. There were some limited points of comparison with a Rogerian style of coun-selling, in that we listened, reflected back, asked questions which encouraged people to reflect on their actions and did not pass judgement. We also dealt with the intimate. We did make it clear that we were researchers, not anything more. . ...

The same protestation is made by Butt *et al.* to the criticism of 'practises therapy without a license'. 'Our position, very simply, is that we do not see ourselves as practising therapy.'

I am not sure that such self-definition and protestation is sufficient in resolving this dilemma. If the co-partners in a collaboration treat sessions as counselling or therapy sessions this has implications for research study. For instance, there are clearly instances where one might not (or indeed might) pursue a line of questioning because of judgements of a more psychoanalytic kind about a person's self-esteem, repressed fear, and so on. Counselling/therapy in short would push us in one direction, research in another. This distinction must be made clear early in the collaborative pact. It is particularly important in the field of teacher development for the aim of professional development likewise can occasionally travel in a different direction to a prior research mission.

In general the ethical and methodological dilemmas I have noted would be best dealt with through clear procedural guidelines. For instance, the counselling/therapy and research distinction should be faced and discussed early in the collaboration between academic and teacher and some procedural guidelines drawn up. Similarly the question of the ownership of the data should be discussed and resolved. For instance, in our own work at RUCCUS (Research Unit on Classroom Learning and Computer Use in Schools) at the University of Western Ontario we have a range of projects studying teachers' lives. In all cases we go through the same procedure of informed consent, followed by feedback and negotiation of all data and reports; teachers have a final power of veto over the data and reports in which they feature.[19]

The requirement of procedural clarification is integral to developing more refined ethical and methodological guidelines in the study of teachers' lives. Working in a more collaborative mode, the study of teachers' lives provides an important arena for reflective and educative research study and ultimately an important, and as yet relatively unexplored, avenue to teacher development.

Ethical, procedural and methodological debate is now vital in this emerging field of study. Certainly a good deal of work is underway aimed at further exploration and clarification in this regard. If our work at RUCCUS is anything to go by this is a painstaking and protracted process based as it is on a continuing exploration and negotiation over values, ethics and procedures. As a collective enterprise of teacher researchers and academic researchers our work remains tentative, an ongoing dialogue. At it's best it resembles research as a grounded conversation between equal partners. But it is still often not at its best.

Finally, we should be aware that, important as it is, procedural and methodological clarification needs to be accompanied by other changes. It remains true that 'major shifts are more likely to arise from changes in political and theoretical preoccupation induced by contemporary social events than from discovery of new sources or methods'.[20] As in other things the story of our research endeavour must be located within a genealogy of context.

NOTES

1 'Reform can't be left to the education establishment', *New York Times*, 26 August 1990, p. 19.
2 For instance, Peter Woods, Mary Lou Holly and Michael Huberman.
3 Bruner, E.M. (1984) 'The opening up of anthropology', pp. 1–18 in Bruner, E.M. *Text, Play and Story: The Construction and Reconstruction of Self and Society*, Washington, D.C.: The American Ethnological Society, p. 7.
4 Denzin, N.K. (1989) *Interpretive Biography*, London and Delhi: Sage, p. 29.
5 Freccero, J. (1986) 'Autobiography and narrative', pp. 16–29 in Heller, T.C., Sosna, M. and Wellbery, D. A. (eds) *Reconstructing Individualism: Autonomy, Individuality, in Western Thought*, Stanford, CA.: Stanford University Press. See also Gilligan, C. (1982) *In A Different Voice: Psychological Theory and Women's Development*, Cambridge, Mass.: Harvard University Press.
6 Denzin, N.K. *Interpretive Biography*, p. 14.
7 Bertaux, D. (ed.) (1981) *Biography and Society: The Life History Approach in the Social Sciences*, California and London: Sage, p. 9.
8 Tripp, D. 'Teacher autobiography and classroom practice', Western Australia: Murdoch University, mimeo, p. 2.
9 Becker, H.S. (1970) *Sociological Work: Method and Substance*, Chicago: Aldine, p. 126.
10 ibid., p. 128.
11 ibid., p. 129.
12 Goodson, I.F. and Walker, R. (1990) *Biography, Identity and Schooling*, London, New York and Philadelphia: Falmer, pp. 148–9.
13 Buruma, I. (1991) 'Signs of life', *New York Review of Books*, Vol. XXXVIII, No. 4, 14 February, p. 3.
14 ibid., p. 4.
15 MacIntyre, A. (1981) *After Virtue: A Study in Moral Theory*, London: Duckworth, pp. 206–7.
16 See Goodson, I.F. (1988) 'Teachers, life histories and studies of curriculum and schooling', in *The Making of Curriculum: Collected Essays*,

London, New York and Philadelphia: Falmer.
17 Becker, H.S. (1952) 'The career of the Chicago public school teacher', *American Journal of Sociology*, Vol. 57, p. 470.
18 Bogdan, R. (1974) *Being Different: The Autobiography of Jane Fry*, New York and Chichester: John Wiley, p. 4.
19 Goodson, I.F and Mangan, J.M. (eds) (1991) *Qualitative Educational Research Studies: Methodologies in Transition*, RUCCUS Occasional Papers Vol. 1, RUCCUS-UWO, London, Ontario.
20 Popular Memory Group (1982) 'Popular memory: theory, politics, method' in Johnson, R., McLennan, G., Schwarz, B. and Sutton, D. (eds) *Making Histories*, Centre for Contemporary Cultural Studies, London: Hutchinson, p. 205–52. My thanks to Kathleen Casey for a number of discussions on inter-textuality and for drawing my attention to the work of the Popular Memory Group.

INDEX